With unusually vivid storytelling un ...., Molly Rettig gives voice to the men and ... .appers and pilots, archeologists and Native elders— ...es trace the history of modern Alaska, and explain why the Great Land exerts such a powerful grip on the national imagination. Molly Rettig is one hell of a writer, and in *Finding True North* she spins one hell of a story.

—*Scott Weidensaul, author of* A World on the Wing *and Pulitzer Prize finalist* Living on the Wind

---

Molly Rettig's is a fun, fresh voice. She is an intelligent, patient observer who makes all her sentences count, like minutes of daylight gained after winter solstice. Through her eyes, we see how Alaska turns our preconceived notions down a gravel road we didn't know was there. We bump along to reach a perfectly imperfect place, in which we might spend the rest of our lives.

—*Ned Rozell, science writer for the University of Alaska Fairbanks' Geophysical Institute and author of more than 1,000 weekly newspaper columns*

Finding True North is a deft, lively mix of personal, historical, and reportorial storytelling. With an inquisitive and compassionate eye, Molly Rettig captures the glamour, the grit, and the contradictions of the 49th state and its people. I'd go with her anywhere.

—*Florence Williams, author,* The Nature Fix: Why Nature Makes us Happier, Healthier, and More Creative

Finding True North

Finding True North

Firsthand Stories of the Booms That Built Modern Alaska

by Molly Rettig

University of Alaska Press
Fairbanks, Alaska

Text © 2021 University of Alaska Press

Published by
University of Alaska Press
P.O. Box 756240
Fairbanks, AK 99775-6240

Cover art by Corey DiRutigliano.
Interior design by Paula Elmes.

Library of Congress Cataloging-in-Publication Data

Names: Rettig, Molly, author.
Title: Finding true north : firsthand stories of the booms that built modern Alaska / by
    Molly Rettig.
Description: Fairbanks, AK : University of Alaska Press, [2021] | Includes index.
Identifiers: LCCN 2020030588 (print) | LCCN 2020030589 (ebook) |
    ISBN 9781602234437 (paperback) | ISBN 9781602234444 (ebook)
Subjects: LCSH: Rettig, Molly. | Gold mines and mining—Alaska—History. |
    Petroleum industry and trade—Alaska—History. | Alaska Natives—Biography. |
    Alaska—History. | Alaska—Description and travel. | Alaska—Biography.
Classification: LCC F904 .R435 2021 (print) | LCC F904 (ebook) | DDC 979.8—dc23
LC record available at https://lccn.loc.gov/2020030588
LC ebook record available at https://lccn.loc.gov/2020030589

Contents

Acknowledgments

will never again skip over the acknowledgments section of a book! This book is truly the work of so many people. First, my deepest thanks to my sources—Clutch Lounsbury, Al Wright, Julie Mahler, Mike and Patty Kunz, and so many others who shared their stories over countless hours and years, and became much more than sources during the writing of this book.

Thanks to the University of Alaska Press for the wonderful editing and design work, particularly Elizabeth Laska for believing in this project and making it better.

Thank you to my mother, Suzanne Donovan, for the gentle (and not-so-gentle) prodding over the years to get these stories on paper, and to keep trucking when I was ready to give up.

Thank you to my writer friends Bonnie-Sue Hitchcock, Ned Rozell, and my journalism school posse, who provided inspiration, critiques, and encouragement along the way.

Thank you to Sara Camilli, who showed me the value of having a "real-life agent" and shared her time and expertise with a novice neighbor.

Thanks to the first and last editor of all my stories, my husband Josh Kunz, as well as my sharp-eyed family members who read so many versions of this over the years.

I'm a different person than when I started this project, and—more than ever—in awe of books.

Introduction

P eople in the Arctic may have been the first to notice something crazy was happening to the global climate. The air here was getting warmer and the land more moist, new plants were springing up, and animal migrations were changing. It may sound like a familiar story to us, mirroring many of the changes we're seeing today. But this was 13,000 years ago, at the end of the last Ice Age, or as my father-in-law would call it, the Pleistocene.

It was also very disruptive to life on the Bering Land Bridge, a massive swath of land connecting Asia and North America—on a modern map, Siberia and Alaska. As the world warmed, woolly mammoths and small prehistoric horses couldn't survive on the shrubby tundra that now crept across the land, meaning hunters and gatherers couldn't survive there either. Like sand swirling in the wind, the world's creatures began to stir. The people of Beringia looked for a better place to go.

With melting ice opening new corridors, people traveled east, toward North America, and found themselves in Alaska, an Aleut word for "Great Land." These were the First Alaskans, this much we know. Of course, there's a lot we don't know about these ancient people, like how they got here or exactly when they arrived. The journey may have taken hundreds of years, or thousands. Ostensibly, they were searching for food, or climate, or refuge from enemies—something that would lead to a better life. And while we learn a little bit more with each bone or projectile point that's discovered, there is much we'll probably never know.

Some of this history lives on, with the Indigenous people of North America and the tribes that span Alaska. Their languages and stories and traditions evolved from these First Peoples. And while they have adapted to modern times, they have also maintained a traditional way of life based on hunting and fishing and a deep connection to the land. The First Alaskans are the ones who cracked the code on how to survive, and thrive, in the harshest environment on earth.

In the long period since then have come the Next Alaskans—those who arrived long after the Bering Land Bridge was submerged under rising seas, but who still found their way here. There were the Russian fur traders who came hunting for sea otters and other rich pelts that were in demand around the world. Then the gold miners and missionaries and soldiers, the restless souls who traveled by foot and train and hand-cobbled boats, over mountain passes and glacial rivers, until they couldn't go any further. These next-comers arrived in waves, driven by major events in world history: The Gold Rush. World War II. The Oil Boom. Events that transformed Alaska and reverberated across the planet. Compared to the hunters and gatherers who preceded them, they had a different approach to living here, carving Alaska's wild spaces into homesteads and frontier towns that looked more like the places they'd come from. But they still shared something in common with their predecessors—the desire for a better life.

A latecomer to Alaska myself, I didn't arrive until 2010, as one of the many twentysomethings flocking here for adventure. By then most of the rivers and trails could be found on Google Earth, and you could get a good latte and a decent cell signal as far north as Fairbanks. Like those who had come before, I was also searching for something, but it was something not easily defined. I had dreams of making a difference, somehow, of making the world a better place, but no idea how to convert those dreams into action. This streak of idealism had led me to a degree in environmental journalism and all the way to a job at the *Fairbanks Daily News-Miner*, where I covered climate change and wildlife and the rugged Alaska lifestyle. As a new cub reporter, suddenly I was writing about oil and gas and mining in one of the world's great resource economies. I learned about Alaska Native culture, visited villages and fish camps, and talked with whaling captains and tribal leaders and Elders who'd grown up in canvas tents and sometimes barely spoke white English.

I learned more than I had in many years of school. But the deeper I went, the more confused I became about my own purpose for coming here. In Alaska, life was so entwined with resources. Enormous deposits of gold and copper and oil and gas lurked under lands that had been used for hunting and fishing for thousands of years. Alaskans depended on both. They needed clean food and water, but they also needed jobs and public services—creating a constant tug-of-war about how best to use the land, about who should get to decide.

The black and white views I had arrived with, of well-defined problems and clear solutions, slowly faded away. Alaska had a love-hate relationship with resource development that dated back a long time. It was a story of booms and busts and reinvention. To understand it fully, I realized, I had to go back in time and see how it had started. To talk to those who lived through the resource booms, to see them up close and hear what had been gained and what had been lost. Maybe that would give me some idea of how we got here and, more importantly, where we are going.

This book is about the resource booms that built modern-day Alaska, through the stories of those who lived them. Starting at the turn of the twentieth century, *Finding True North* is a journey through the gold rush, World War II, and the oil boom. While there are certainly other major events that have defined Alaska over its history, including especially the Russian trappers who arrived in the 1700s, these stories begin with gold because it seemed like the closest thing to the birth of modern-day Alaska. Additionally, it was fairly easy to find descendants of the gold rush pioneers who could share their family history first-hand.

This book is a culmination of more than five years of research and interviews with more than thirty long-time Alaskans, from trappers and gold miners to professors and political leaders. For the sake of the narrative, I whittled the list down to four main characters. The first three each represent a major chapter in Alaska's history: the gold rush, the airplane age ushered in by World War Two, and the oil boom, eras that transformed the state forever and are still very present today. The final character brings us back to the Indigenous knowledge that existed before all that, and that survived the seismic changes of the past century to come face to face with the modern world. This book does not attempt to provide a comprehensive history of Alaska, or even a complete look at the events themselves. It simply presents my own journey through history with four Alaskans who have shown me how this place was transformed from a land of subsistence to a land of resource development, where survival seems to hinge less on wilderness skills than on the price of a barrel of oil.

I have done my best to include the diverse voices of Alaska. The main characters in this book include a third-generation Fairbanks gold miner, an Athabascan bush pilot, a pipeliner from New York, and a Gwich'in mother and trapper. I hope you enjoy their stories as much as I did.

PART ONE
GOLD

Sourdough:

Sour on Alaska, not enough dough to get out.

Also refers to the early gold miners in Alaska, who
wore a leather pouch of sourdough starter around
their neck to keep it from freezing.

1

A Gold Rush Town

The tunnel is darker than a moonless night, the type of darkness that reaches inside of you, sucking out everything except your fear. I fumble with my headlamp and finally press the button, creating a cone of light that shatters the spell. The walls are not black at all. In fact, they're made up of brown, shimmering schist. As I walk through, slightly hunched over, I think of the treasure contained in these walls, dragged out of here nearly a hundred years ago, one bucket at a time. The chunks of quartz glittering with gold that the whole world desired. This isn't an empty void but a trail to treasure. It's hard to believe I've probably skied over it a hundred times without even knowing it was here.

Ahead of me an old man shuffles down the tunnel, his gait stiffened by years of mining. His baritone voice echoes off the dank walls.

"Some people follow these veins forever and never find any gold."

Clutch Lounsbury practically grew up in this tunnel. With a round belly and a white bushy beard, he could easily be mistaken for Santa Claus, if it weren't for the chocolate-brown Carhartt bibs and Alaska Miners Association cap.

As we head deeper into the void, Clutch tells me how this tunnel was formed. How hot fluids surged up from the earth's core millions of years ago and deposited a thick vein of ore in this crack. How researchers

— 1 —

installed sensors down here during the Cold War to monitor nuclear activity in Russia. The time they filmed an episode of the reality show "Gold Rush Alaska" in this very spot. Stories are Clutch's currency, and he never seems to run out. He flows from one subject to the next like a wide, braided river, always changing direction but never running dry.

The hill we're walking through is one of many rising up from the Tanana River Valley in interior Alaska. Not quite a mountain, Ester Dome is one of the most prominent hills around Fairbanks, a spot so rich in gold that it has been mined almost continuously for more than a century. Most of the mine shafts that once crisscrossed underneath the dome have collapsed, taken out by time or explosives. But after eighty years, this one still stands, an underground tribute to the last great gold rush.

Not that the neighbors would ever know it was here. Less than two miles from my house, I've flown by it countless times on skis and bikes and snow machines without ever having a clue. There's no scaffolding, no safety tape, no "Active Mining" signs. In fact, you would never suspect anything at all unless you walked through the trees, down the hill, and right through the front door of Clutch's cabin. At first glance, the Arctic entryway would resemble any old house in Fairbanks. To the right—a living room, with an old floral sofa and a small wood stove, a stack of kindling ready to go. Then you would look to the left and see a wall of yellow spray foam, as bumpy and porous as exotic sea coral. And a gaping black hole shooting into the side of the hill, like a portal to another world. A Dall sheep head guards the entrance to the mine, next to a sign that says, "If it can't be grown it must be mined."

That's where Clutch had handed me a yellow hard hat and asked if I was claustrophobic.

I'm not, but as we go deeper, I can feel my stomach tighten. I've never been in a gold mine before, let alone an eight-hundred-foot tunnel blasted into a Subarctic hillside. As a starry-eyed grad student, I came to Alaska to live in the woods, surrounded by trees and wildlife. To write stories about melting sea ice and hungry polar bears, showing the effects of climate change to the outside world. When I first arrived, I marveled at the wilderness that stretched in every direction, the moose browsing through the woods in the backyard and all the little footprints etched in the snow. A slice of nature in the raw, just as I'd imagined. This was before I learned my next-door neighbor had a gold mine in his living room.

As I look up, I notice there's no wooden cribbing around the tunnel anymore. After the first sixty feet, the entire support structure has disappeared.

"This is all freestanding ground," Clutch says breezily, waving a hand at the ceiling.

Great, I think, eyeing the jagged edges of schist just a few inches from my head. Above that, fifty feet of rock and soil separate us from the forest floor, and the fresh and airy world I'm used to. I try not to think of the weight of all that earth, held up by nothing but its own internal strength. This tunnel was gouged out of the rock with a chisel, a hammer, and a healthy dose of dynamite. By a single man with a carbide headlamp, chasing a childhood dream.

Clutch stops and places a large, meaty hand against the wall. This must be the spot.

"See that white milky stuff?" He rubs his thumb along a pale streak of minerals. "That's what you're lookin for when you're mining."

The stripe of quartz is only a couple inches wide, so subtle I wouldn't have noticed it without the extra lumens of Clutch's flashlight. The flecks of gold lodged inside are too miniscule for my eye. Only a miner would know they were there. I touch the rock gently, as if it's a piece of my mom's china.

"Where did it come from?" Even to my own ear, I sound like an awestruck kid on a geology field trip. And just like my fifth-grade teacher Mr. Dickson would have done, Clutch seizes the question like a loose football, setting off on a rambling explanation that I try my best to follow. He describes faults in the earth's crust that sometimes move, like earthquakes, sliding his palms against each other roughly in opposite directions.

"It's a lotta heat and pressure. Grinds the rock right into a clay, see?"

He rubs a reddish powder between his thumb and forefinger, and I think of rouge eye shadow. As the earth's plates shift, it gives hot lava an opportunity to flow upward, dissolving minerals like gold and quartz from the rocks and carrying them toward the surface. As the molten liquid cools, it looks for a place to settle—in the various faults, cracks, nooks, and crannies under our feet—creating bodies of ore that have tantalized humans for thousands of years.

Buried in the quartz is a small hole, about the size of a silver dollar. Clutch leans toward it, as if peering into the past.

"That's where I drilled a hole, 115 feet, lookin for values," he says.

Using his dad's old generator and a diamond-tipped drill bit, he took core samples of this entire tunnel, sending out feelers for gold in every direction.

"Got a ninety-eight percent core recovery on that."

I have no idea what that means, but can tell by his tone that it must be quite a feat.

"Wow."

A few hundred feet in, Clutch flicks his flashlight above our heads. I look up at a little hatch in the ceiling.

"What's that? An escape tunnel?"

"Nope. It's not a way out," he explains. "It's a way in." Above the wooden door is a chute. The chute runs up, like a man hole, through thirty feet of rock, and terminates at a very special pocket of ground. The type that keeps miners awake at night—quartz speckled with high-grade ore.

"This was really rich in here, 26.9 ounces to the ton," he said, a number that must speak for itself among miners. I nod to show I'm impressed.

As we continue walking, the tunnel feels like it will never end. Halfway to China, as Clutch likes to say. But we finally run into a wall of solid rock. The end of the vein, and of the dream that ran alongside it. This mine has lived through nearly a hundred years of history— through booms and busts, through wars, earthquakes, and floods. It was built right after the Great Depression, when people were hungry for opportunity, not above burrowing into the frozen earth looking for pay. Thousands of tons of ore were shuttled out of here in a hand-pushed cart, crushed, leached, and melted into gold sponges, then sold to the U.S. Treasury, which was collecting all the nation's gold in a desperate attempt to resuscitate the economy.

As we walk back toward his living room, Clutch tells me how his father chased this vein into the mountain, following the gold flecks wherever they led. Like the old pans and iron pipe scattered around Ester Creek, Clutch is a product of the Gold Rush—an example of just how far people would go for something shiny.

I first met Clutch at the Golden Eagle, a smoky saloon slouched under the birch trees outside of Fairbanks. It sits at the foot of a hill like a ski lodge, except one corner of the porch is sagging, and the bathroom stalls don't have doors. On the other hand, the beer is cheap and you can cook your own burgers the way you like them on the grill.

On a warm evening during my first summer in Alaska, I climbed the rickety wooden stairs. A group of bearded locals chatted on the porch, looking up to see if they recognized me. Three sled dogs rushed over, greeting me with a few quick sniffs before returning to their spots in the sun. It wasn't every day a new person showed up, I guessed, especially a female. As I reached for the heavy pine door, I felt the buzz of finding myself somewhere new, of not knowing what was inside. An acrid smell hit me first. I saw the culprit in the middle of the room, a pot-bellied coal stove coated in black dust. There was a pool table in one corner and a piano in the other, the walls collaged like a teenager's bedroom in pictures of dances, plays, and community parades. The wooden bar ran the length of the building, sturdy and no-nonsense, like the ones from old western movies. At the far end, two men with bushy beards huddled over their beers. I could almost see the stories on the tips of their tongues, just waiting for a fresh ear to sit down beside them. A woman with blond dreadlocks refilled a pint from the tap and handed it to a man who looked like Paul Bunyan.

Behind her, sunlight filtered through the windows stained yellow from cigarette smoke, illuminating rows of bottles like colorful Christmas lights. Though it appeared to be held together by little more than string, this bar had more character than the ones from my favorite TV shows.

The bartender turned to me.

"What can I get ya?"

Copying the customer in front me, I ordered a $2 "mystery beer."

I hardly knew anyone in town yet. After finishing journalism school in Colorado, I had landed a job at the Fairbanks Daily News-Miner, a small newspaper in the center of Alaska. Though it was thousands of miles away from any major media market, it seemed like the perfect place to cut my teeth as a science writer. As I'd sat in an organic coffee shop in downtown Boulder filling out the application, I daydreamed about the stories I would find in Alaska—stories of caribou herds and Indigenous hunters, climate change and offshore drilling. As I updated my resume, searching for different euphemisms for the word "intern," in my mind I was already soaring around in bush planes and chasing sled dog races across the tundra. After a childhood of building lean-tos and snow forts in central Pennsylvania, this was a chance to experience the real thing. The more I thought about it, the clearer it became: I had to go to Alaska, for all the reasons I'd wanted to become a journalist in the first place.

I knew it would be a sharp contrast to Boulder, a college town at the foot of the Rockies, where a group of nature-lovers had created a bubble of wilderness around themselves. But after three years Boulder was starting to feel too perfect, too insulated from the problems of the outside world by Priuses and Patagonia puffy jackets (incidentally, the city had just passed the United States' first self-imposed municipal carbon tax). I expected Alaska to be the opposite—a vast, all-encompassing wilderness dotted with a few outcrops of civilization, where people battled against the elements to scratch a living from the land. I knew I could handle the sunny slopes of Colorado, but would I be able to hack it in Alaska?

It would only be for a year, I figured, as I packed up my red Subaru wagon and loaded three pairs of skis onto the roof. I was aiming for an adventure just long enough to rack up some bylines and exploits before moving on to bigger and better things. As the ferry cut through the whale-laden waters of the Inside Passage, I thought of the stories that awaited me, stories of whale hunting and polar ice expeditions. It was early May when I cruised into Ester, a quirky village about ten miles from Fairbanks, where I'd be sharing a house with two biologists from the National Park Service.

Unlike the hippy paradise I had come from, Ester was a potpourri of miners, artists, professors, and dog mushers. It retained a backwoods feel, a smattering of homesteads wedged into the hillside with neat cords of firewood stacked outside—long piles for long winters. Four wheelers and snowmachines zipped up and down steep dirt roads named for minerals: Sapphire, Amethyst, Azurite. My house on Stone Road looked like it had been clipped from a postcard, built from giant Lincoln logs and tucked into the trees. And, at the bottom of the hill, just a five-minute walk from home, was our very own pub.

So far, Alaska was living up to my expectations. And so was the Golden Eagle bar. I grabbed a stool and spun it around. In a corner next to the dart boards, a dozen people sat around a wobbly table made from an old cable spool playing folk music. It was a weekly tradition at the Golden Eagle, according to my new roommates. Every Sunday, locals showed up with guitars, banjos, and harmonicas, and jammed into the night, while everyone else ate moose chili or homemade blueberry pie and tapped their feet to the music. Mustaches, flowy skirts, Harley-Davidson T-shirts—they made quite the ensemble, moving from Led Zeppelin to Bob Dylan without skipping a beat.

Parked in the corner, one person stood out among the colorful band. Clutch wore a tie-dyed necktie over tan Carhartt bibs. He was playing an instrument I'd never seen before, an upside-down metal washtub with a string attached to a sawed-off hockey stick. He held it upright on top of the tub, keeping the string taut like a bow. Sitting on a stool with both feet resting on the tub, he plucked the cord with his thumb, sipping Scotch on ice with the other hand. His fuzzy white beard framed a bulbous nose and round face tipped slightly into a smile, as if cooking up a new joke. He looked like a gold miner from a cartoon that had sprung to life. He looked...Alaskan.

During a break in the music, the group drifted to the bar and I wandered over to get a closer look at the washtub. It was painted blue with "Ester City Limits" blazed on the side in bright yellow. Clutch reappeared with a fresh Johnnie Walker.

"Do you play tub bass?"

He sounded so hopeful I felt bad saying no, I had no musical ability whatsoever.

"Oh, there's nothin to it," he said, setting his glass on the table and picking up the hockey stick. I could tell by the frayed grip that it had seen plenty of ice time.

"You set the pitch by changing the tension of the string. See? Like this."

He moved the stick forward and backward as if shifting gears in a truck. When he strummed, the tub acted as a resonator, amplifying the vibration like the sound box of a guitar.

"There's only one chord. You can't mess it up." And with that, he handed me the stick.

I started running into Clutch regularly on Sundays. His wife Lorna was usually there too, a petite lady with a head of white curls, a feisty fiddle player. Even without any musical skill, it didn't take long to become part of the band. When Clutch saw me come in, he would hand me the hockey stick and head to the bar, returning with a glass of red wine for Lorna and a fresh batch of stories for me. His family had been mining in Fairbanks since the gold rush days, he told me. His grandparents came up by horse and sleigh, traveling hundreds of miles through the frozen, windblown wilderness, to pan the creeks for gold. His dad carried on the tradition, tunneling into the hillside to extract rich chunks of ore.

The mine was still there, carved into the back of his old cabin, not far from me.

"Wait." I must have heard him wrong. "Inside your house, you mean?"

He chuckled, as if it were just the reaction he was going for.

"Yep, my dad ran a drift right behind the cabin. There was a little pinch of value and he just made a ninety and went up the hill and he did fairly good. There was some high-grade gold in there."

Wow. Even for Fairbanks, that seemed pretty crazy. In Boulder, you couldn't build a garage without a permit. Imagine what they'd say about a mine.

"Do you still mine it?"

"Oh, not anymore." The glint in his eye faded. "It's not really worth it."

"Really? I thought gold prices were up these days," I said, revealing everything I knew about mining in one quick burst.

"Well, first I'd have to get through the government."

He spit out the last word like a sip of bad beer, and continued.

"They're tightenin the screws and makin it really hard for a guy to do anything. They'd only let me move so much rock a week. I think I'd be dead and gone before I got it goin."

I offered a sympathetic grunt, not sure what to say. I had never had a soft spot for miners. I was raised to recycle, compost, and do my part to save the planet. Growing up in central Pennsylvania, coal mining was everywhere. Not drifts dug into the side of houses, but underground tunnels that stretched for miles, winding beneath roads, yards, and soccer fields like vast secret rivers. Mountains that literally had their tops blown off to expose the coal seams inside. Pennsylvania was home to the largest deposit of anthracite coal in North America. We had studied it extensively in school, learned about steam shovels and strip mining, about the town that had a coal fire burning beneath it for more than fifty years. The pictures of soot-faced men carrying picks and lunch pails, queuing up to take the elevator deep underground, were still etched in my mind. Driving home from soccer tournaments, we'd seen culm banks on the side of the road, mounds of mining waste that had been left behind in the insatiable search for coal. These large mining companies were polluting the earth, my mom would say to a minivan full of kids in soccer cleats. Regulation was the only way to keep them in check: the more, the better. Though I had left coal country behind, the sentiment had stayed with me. It had followed me across the country, as I earned a master's degree in environmental journalism, and all the way to Alaska.

Yet now, standing in a smoky bar on top of a massive gold deposit, I found myself feeling kind of bad for Clutch, unable to work the mine he grew up in. The seventy-year-old bass player, who coached women's hockey and taught children how to pan for gold, just didn't fit my image of the greedy miner. I could feel the stereotypes clashing in my mind, ramming into one another like hockey players.

Clutch took a sip of his drink.

"It's a shame, because if it weren't for gold, Alaska wouldn't be here."

It took a while to sink in, but Clutch was right in a way. Alaska wouldn't be here, at least not this version of it. The more I looked around, the more evidence I saw. In downtown Ester, piles of mine tailings lumped the edge of the streets like sand dunes, trees shooting out at haphazard angles like something from a Dr. Seuss book. Old steam boilers littered the ski trails, tangled in ferns and alder branches. In fact, the bluff that ran past my house had been formed not by the steady hand of erosion but by draglines that had ripped the valley open looking for gold. And it wasn't just a thing of the past; you could still hear the bulldozers clawing away at the open-pit mine on Main Street.

It turns out my new neighborhood sat on top of one of the richest gold veins on the continent, stretching from Ester Creek to the hills above Fairbanks in an arc forty miles long and eight miles wide. When it was discovered in 1902, it turned life upside down in Alaska, triggering the last great North American gold rush.

Nothing would ever be the same. An Indigenous land of some 30,000 people, who had hunted across great distances and culled every bit of nourishment from the earth, gave way to a western frontier. Towns popped up in the middle of the wilderness and the population doubled almost overnight. Millions of ounces of gold were gouged from the ground, the water, and the rock. Fortunes were made and lost in an instant. When the fever died down, most of the towns did too, fading back into wilderness. But some survived.

Gold was the only reason Ester was here. If those nuggets had never been found, Alaska might still be an anonymous landmass sitting quietly at the top of the globe, across the strait from Siberia. With no newspapers, no roads, no stores or saloons, none of the things that enabled me to live here today.

A conundrum, indeed. Suddenly the story I had built my new life upon didn't quite add up, and I felt the ground shift beneath me a little. Which one was it? Was Alaska the place of the American imagination, where polar bears roamed the ice-fringed tundra and the northern lights danced overhead, a land that seemed designed to awe and inspire, to remind us how small we were? Or was it just a big bucket of resources—a

Clutch Lounsbury in front of his gold mine in Ester, Alaska. The hard rock mine is accessed from the arctic entryway of his cabin.

repository of gold and fish and wood and oil to feed our modern lifestyle? Could it be both? It didn't seem possible.

One thing was certain. I wouldn't find the answers written in a book or lying at the bottom of Ester Creek. If I wanted to see a true frontier, I had to go back to an earlier time, a time before our thirst for resources had transformed Alaska into the place it was today—where a friendly visit to a neighbor could lead you deep into an underground gold mine.

And what better place to start than the center of Gold Rush history? Ever since a nugget was discovered glimmering in the bottom of a creek more than a hundred years ago, Alaska's history had been a rollercoaster of booms and busts, of explosive growth followed by sudden collapse.

Gold. War. Oil.

All leading to the summer of 2010, when the entire economy of Alaska rested on a 48-inch-diameter pipeline that carried crude black oil across the state, delivering this Arctic treasure to the world market. When a young journalist moved to Alaska, eager to fight for sustainability.

Luckily, the people who lived through these booms were still alive, people like Clutch and Lorna. They could show me what Alaska was like before the world discovered its incredible riches, and what happened when they dried up.

After a century of intensive resource extraction, maybe the idea of wilderness persisted only in the imagination. Or maybe there was still something left that needed protection.

2
The Stampede

Fairbanks was still pretty feral when the first issue of the *Daily News-Miner* rolled off the press in 1903. Gold prospectors trolled the dirt streets, where the bitter tinge of coal mingled with the stench of horse dung. The wooden bridge over the Chena River rattled day and night with the clip clop of horses' hooves, while steamboats with giant wooden sternwheels pulled up to the dock on Front Street, exchanging pallets of flour and bacon for bags of gold dust. Most buildings were made of log, crudely fitted together with slabs of sod stuffed between—except for the dance halls and casinos, whose elaborate wooden facades echoed the frontier towns of the Wild West. Loose dogs ran through the streets, sleeping under doorways and fighting for scraps. Every so often a fight would break out between men, too, outside the bars or in the shadowy streets of the Red Light district—over gold claims, gambling debts, or women, the main objects of value in the dusty mining town. In the center of this, a new church popped up on Third Avenue and Cushman Street, a smudge of morality in the rough-and-tumble town.

By the time I began working at the newspaper in 2010, Fairbanks was a bit more civilized. The streets were paved, clean, and trimmed with flowers. Architecturally modest but not without character, a few stately buildings mixed in with the concrete boxes and old log cabins. Though there was no sign of the brothels that once lined Fourth Avenue or the piles of timber stacked up on the shore, the general layout remained the same. The Chena River still flowed past First Avenue, in no great rush to join the Tanana River a few miles south. The *News-Miner* newsroom had moved across the river from its original location to accommodate a large printing press, purchased in the sixties. There, among a floor of reporters, with no walls or windows, was my desk.

It was a great place to work. During the summer, I could stroll across the footbridge to the courthouse, eat lunch in the city square, or duck in for coffee at McCafferty's cafe. Every day was a crash course in something new: hunting regulations, military affairs, Indigenous rights, and the biggest part of my beat: resources. While other newspapers brimmed with stories of technology and health care and international policy, Alaska's headlines were dominated by more tangible commodities: gold, fish, copper, oil. Without these natural resources, it seemed, the state would have no economy at all. Being a reporter was fun, like going to a different class every day and turning in my homework before dinner. Though I wasn't covering quite as much science as I'd hoped, it was exciting to learn about the things that made the state go round. And, because of Alaska's outsized influence, the world.

Then winter came, and the temperature dropped like a hammer. The river froze, first forming delicate pans of ice that floated on the surface, then solidifying into a thick white crust that masked any movement. It was fascinating to watch the progression. The sun retreated, gradually at first, just a few minutes each day, then precipitously, like the last gasp of a dying lamp. By early December, we were down to a few hours of sun each day, not enough to exude any real heat. It dropped to minus-20. Then minus-30, and minus-40. I was still intrigued. I wanted to see how cold it would get, what it was like at this extreme end of the earth, and how civilization could manage to hang on.

During that first cold snap, I had no idea what to expect. Did people still go grocery shopping? Would school be cancelled? What about the public meetings I was supposed to cover? I was surprised to learn that, in conditions where most cars won't even start, life went on pretty much as usual.

On a Monday night shortly after Thanksgiving, I left the fluorescent glare of the newsroom and walked to a city council meeting. Across the street, a white bell tower punctured the hazy Fairbanks sky. The Catholic church dated back to 1904, when the local priest had traveled from gold camp to gold camp collecting donations from miners. Next door, the sign outside the bank flashed "–35F" in bright red lights, as if warning that it had exceeded its operating temperatures and was about to shut down. I huddled into my pink puff coat as I crossed the Cushman Street Bridge. The river was covered in a frozen blanket of smog that instantly brought tears to my eyes. I had learned about this phenomenon, called "ice fog," during a recent interview with a chemistry professor: when the air was too cold to hold moisture, the vapor produced from breathing or burning wood turned directly into ice, leaving little particles suspended in the air like stardust. A fascinating concept, I thought, but really gross to inhale. Through the slits of my frosted eyelashes, I looked out at the white city—the buildings, sidewalks, and trees outlined in snow, with little puffs of steam slithering from chimneys, tailpipes, and underground utilidors. A few blocks west, the coal plant belched a thick plume over the city. It was a cross between a winter wonderland and the set of a post-Apocalypse movie, both beautiful and ugly at the same time.

I passed the Masonic Temple on First Avenue, a red building with fancy Renaissance columns where the Freemasons held their meetings a hundred years ago. I tried to imagine living here back then, when you had to cut down every tree you could find to stay warm. When the pioneers showed up, none of this was here—no steam heat or public buses or conveniently placed kiosks where you could plug in your car. Most settlers had to figure out how to survive using only their hands and their wits.

Even in full winter regalia from REI, the air outside felt like dry ice. It burned the tip of my nose, drove through the seams of my jacket, slipped under my sleeves and mittens, finding every weak point in my layers of wool and goose down armor. Shoving my hands deeper in my pockets, I picked up the pace. City hall was a few blocks ahead on the corner of Eighth and Cushman Street. With large bay windows and concrete piers, it looked more like it belonged in Chicago's historic district than in downtown Fairbanks. The handsome Art Deco building was the old schoolhouse, built in 1932. Before that another school had stood in the same place, a two-story wooden building with a belfry and a tall flag tower. It was fairly modern for its day, with electricity, lots of windows, and a heated basement where kids could run around on really cold days. Each morning, around a hundred fifty students poured in from the surrounding village, and were herded into classrooms by a handful of teachers. One, a young woman from Oregon, began working there in 1907, the year the school opened. At twenty-one years old, she had just finished her teaching degree—quite an accomplishment for a woman in those days. But then, she wasn't an average woman. She played hockey and basketball, hunted and fished. She wasn't afraid of the cold or the dark, or the prospect of living in a frontier town that could go belly up any day. Clutch's grandmother had traveled a long way to get her first teaching job.

Nellie Parsons had long dark hair and wide-set brown eyes that seemed to grow to the size of walnuts when she heard something interesting. And she had always been curious. After finishing high school in Oregon, she began taking classes at Willamette University in Salem. Located across the street from the copper-domed state capitol, Willamette was one of the oldest universities in the western US, founded by Methodist missionaries in 1867. At the time there were only a few women strolling around the handsome brick buildings and grassy lawns. And Nellie was there to learn, not to find a man.

But that didn't stop them from finding her. Somewhere on campus she caught the eye of a star football player named George Lounsbury. GL to his teammates, he had thick brown hair and chiseled features that turned heads as he walked to class. GL had grown up on a farm in Iowa and moved west looking for opportunity. But his story had a tragic side as well—when he was in high school, his mother and brother were coming home from church when their horse and buggy was hit by a speeding train, killing them both on the spot. GL was devastated, left with only a father he didn't get along with. Using the lifetime rail pass they had received as part of the settlement, he took the train across the country and ended up at a farm in Salem, working for a state senator.

It was a welcome change of scenery from Iowa. Horses roamed the lush Salem countryside, and the air tasted like the sea. One day GL's boss was sitting on the patio when he saw the young man leap a fence on his way to the barn. He couldn't believe his eyes—the Iowa farm kid had the grace of a gazelle, even with his hands full of milk buckets.

The senator called him over.

"I've never seen anyone jump like that before! What do you think about track, son?"

A standout athlete in high school, GL missed playing sports—the adrenaline, the competition, but most of all being part of a team. The senator took him over to the athletics department at Willamette, where his son went to school, and signed him up for track and field. It turned out to be quite the gift to his alma mater. Within a year GL broke the Oregon state record for high jump and long jump, and before long he was picked up by the football team too.

While Nellie was attracted to GL, she was on a slightly different track. Her weekends were spent not at the football field but at the campus church, where her father, John Parsons, was the minister. She was still finishing her studies when her dad took off for Alaska. As new towns were popping up across the north, churches were scrambling to keep up, to temper the crime and greed that were flourishing on the frontier while gaining some followers in the process. Dr. Parsons rode a ship up through the Inside Passage, climbed over the coastal mountains, and floated down the Yukon River, all the way to the gold fields in Fairbanks. He built a Methodist church on Third Avenue and Cushman Street, right in the center of the action.

When Nellie graduated in 1906, she moved north to join her family. But GL wasn't done with football yet. The next year, he transferred to Oregon State University and played for the Beavers in the Pacific Northwest league. For a time, it seemed like their paths would not reconnect. After college, GL faced a crossroads: should he go back to the farm in Iowa, look for a job in Seattle, or try something else entirely? There were plenty of options for an educated young man, as electricity transformed the nation and the railroad sprouted across the west. But those opportunities didn't excite him.

There was one thing that did, however. When GL heard about a sports contest in Fairbanks over the Fourth of July, he saw a chance to test his athletic prowess in the north and see the girl who still held his heart. So he borrowed money for a boat ticket and made the long journey north. Downtown Fairbanks was decked out in red, white, and blue for the occasion, with American flags waving in the breeze and triangle bunting crisscrossing the streets. Though Alaska was not yet a state at the time, that didn't diminish the patriotism of Fairbanks' mostly American populace. The whole town showed up in their finest dresses and suits to watch the parade weave through the dusty streets.

Ladies in frilly white hats perched atop carriages, festooned with ribbons and doves. Though fashion was a year or two behind New York, no one seemed to mind. Spectators swarmed Front Street and crowded onto bleachers stacked ten rows high. The main attraction, however, was not the parade or the music but the sporting events happening right along the river, the running and jumping and wrestling and shot-putting taking place all throughout the day. The Arcade Cafe swung its doors open to the commotion of the street. Children wolfed down hot dogs and ice cream along the edges of the track as they cheered on their favorite athletes.

GL signed up for the footrace, the pole vault, and his specialty—the long jump. Most of his opponents were prospectors who were working the surrounding creeks, young guys in their physical prime. But they were no match for the multisport college athlete. GL earned $155 in prize money on his first day in Alaska, more than enough to pay for his fare. As he launched through the air like a spinner dolphin, Nellie was watching. Feeling flush from this auspicious start, he stayed and found a job at a mine outside town.

Meanwhile, Nellie was busy in town as summer hardened into winter. When she wasn't teaching, she played hockey on the river and organized games for the city basketball league. On Sundays, she traveled to the outlying mining camps to sing and play piano at her father's services. She often stayed to mingle at the ice cream socials that followed. There were plenty of single miners eager for a conversation or a dance. Nellie was a rare catch in those days, a college-educated woman who also loved sports, and GL knew it. Though he worked ten miles away, every week he would run into town to see her, showing up at her parents' doorstep covered in snow.

The miles paid off. GL and Nellie got married in Portland on November 6, 1909. After a honeymoon in Colorado, they headed back to Alaska shortly after the New Year. While the distance between them had finally closed, the greatest test still lay ahead. The journey back to Fairbanks was no easy feat—in fact, most couples would never have survived it. Puget Sound was calm and glassy as they boarded the steamship in Seattle, but the air got colder and the waters rougher as they cruised north into the Gulf of Alaska. The scenery was so splendid it was hard to believe—glaciers decorating the valleys like sapphire earrings, waterfalls pouring off rocky cliffs and splashing into the sea. They passed old shipwrecks littering the channels and Alaska Native camps dotting the shore, inhaled the salty ocean breeze as they stood on the deck, snapping pictures with their new Kodak and talking about the future.

After days on the open sea, their boat slid past icebergs the size of barns and pulled into the dark waters of Prince William Sound. The town of Valdez sits there, at the head of a deep fjord carved by glaciers. It's the Alaska that dreams are made of, with steep snow-tipped summits rising out of the blue bay, lush rainforest crawling down to the coast, and huge tidal glaciers calving into the ocean. Sitting next to the storm factory that is the Gulf of Alaska, Valdez is as wet as Fairbanks is cold, receiving more snow than any other coastal community in North America.

It was almost like the town itself had blown in with a snowstorm. Before the gold rush, there was very little on the shore except black bears and a lot of kelp. Valdez was traditionally a trading spot, a point where Athabascans from the Copper River had met up with the coastal Chugach people to exchange copper, jade, furs, and other essentials. But they didn't need a lot of infrastructure to do it. Now it had exploded into a port town, with shops and inns, bowling alleys and breweries, cropping up at the toe of the mountains. It was the gateway to the new gold strike, the only way to Fairbanks on American soil. Steamships arrived daily, disgorging starry-eyed prospectors onto the rocky beach. Most knew nothing about gold mining or cold weather, or even about the outdoors in general. But that certainly didn't stop them. They flooded the little town, buying maps and tools and food to prepare their outfit for the final push to Fairbanks.

As GL and Nellie shopped for last-minute supplies, they were careful to avoid the scams that seemed to lurk on every street corner. Miners weren't the only ones who were drawn to the gold rush. Businessmen could smell the opportunity as well. They came en masse to feed on the frenzy, selling boots and rifles and gold-finding gadgets, alcohol and jewelry and entertainment. The vast majority of prospectors were single young men, strong in build but often lacking in worldliness. As they poured into Valdez and the other boomtowns, they made an easy target for seasoned salesmen, who quickly learned they could make more money "mining the miners" than actually digging for gold.

One merchant named Soapy Smith left quite a legacy as he flitted from one boomtown to the next in a cloud of shady businesses and cheap cons. In Skagway, for example, he opened a telegraph office and charged $5 per note. Stampeders eagerly forked over cash to send messages to their loved ones back home, unaware that there was actually no telegraph line within one hundred miles. To cover his tracks, Smith even forged fake replies from parents and wives. There wasn't much law enforcement in these towns, after all, which had pretty much materialized overnight. Justice, instead, was left to townspeople and vigilantes. As Smith's crimes mounted, the villagers grew wary, worried he was scaring away new business. When he showed up at a town hall to protest, the guard wasn't happy to see him carrying a shotgun, and the ensuing shootout left them both dead.

Valdez attracted the same gritty characters as Skagway, Juneau, and the other Klondike towns. Clutch's grandparents Nellie and George saw no reason to linger there. They had four hundred miles ahead of them, and the trip north needed to be made in winter, when the rivers and tundra were frozen thick enough to pass. They loaded their life's possessions onto a double-ender sled and hitched it to their new horse, Buck, a brown gelding with a white blaze running down his nose. Though slightly knock-kneed, Buck was good-natured and dependable. GL and

Nellie followed along by foot, strapping wooden snowshoes to their boots when the drifts became too deep.

The Valdez Trail had been built by the U.S. government just a couple years earlier because the only other access to Fairbanks—the Yukon River—was frozen most of the year. If people wanted to go to the end of the earth for gold, the government would at least pave the way. Army surveyors had scouted the country for the least treacherous path, following old trading routes and game trails whenever possible. But in the land of permanently frozen ground, or permafrost, there was no such thing as easy passage. Engineers knew that melting the ground would be a nightmare, turning the trail into a hopeless swamp. So they built "corduroy roads" over it, placing crisscrossed layers of logs over the permafrost to insulate it from the traffic above. The surface was topped with gravel, which had been steadily manufactured by the surrounding glaciers over thousands of years. While the single-lane wagon trail may have looked crude by today's standards, in 1910 it was an engineering marvel. Built before tractors, graders, or gravel crushers, it crossed two giant mountain ranges, threaded through six-hundred-foot canyons, and bridged raging glacial rivers. A four hundred-mile testament of the government's desire to settle an unruly land.

GL and Nellie followed the Lowe River out of Valdez. GL walked ahead, wearing a canvas overcoat with a fur ruff and leather boots that laced up to his calves. He guided Buck down the trail, making sure the sleigh stayed upright on steep drops, banked turns, and awkward side hills. In some places, the trail was nothing more than a chute blazing through walls of snow, barely wide enough for the sled to slip through. Nellie followed behind, bundled in a beaver hat and a fur coat that fell to her ankles. She walked most of the way, occasionally sitting on the sled when she needed to rest, perched on a bale of hay.

Their very first obstacle was the Chugach Range, a chain of rugged mountains towering over Valdez, holding over a hundred glaciers in its folds. The sun vanished as they entered Keystone Canyon, where a river had blasted a hole through a mountain of slate. The walls of the canyon were nearly perpendicular. Nellie looked up at torrents of ice plunging

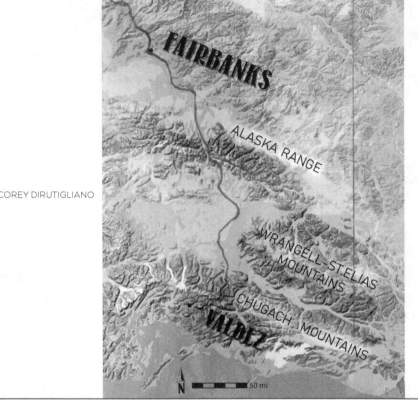

MAP BY COREY DIRUTIGLIANO

hundreds of feet off of cliffs, frozen in motion. She had seen waterfalls in the Cascades before, but not like this. The stunning sculptures of ice were as sharp as daggers in some places, as smooth as marble in others, the same exquisite blue as the windows in her father's church.

From there, the wagon trail climbed into the mountains, young peaks pricking the sky like shards of glass. At times there were so many travelers waiting to cross that an assembly line formed at the bottom, but it was relatively clear on the day GL and Nellie approached, making the mountain loom even taller. Even Buck was nervous as they traced a steep ridge up to the summit. Thompson Pass was a small gap in the Chugach

Range, the lowest point to sneak across the mountains. But it was still incredibly exposed. The weather changed fast. It could snow five feet in a single day, and avalanches came out of nowhere, as if hurled down from the heavens above. Even sunny days were dangerous, as the reflection off the brilliant snow could leave a person's corneas burning for days. The wind kicked up as they crossed the pass, blowing snow in sheets and swirls, transforming it into a million tiny daggers. GL huddled into his coat and wrapped the reigns around his forearm, trying to keep their whole outfit from blowing off the trail.

Many years later, Clutch's grandfather told him about a prospector from Seattle who was traveling on the trail around the same time, responding to an ad for miners in the Seattle Times. As he crossed Thompson Pass, an avalanche broke loose and flushed his horse down the mountain in a wave of powder the consistency of wet cement.

"Buried 'em up to his nostrils," Clutch said. "They dug it out and dragged it back up to the trail."

GL and Nellie passed other eclectic travelers on their way to Fairbanks, dog sleds loaded with mining equipment, horse-drawn bobsleds, and luxury carriages complete with foot warmers for the first-class passengers. They saw the full gamut of weather conditions, too, from blizzards that whipped off the ground like evil spirits to blue sky and bone-chilling cold. There was no alternative, after all. There was no train to Fairbanks yet, and the first ships wouldn't be leaving for months, when all the good ground was likely to be staked. After walking through twenty miles of snow and wind, GL and Nellie would stumble into the next roadhouse, exhausted, to catch a few hours of rest. Sometimes they found a cozy inn with hot roasts and fresh vegetables, other times a canvas lean-to that barely blocked the winter wind. The Valdez Trail was not for the faint of heart. Clutch's grandparents made the trip before the road was crowned, ditched, or drained, plowing ahead where many had turned back. Within ten years, the automobile had taken over, turning the route into a scenic highway.

The landscape softened as they crossed the Alaska Range and approached Fairbanks, "the Golden Heart City." But the greatest challenge still lay ahead. Now the search for gold would begin.

GL & Nellie on board the steamship traveling from Seattle to Alaska in 1910. PHOTO FROM LOUNSBURY FAMILY COLLECTION.

The mayor spoke and snapped my attention back to the present. After sitting through the City Council meeting the past three hours, it was finally time for a vote: the part I had really come for. Would they authorize funding for a new bridge? The city engineer had made his case—Barnette Street would provide another path across the river and ease congestion on the main street. But it would also add several hundred thousand dollars to an already-strained budget, which relied on a small and stingy tax base to keep the city running.

After covering city government the past six months, occasionally struggling to stay awake in a drone of speed bumps and zoning debates, I realized how much I actually took for granted. Here I was, less than two hundred miles from the Arctic Circle, living with almost every luxury my brother enjoyed in Manhattan. Roads, power, water, sewer. The Internet might be a little slow sometimes, but it was amazing it even reached this far. I thought about how long it would have taken Nellie

GL & Nellie begin the ascent of Thompson Pass on the Valdez Trail, one of the most difficult sections of the 400-mile hike to Fairbanks.
PHOTO FROM LOUNSBURY FAMILY COLLECTION

to send a letter in her day, to assure her mother she'd made it safely to Alaska.

As I had learned Clutch's family history, I realized what I owed to the pioneers. They weren't the first ones here, no doubt, and their arrival must have been extremely disruptive. But they had built a community in one of the harshest lands on earth. They came chasing opportunity, and they weren't scared off by the punishing winters or ungodly mosquitoes. At first, they knew nothing about how to live in the Far North, but they made mistakes and learned—figuring out how to thrive in this country, and paving the way for others to follow. As the rest of the nation modernized and left rustic life behind, Alaska had continued to attract the oddballs who didn't mind cold snaps, outhouses, or fending for themselves. The type of culture that still draws people today.

While I remained conflicted about resource development, I had to admit that none of these things would be here if it weren't for the miners. And the yellow metal that brought them here.

3
Frozen Gold

The biggest nugget Clutch ever found was about the size of his fingernail.

"It's not very big but it's kinda cute," he said, holding up his thumb in the dim light.

It went missing for five years, back in the eighties, then showed up in his shaving kit one day.

"My wife has never seen me without a beard. That'd be the last place I'd look for my nugget."

Clutch chuckled as he stroked the white fuzz that enveloped his face.

Beside us, the coal stove chugged away, filling the bar with a black haze. The thermometer hadn't budged from minus forty since yesterday, and after two days stuck inside, cabin fever had set in with a fury. So I had turned off Netflix, put on every layer I owned, and walked down to the Golden Eagle for some Sunday entertainment.

Clutch came over to say hello when I entered in a cloud of steam. "Got a good story from my brother yesterday," he said, as if we were in the middle of a conversation. "He was sittin on the couch one day when my dad came outta the drift with his head torch still on. Caught the whole laundry line on fire."

He broke into laughter that shook half his body. Picturing a clothes-line of flaming underwear, I couldn't help but join in. I ordered a mystery beer and took the stool beside him, feeling the coziness of the bar thaw me—the sounds, the smells, the neighbors who had become friends. In the back corner, Lorna was on the fiddle, her bow dancing over the strings. Against the other wall, my boyfriend Josh flipped a burger at the Do-It-Yourself grill. We had met at a soccer tournament over the summer and started dating soon after. It seemed like a long shot at first—an east coast girl who could barely chop wood and a wildland firefighter from Alaska. Josh's parents had moved to Fairbanks during the oil boom of the 1970s. He grew up in a dry cabin outside of town, and was a typical do-it-all Alaskan. We both liked soccer, skiing, and hanging out at the Golden Eagle. So far, it had gone pretty well.

While Josh tended the grill, Clutch and I chatted at the bar. I was happy he had come tonight, because I had some rather pressing questions. I'd been assigned to write a story about Pebble Mine, a massive gold and copper mine planned for southwest Alaska. It was going to be the largest open-pit mine in the world, twenty square miles and nearly as deep as the Grand Canyon. To thicken the plot, it would be built right next to Bristol Bay—the largest red salmon fishery in the world, and basically the crown jewel in Alaska. It was the type of project that riled everyone up—fishermen and environmentalists as well as miners and geologists. The kind that made my hackles rise, stretching my journalistic objectivity to its elastic limit. Before diving into the controversy, though, I wanted to get a miner's point of view.

"So Pebble Mine is a big deal. You think it'll happen?" I asked Clutch. His eyes lit up.

"Oh, it'd be a boon for the state of Alaska. More jobs, more income. Almost no industry down in those parts."

It was true. Southwest Alaska was the poorest region of the state. In many of the villages, there were very few jobs or services to speak of, almost no economy in the modern sense. I had seen it firsthand, had visited communities where residents drank water from the same rivers where they dumped buckets of raw sewage. The one thing they did have was wild salmon, which had supported the Native people for thousands of years. The mine would carve right through streams and wetlands where thirty million fish came to spawn every summer. And now $300 billion worth of gold and copper had been discovered right beneath them. The fishermen were desperate, crying out for help and suing the federal government to try to block the mine. Native communities had joined forces with sportsmen and national conservation groups, re-drawing the typical lines on the battlefield. It was democracy in action, and it seemed to be working, at least for the moment. The EPA had pushed the pause button until it could determine how the mine would impact the fishery. On the other side, miners were frustrated.

"The government, the BLM is kowtowing to these Sierra Club people, they're settin the rules for miners," Clutch said, falling back on an argument as comfortable and worn as our wooden stools. "They were stringent before and they're gettin worse yet."

I nodded along, but pressed on.

"But what if there's a spill?"

I hated to give the classic environmentalist reaction, screeching panic in the face of any kind of development. But it was a valid question. In one of my journalism classes, we had learned about the two hundred abandoned mines scattered around Colorado, leaking toxic lead and zinc into some of the same waters I had paddled through. Some of my favorite ski towns had been fighting acid mine drainage for more than a century.

It was also nothing new for people in the North. Just recently, a dam had burst at a massive gold and copper mine in British Columbia, spewing millions of cubic meters of toxic waste into the watershed. Lakes turned green and salmon streams glistened with slime as the mining company assured locals that everything was fine.

Clutch clinked the ice cubes around in his glass, as if swirling away my worries.

"Oh, technology is so good these days. With those cut and fill techniques, the fish will never even know they're there."

It was the type of response I'd expected. Minerals first, environment later. But then, Clutch saw the world through gold-tinted glasses, came from two generations of miners who had seen regulations erode their industry like the Tanana River had eaten away at its banks. Minerals are what brought his grandparents here, and all the other pioneers as well.

If I really listened, he wasn't saying that he didn't care about the environment, or the fish, or the Native people. Just that the door swung both ways. The mine was a risk, sure, but so was not building it, depriving a poor region of needed jobs, putting handcuffs on a resource-based state.

He didn't see regulation as just annoying, but harmful.

The question tumbled around my mind like a loose rock, searching for a smooth place to rest.

Man, I thought, as Josh walked over with two paper plates. This was a heavy topic for burger night at the Golden Eagle.

"Dinner is served." Josh set a burger down in front of me topped with lettuce and tomato and a generous blend of condiments.

"Ooooh, thank you." I spun my stool to square up to it.

As Clutch returned to his washtub, I took a lavish bite. Mmm, Josh had even caramelized the onion. But as I savored my food, I couldn't keep my thoughts from the salmon.

Pebble Mine was a battle between food and minerals, at least in my eyes. I had come to Alaska with certain values, believing some things were worth more than money, that we only had one planet and we should protect every bit of it, at any cost. In twenty-six years, I hadn't questioned those ideas. Now, barely six months into living here, I was already starting to feel challenged. Maybe it was easier to be an environmentalist when you lived on the east coast or in a solar-powered city like Boulder, but it was different in Alaska, where resources directly translated into jobs and tax revenues, and our very ability to live up here. Where the regulations cooked up by committees thousands of miles away were actually felt. Was I one of those out-of-touch liberals whom people like Clutch despised—more sympathetic to birds and fish than actual human beings?

I thought about my upcoming newspaper article, about how to frame the issues fairly and yet say something decisive. I clearly had a different worldview than Clutch, but it bothered me that there was such a gap between us. Was regulation more harmful than I realized? Where had these rules come from in the first place, and who were they really protecting?

———————

Those rules certainly didn't exist when Clutch's grandparents arrived in Fairbanks a hundred years ago, towing a sleigh full of mining equipment. Regulations were no way to settle a frontier, and that's what the government was trying to do. As GL and Nellie walked through the wide gates of the Tanana Valley and followed the Chena River north, it was clear they were getting close to gold country. They passed streams that had been turned inside out, and gravel piles that reached taller than any building they'd seen in Alaska. There were no crews restoring the banks or cleaning up debris, no officials running around with orange vests or clipboards. The only limit on where you could go was the miner on the creek beside you.

GL and Nellie staked some land north of town in the mining outpost of Fox. Compared to the soaring mountains and sparkling glaciers they'd been traveling through for the past month, the Tanana Valley was more subdued: lazy rivers flowing through green domes, ridges thick with spruce trees. They set up a canvas wall tent on Engineer Creek while they built their log cabin, harvesting a few dozen trees from the ocean of white spruce surrounding them.

They were in the heart of gold country, just a few valleys over from the creek that gave birth to Fairbanks. When an Italian immigrant named Felix Pedro plucked a nugget from the gravel in 1902, it set off a stampede from around the world.

Hundreds of miles from the nearest coast, Fairbanks is walled by mountains on three sides. Getting here was no easy trip—but gold has a powerful draw, and people came from every direction, from the streets of New York City, the mountains of Japan, and the olive orchards of the Mediterranean. Gold fever didn't discriminate, sweeping up doctors and lawyers as well as blacksmiths and bankers. They left behind farms, families, and predictable futures to take their chances in Alaska, just the latest in a series of gold strikes that rippled through the nation at the turn of the twentieth century, remaking the culture and economy of America forever.

It was a desperate time in the States, after all. The nation was still reeling from the Panic of 1893, caused by overbuilding and speculation on railroads. When the bubble burst, Americans everywhere flooded the banks to withdraw cash, creating a credit crunch that wiped out hundreds of banks and thousands of businesses. Unemployment soared to forty percent in parts of the country, and soup kitchens scrambled to feed all the hungry mouths. It was the worst depression the United States had ever seen, and it was fuel for a furious gold rush to the end of the earth.

When the ice melted, GL rolled up his trousers and waded into water that was just barely above freezing. Using what was essentially a large metal pie dish, he scooped gravel from the bottom and swished it around the gold pan, looking for "colors" that might change the course of his life. The technical term was placer gold (pronounced plah-sir), the little grains of gold that are flushed out of the mountains and captured down in the drainages.

Though gold originates in bodies of ore like the one behind Clutch's cabin, over time it's slowly liberated by rain, wind, and flooding. Slow and insidious, these natural forces work away at the rock, breaking it into tiny pieces of gold and sediment and carrying them down into creek bottoms, where they settle in the gravel. Gradually, at the leisurely pace of geologic time, these creeks fill in with dirt, burying streaks of gold-bearing gravel under layers of soil and vegetation. Prospectors called these "pay streaks," and to get to them, they dug vertical holes down to bedrock and ran horizontal "drifts" outward, following the pay wherever it led. These underground mazes were called drift mines, and they were scattered up and down the creeks of Alaska like the budding Subway system of New York.

GL got a job at a drift mine in Fox, a dusty creek bed dotted with enormous gravel piles. While the early prospectors had to dig by hand, new technology was expediting the process, making life a little easier for guys in the mines. Using a steam-powered shovel, they punched a hole in the ground the size of an elevator shaft, clawing away at the frozen soils until they hit bedrock. It was important to do this in the winter, when the ground was colder and less likely to collapse. Dozens of feet down, sometimes more, is where the elbow grease took over. Men hacked at the walls with picks and pushed loads of gravel through dark passage-ways like sweaty super-powered voles. The average worker walked ten miles per shift behind the wobbly arms of a wheelbarrow.

GL had one of the enviable jobs, stationed above ground. He was the hoist engineer, in charge of scooping gravel out of the mine with a large bucket and arranging it on the surface. It was a skilled job, requiring a keen eye and a gentle hand, and paid better than the average under-ground grunt. He used a windlass, the same technology used to get water from a well: a large ore bucket attached to a cable ran up and down the shaft, rotated by a steam-powered winch. When it reached the top of the gin pole, which stood above the shaft like a telephone pole, it triggered a carrier mechanism and dumped its load. The roar of falling rocks could be heard several valleys over.

Up and down, day and night, GL kept the bucket running smoothly from the control booth. He was also in charge of power, which meant every hour or so he had to stop what he was doing and go stuff rounds of firewood into a giant locomotive boiler that looked like it had been pulled off the front of a train. It burned hot and fast, converting massive amounts of wood into steam to turn the hoist and flip the bucket, all in the pursuit of gold.

As GL moved gravel, he had to keep an eye on a bunch of other details too, the many minute actions that had life or death consequences—making sure the bucket didn't get overloaded, the boiler didn't overheat, or that he didn't wander into one of the open shafts scattered around the creek bed. Drift mining was a dangerous profession. These were the days before labor unions, before safety meetings or workplace inspections. If you had the poor fortune of getting hurt on the job, it only meant you wouldn't get paid the next day. Prospectors tried to minimize the risk, but it was always there, lurking in the tunnel like invisible dust. Chunks of ceiling could thaw and crumble without warning. Every strike of the pick could release a deadly rush of groundwater. Accidents were part of life, and men were killed in falls, cave-ins, and fires. Some corpses never made it out of the tunnels. It was a lot of risk for such a low return. The average worker could only move a hundred wheelbarrow loads of gravel a day, and it was hard to make money at such a low volume.

They spent the whole winter stockpiling pay dirt, the cold soils they hoped would contain enough gold to turn a profit, or at least pay off their creditors. These piles of dirt sat all over Fairbanks, like ant hills the size of four-story buildings. "They were called 'winter dumps.' You didn't know what you were gonna get 'til spring. There was no guarantee," Clutch said.

In May, when the snow melted and water came pouring off the hills, GL's crew harnessed the hydropower. They dammed up the creeks and carved the earth into a water park, building an elaborate system of ditches, chutes, and flumes to channel the flow toward their dumps. When they lifted the gate of the dam, water gushed out like a flash flood, pushing gravel into long sloping sluice boxes. These metal cages were designed to simulate a real stream, creating eddies in the water that allowed heavier particles to settle out in the bottom of the tray. That's where the nuggets and flakes washed up, lodged in the bristly black turf, like jewels in the bath drain—the cold, hard fruits of an entire winter's worth of labor.

The rest of the gravel they were less concerned with. All the extra rocks and sediment ran back into the streams, back into the rivers, changing the ecology of the whole watershed. It wasn't a big deal at first, when prospectors dug their holes by hand, shoveling just a few cubic yards per day. But as more miners showed up, they brought the latest technology and gadgets with them. Rather than melting the permafrost one fire at a time, soon they were driving hundred-foot-long steel pipes into the earth and pumping steam through them, thawing football fields worth of ground every few weeks. Five-gallon buckets turned into five-yard hoppers, wooden-handled shovels were replaced with hydraulic canons. The dumps grew bigger and bigger.

Sluicing these huge stacks of paydirt washed an enormous amount of gravel into the rivers, muddying up the water and killing fish and plants downstream. The forests took a hit too, as miners harvested wood for their boilers until there were no trees left, until the hills stood naked and the wind whistled through the valleys. All these workers needed to eat, too. They shot moose, sheep, caribou, and smaller critters, putting pressure on some areas and hunting out others.

This wasn't so great for the Indigenous people who depended on those fish and game populations to survive. But the economy was booming. By 1910, more than thirty million dollars' worth of gold had been gathered from the creeks around Fairbanks. Some men were made into millionaires, upgrading equipment and flipping claims as they siphoned Alaska's riches into the world market. But there were many others who never saw a hint of the wealth they'd dreamed of. After a year or two of trying, most stampeders gave up and headed home, with nothing but a pill box full of gold flakes and some shiny memories.

GL and Nellie never struck it rich in Alaska—not in gold, at least. But they hunted sheep, ran dogs, and fished the gravel bars of the Tanana River. Their first son, Lloyd, was born on Engineer Creek in 1910. In January, when the days had shrunk to the length of a football game and the average temperature hovered around twenty-below, Nellie sent a postcard to her in-laws reporting, "It's a pleasure to be in Alaska at present. The weather is so fine."

———————————

I washed down the last bite of my burger with a sip of mystery beer, so full I could barely move. Clutch reappeared to pay his tab. The jam session was wrapping up, and Josh had been sucked into a game of pool.

"I wanna show you something," Clutch said.

I plopped off my stool and followed him to the front of the bar, by the door. He pointed to a black and white photograph on the wall, edges slightly crinkled, of a group of women playing hockey on the Chena River.

"That's Nellie, right there in the middle."

"Wow." I leaned in close to study this woman who lived a century before me, yet almost felt like a friend. In the photo, Clutch's grandmother was about my same age, dressed in a long tailored wool coat, a white bell-shaped cap, and ice skates. Though wrapped in the fashion of her time, I could tell she was a modern woman. A teacher, hunter, musician, and mother, she had traversed Alaska in the dead of winter and built a home in the wilderness. Behind her, Front Street was lined with cafes, hotels, and saloons, with horse-drawn carriages plodding along wide dirt roads, the rough mining camp that had blossomed into a city.

Ever since learning about the Gold Rush, I'd had my doubts about the pioneers. They had raced north to get rich, taking over a land and culture that wasn't their own—the settlement story heard around the world, since the first Europeans set sail to the west. They had filtered into every major river valley of Alaska, staking claims and building cabins on lands where native people had hunted and fished for thousands of years. It was the frontier, after all—wide open for the taking, with the full blessing of the U.S. government. While Alaska was huge, it was a tough place to live, a place where every scrap of food and firewood counted. Mining touched the water, the trees, the plants and animals—virtually every element of the natural world. The scars were still visible today right outside my backdoor.

As technology enabled us to suck gold from the ground at ever greater scales, the environment always seemed to take a backseat. Horrible things happened before protections were put in place, before we realized we couldn't exploit the land forever and still expect it to provide. The gold rush had taught a hard lesson, one I wish we didn't have to learn again and again: while booms may seem like free money, we pay for them eventually.

I thought about Pebble Mine, about the prospect of digging a massive pit at the headwaters of Alaska's prize fishery. Counting on an earthen dam to protect the world's greatest run of wild salmon. Some things were too precious to measure in ounces or dollars. No matter how many jobs it created, as Clutch said, I just couldn't swallow the risk.

I looked at Nellie, seeking for some answers on her flushed face. What would she have thought about Pebble Mine? And what about her husband, GL? After working so hard with his pan and bucket, how would it feel to stand on the rim of a man-made crater, watching dump trucks running up and down the spiraling roads like Tonka toys? I would never get to ask them.

Back in 1910 the young couple had their own bigger problems. Fairbanks was about to be rocked by a scandal that would threaten everything Clutch's grandparents had worked for, that would send the gold miners fleeing from their holes and scurrying back to the towns they came from.

Though if that unfortunate incident hadn't happened, I may never have made it to Fairbanks, may never have known Clutch at all.

4
Going Home

When I opened the front door, I was momentarily blinded. The sun reflected off the white snow like a laser, stopping me in my tracks. Blinking slowly to let my eyes adjust, I heard Josh's voice from the yard.

"You coming?"

When Josh came into focus, he was putting on his cross country skis. I stepped off the porch and dropped my own skis on the snow next to his. Long and ridiculously skinny, they looked more like matchsticks than the fat downhill skis I was used to.

Josh tilted his head up and closed his eyes in a moment of sun worship. His face was starting to tan up, making his eyes look extra green.

It was spring in Fairbanks—a force strong enough to eviscerate the snowpack, draw geese from across the earth, and send the whole community into a state of euphoria I had never quite seen before. The town was plastered in smiles—inexplicable, gratuitous smiles where you would typically see blank stares—standing in line at the post office, for example, or waiting at traffic lights. Even though the world outside was still frozen, people walked around the supermarket in flip flops and boardshorts splashed with Hawaiian flowers. It was like the whole town was in a giddy stupor, drunk on the energy of the sun. Spring is always cause for celebration, even in lower latitudes (Pennsylvania built an entire holiday around a groundhog, after all). But this was something different. It was delirious, infectious, almost magical.

It had been a long winter, for sure. I had felt the hard slap of forty below, had frost-nipped my nose and almost destroyed my car in a single moment of stupidity. I knew I shouldn't have cold-started it after letting it sit for so long. That's what the mechanic warned me when I had taken it to get winterized, which entailed adding an oil pan heater, a battery blanket, and a trickle charger under the hood. When I picked it up, there was a cute little three-prong plug hanging out of the grill, matching every other car in town.

"Technically you should plug in at zero," he told me, in the patient voice of a kindergarten teacher. "But definitely minus-twenty or colder."

Apparently that's when batteries lose their charge and motor oil starts to turn to gravy. I'd followed his advice diligently, always looking for a head bolt heater when I went to school board meetings, the gym, or the grocery store. But when I got back to town after Christmas vacation and went to pick up my car up at the newspaper, someone had unplugged it and moved it behind the building, far away from any outlet. I could have tracked down an extension cord and plugged it in for an hour, I suppose, but it was late, and cold, and I really wanted to get home. I let out a big sigh of relief when it started right up, and another one when I pulled into my driveway. No harm, no foul. But what I didn't know at the time was that turning the ignition had caused cold, gloopy oil to start pushing the seals from the cylinder. I wouldn't find out until a couple months later, when the seals had finally wriggled their way out and oil had gushed through the holes, nearly draining my oil pan. Luckily, I made it to the shop before my engine seized up, but it was a sobering reminder to always plug in that I would not soon forget.

The hard lessons and close calls had certainly been educational. I felt humble, less naive. Smarter.

After a long winter, this was our reward.

March was a gift that came wrapped in soft snow and sunshine, with temperatures that might even break freezing some days. In Alaska, March wasn't just a lunar cycle, a page on the calendar with four weekends to play with. It was more like a festival, like the last day of school when you get to play Capture the Flag all day instead of sitting in class, dreaming of summer. March was a month made for ice fishing, winter camping, and long-distance sled dog races. The elusive sweet spot when all my favorite ingredients lined up: snow, sun, and the beautiful playground of Alaska.

We were gaining seven minutes of light each day, fifty minutes a week, meaning I could actually see out the window as I sipped my morning coffee or go skiing after work without a headlamp. It created a strange feeling that time was infinite, that a world of possibilities lay out before us.

Josh and I skied to the top of the driveway, turned right and shuffled about a hundred yards uphill to the big S curve, where the trail dove off the edge of the road. We called it "the wall," a short but nearly vertical hill that led us to the main trail system.

"Your turn, I went first last time," I said, poking Josh with my ski pole.

He lined up so his skis were hanging over the edge and dropped in. The hill wasn't big, but steep enough to be exciting on skinny skis with no edges. A tad rough too. Before I could drop in behind him, his ski caught a branch and plunged him headfirst into the snow.

"Oof." When Josh raised his head, his hat and sandy goatee were covered in white fluff, but he was laughing. Whew, I thought, trying to hide my own amusement as I sidestepped down after him.

"It's soft, at least," I said, extending a mittened hand. A storm had come through a couple days earlier and dropped six inches of powder on the trails. Then it had cleared up and dipped to a pleasant twenty degrees.

When Josh had untangled himself, we skied down alongside the power line and turned left into the forest. The tall aspen trees extended their beautiful lady fingers, each twig frosted in snow. This was my favorite trail in Fairbanks. Weaving like silly string up, down, and around Ester Dome, the trail was originally established during the gold rush days to haul equipment to the drift mines scattered around the hillside. We skied past an old wooden hoist slumped under the snow, and I tried to picture George Lounsbury unwinding cable from the wheel.

As I glided along, listening to the soft rise and fall of my skis on the trail, my mind drifted to the future. My first year in Alaska was almost up. According to the original plan, it was time to go back to the real world—to get serious about a career and settle down closer to my family. Not "east coast" serious, though—even my mom had accepted the fact that I would probably never come back to Pennsylvania. I was too addicted to the mountains. But we were trying to find a compromise, and all arrows seemed to point back to the large sunny state of Colorado. Perfect weather, lots of snow, and just a quick flight from Philadelphia: an all-around easy place to live.

Alaska, on the other hand, was the opposite of easy. Cold, dark, and isolated for much of the time. Far away from family and friends. In just one year, I had missed weddings, baby showers, and graduations of people I cared about. I had missed opportunities that would have propelled my career—Alaska wasn't exactly the nerve center of the mainstream media. In spite of that, I was really happy. There were no sleepless nights questioning my path in life. No anxiety over money or status. I went to bed tired, watching snow fall outside the window, thankful for the blankets and logs and, yes, even the oil boiler that were keeping me warm. The wisdom of my parents and mentors had truly sunk in—it was the simple things that mattered. My life here revolved around food, shelter, friends, and fresh air. And it was full.

I looked to the south, where the ragged edge of the Alaska Range peeked through the tall spindly aspen trees. There was nothing between us but a hundred miles of mystery. Could I really leave when there was so much left to see?

A hundred years earlier, GL and Nellie were likely feeling the same way. They had a nice home on Engineer Creek, and had just started a family. Living in Alaska required a lot of work, but it was work they truly enjoyed. They talked of moving into town one day, and had even started saving for land.

Their nest egg was tucked away at one of the main institutions— the Washington-Alaska Bank, owned by E.T. Barnette, the father of Fairbanks. As gold dust flowed in from the creeks around town, the two-story building on First Avenue advertised attractive interest rates, encouraging miners to sock away their newfound wealth and watch it grow.

In 1911, just a few days into the new year, the bank shut its doors with no explanation. As GL and Nellie panicked about their savings, along with all their account-holding neighbors, they learned Barnette had fled town overnight with his pockets full of cash. He was arrested in California for embezzlement and hauled back to Alaska for trial. Needless to say, the miners wanted his head on a stake, and GL traveled into Fairbanks with several others to hear the verdict. When Barnette was acquitted on all charges, the town went wild, raging from the court-house to the streets of downtown to burn effigies of the judge. The bank's customers had lost over $20 million in today's dollars.

With no path to justice, GL took what was left of their savings and booked fares on the next ship south. With three-year-old Lloyd in tow, he and Nellie moved back to the family farm in Iowa and had two more boys. Lloyd and his brothers grew up in America's breadbasket. It was a sharp contrast from the frozen tundra, with fields stretching in every direction in wavy green carpets of corn. There was no hustle to scratch paydirt from the ground in the winter, no thrill of sluicing the dump in the spring. It was a quiet life, with a steady stream of chores throughout the seasons, focused not on extracting earth but on cultivating it. The climate was an adjustment too. You could dress for the cold, but there was no escaping the sticky heat that covered the fields like a wool blanket. During the summer harvest, Nellie brought out pitchers of ice water as Lloyd and his brothers picked corn under the sweltering sun.

By the time he was a teenager, Lloyd Lounsbury had square features and a boxy frame. He was the classic Iowa farm boy in many regards, doing farm chores in the morning and going to football practice after school. But he also had an itch that the Midwest just couldn't seem to scratch, one that transcended the rolling hills and hay fields of rural Iowa. Maybe it came from spending the first three years of his life on Engineer Creek, or from his parents' endless stories of Alaska. As he oiled the tractor and fed the horses, he imagined a totally different kind of life.

Like his father, Lloyd's athletic ability opened new doors. After gradu-ating from high school, he joined the football team at Iowa State, scoring a starting spot his freshman year. But by the time football season rolled around the next year, the Great Depression had descended like a plague of locusts. As stock prices tumbled toward an unknowable bottom, Lloyd and his classmates watched their hopes and dreams shrivel up like last year's stalks. Football suddenly seemed like a distant worry as homes, farms, and life savings collapsed at their feet. Seeing no future for himself in Iowa, Lloyd again felt his eyes drifting north. So he borrowed $50 from his parents and decided to try his luck in Alaska. Walking off the farm in his Big "I" sweater, carrying nothing but a backpack and a bedroll, the young lineman hitchhiked across the country, jumped on a boat in Seattle, and made his way back to his birthplace.

While bread lines formed in the rest of the country, Alaska's economy was going strong, thanks to the vast reservoir of yellow metal still lurking under its surface. In 1933, FDR raised the price of gold from $17 to $35 an ounce, in an effort to spark inflation and jumpstart the economy. Four thousand miles away, mining companies revved up production in Alaska. But the scene had changed in the sixteen years since Lloyd had left. When he got back to Fairbanks, there were no men tunneling through the ground or "winter dumps" dotting the landscape. Rather, it was hillsides being stripped away and giant machines thundering through the valleys.

By 1930, small-scale mining had dwindled, as much of the easily accessible placer deposits had dried up. But a second gold rush was in full swing—this one louder and dirtier. Gold dredges had moved in, breathing new life into the economy while completely transforming the environment. Large boats cruised through the valleys, devouring the ground with their long, prominent digging ladders. Owned by a major Boston conglomerate, the Fairbanks Exploration Company bought out all the little prospectors working the creeks and went after low-grade ground on a massive scale. They built power plants and pipelines, imported dredges the size of ocean liners from California and reassembled them in Alaska. The F.E. Company employed a third of the population of Fairbanks at its height and operated eight dredges across the Interior, churning up an area nearly the size of Iowa. But most of the gold was located at the foot of a large dome just outside Fairbanks.

Ester sat on a treasure that would have made King Tut jealous, where a nexus of streams and underground faults had created ground so rich that General Dwight Eisenhower came all the way from D.C. to see it for himself. Lloyd got a job drilling test holes in the ground to pinpoint the pay streak. With a strength honed from years of football and farming, he drilled through hundreds of feet of frozen gravel with a gas-powered drill. He had seen cold weather in Iowa, but nothing could have prepared him for this. When it hit sixty-two degrees below zero, he had to take breaks every thirty minutes to keep his fingers from freezing to the drill handle.

On his day off, Lloyd went to a skating party on the Chena River. A hockey game had formed below the bridge, but Lloyd barely noticed. Instead, he was paying attention to a pretty girl with a curly red bob skating around with her friend. Fay Jennings was seventeen years old. Fay's dad was the agent for the Alaska Railroad, and they lived in an apartment above the train depot.

After a pleasant chat on the ice, Lloyd was intrigued with the auburn-haired Alaskan. Like his mom, she was no girly girl. Fay grew up swimming in gravel pits and roaming the woods around town with her brother. One time they caught a black bear cub and kept it in their backyard as a pet. Though Fay had always been happier in a pair of Levi's than a dress, she had enough of a feminine streak to win first place in a high school beauty contest. The prize was a free airplane ride with Ed Young, a local bush pilot, sparking a love for flying that would last for years (she later became the first female to fly solo in the Interior).

After the party, Lloyd swung by the train depot to pay her a visit. As they chatted in the parlor, Fay barely noticed the disapproving glances cast in their direction. Her parents were hoping for a more distinguished suitor—a lawyer or a banker, perhaps—someone who didn't tunnel through the dirt for a living.

Lloyd, for his part, didn't want to run a drill forever. That's why he was taking classes at the Alaska Agricultural College and School of Mines, a new university that had been built on a high ridge west of Fairbanks. As he sat in class learning about the different types of ore, he was especially intrigued by hard rock mining. Unlike the placer mining GL had done, which goes after little particles of gold washed up in the creeks, hard rock mining targets the original source: the bodies of ore zigzagging through the mountains. These were called gold veins.

Lloyd was determined to get his hands on one. He had seen the power of gold, its ability to flip fortunes and make men into kings. He didn't expect to be the next Joe Juneau, but even a modest discovery would bring him some measure of security, and surely win over Fay's parents. He started helping out an older couple who was prospecting in Ester, coming out on the weekends to take samples of the creek bed. It was hard work, drilling cores from the rock and grinding them into a flour with mortar and pestle. When the old-timers announced their plans to retire, Lloyd considered his options. He wasn't ready to return to Iowa, and he had no desire to be a company man. Plus, the results of the acid tests looked promising. So he counted up his money and bought the claims in the tree-filled gulch on Eva Creek.

Eva Creek cut across the trail ahead of us, gurgling as it ran under a slab of ice, forcing itself downhill. The snow beside me was dented with the little triangles of ptarmigan feet. I could hear my breath as I kicked up the hill, trying to focus on my technique. I could also hear the words of my friend Anna, a former competitive skier at the University of Alaska: "Keep those toes, knees, and nose lined up." Cross country skiing was a graceful choreography of kicks and glides. Or at least, it could be. I hadn't quite mastered it yet. Before Alaska, my time on skis had mainly been focused on going down hills, fast. Steeps, moguls, trees—I loved everything about downhill skiing. Especially the gravity. Yet the slender strips of plastic under my feet now were designed not for dropping into powdery bowls or carving through tall pines but for cruising up and down the gentle hills of Fairbanks.

I would be lying if I said I didn't miss downhill skiing. After all, I had spent three years after college working as a hotel concierge in Vail just so I could ski every day. Being a ski bum was one of the best times of my life—a carefree blur of powder turns, margaritas, and chairlift banter that had forever sealed my love of the Rockies.

And now I had a chance to go back, and not just as a ski bum. I'd been scrolling through Facebook a few weeks ago when I saw the job posting for *High Country News*. The magazine was the bible for environmentalists in the west, covering oil, gas, fish and wildlife with incredible nuance and detail. I had read it religiously in grad school, had sat in the student lounge devouring stories about logging and fracking, about cowboys and miners and Native Americans, and all the conflicting interests that collided in the dusty foothills of the Rockies. It was the type of writing that had inspired me to go to school for environmental journalism in the first place.

And now they were hiring an online editor. Even more surprising, I was actually qualified. As a reporter at the *Fairbanks Daily News-Miner*, I had been living and breathing resources for the past year. I had interviewed oil executives, tribal chiefs, and senators, studied these issues from different angles, and worked on deadline every day for ten months straight. I checked all the boxes on the job description.

The Skype call had gone really well, and they wanted to fly me down for a final interview. Just me. As long as I didn't show up wearing a jacket with a giant BP logo on the chest, it seemed like it was in the bag.

The magazine was based in Paonia, a small town in western Colorado. According to Google Earth, it sat at the foot of an 11,000-foot peak, surrounded by peach orchards and vineyards. It was one of those dreamy climates where you could bike to work all winter and still go skiing up high. You didn't need fur hats or puffy pants or three extra heaters in your car engine just to stay alive. From all indications, it was the perfect next step. So what was I waiting for?

At the top of the hill, Josh stood next to a peeling white birch tree holding a bar of chocolate.

"Want some?"

I grabbed a chunk from his hand, dark chocolate with sea salt. It was cold and crunchy, incredibly satisfying.

In less than a year, Josh had figured out a surprising number of little tricks to keep me going. I hadn't planned to meet someone in Alaska—in fact, it kind of clashed with the plan. But since our very first date at the State Fair, I knew it was something special. Josh could do anything: cut down a hundred-foot tree, butcher a moose, fix a stove or a tire or a frozen ski binding. He even knew how to cook (caribou curry was his signature dish). He was quiet and steady, a contrast to my big bursts of energy, but always up for anything.

Except, that is, moving to Colorado. At least not right now. He was halfway through an engineering degree at the University of Alaska. After getting his first degree in natural resources, he'd worked as a firefighter for five years and then as an arborist for the local electric company. But he was ready to put down his chainsaw and do something different. With two years of classes left, he just wasn't in a position to leave Fairbanks. So taking my dream job in Colorado would mean a long distance relationship, at best. And I knew how those usually turned out.

Josh offered me the last bite of chocolate, then crumpled up the empty wrapper and stuffed it in his backpack. Another hill spooled out before us, this one long and curvy, tilted downhill, with angry-looking glare ice over Eva Creek.

"You're up," he said, tapping my leg with his pole.

I jumped up and down on my skis a couple times, trying to find my center of gravity. The fresh snow slowed me down at first, a welcome bit of inertia. Then I started picking up speed, going a little faster with every foot of elevation I lost.

"Open it up!" I heard from behind me.

I straightened out my skis and gripped my poles a little tighter, surrendering to gravity. I didn't know where this adventure was going, but I wasn't ready for it to be over.

Fay and Lloyd were happily in love, but not everyone was happy about it. Her parents had nothing against the young miner, but he was something of a wild card. They didn't know where was he going in life, or how it might affect their only daughter. Tough questions for any parents, especially ones who lived according to the strict timetables of the railroad. So it was with Fay's best interests at heart that they decided to send her to California to live with relatives. Surely the white sandy beaches and Pacific breeze would make her forget about her Fairbanks flame. And she did enjoy it. Living on the outskirts of Los Angeles, she enrolled at the University of Southern California. After class, she would stroll the Santa Monica pier and watch the sun drop into the ocean. But like many efforts to thwart young love, the scheme didn't work. In fact, it backfired. Lloyd's love letters had followed her move, and when he finished work in the fall he made his own way down to California, picked her up, and continued south. They got married on the Mexican border, far away from any objections.

After the honeymoon, they moved to a neighborhood outside L.A. Lloyd got a job at the Boeing aircraft factory, and they both continued flying lessons. California was new and exciting, with the chance to see movie stars walking on the street and eat oranges that tasted like sunshine. But people were also in large supply, fanning out from the Pacific coast to the mountains in a solid wave of civilization. As the state's economy grew, more people were moving there every day.

It was a far cry from the peaceful forest on Ester Dome. As Lloyd rode the bus home from the factory at night, he thought about the friendly chatter of the ravens. The trees swishing in the wind. Back in Fairbanks, Fay's parents missed their only daughter badly. Playing their trump card, they bought the newlyweds a brand-new car with a clear message: please come home.

In 1935, when winter was just starting to loosen its grip in Fairbanks, Fay and Lloyd packed up the town car and took Highway 1 north, past the pointy peaks of the Sierras and the Cascades. They boarded the ferry in Seattle, just like Lloyd's parents had done twenty years earlier, and set off into the blue horizon—toward her family and away from his, into the familiar and the unknown.

The ski trail dead-ended at an old dirt road. Off to the right, a brown house was banked into the hillside, a wisp of steam rising from the chimney. Behind it, spruce-covered ridges layered the horizon as far as the eye could see, backed by the ghostly silhouette of the Alaska Range. Clutch's white F-150 truck was parked in the driveway, next to Lorna's matching one.

"Should we stop and say hi?" I said.

Just two miles from my house, we had discovered Clutch and Lorna's was the perfect place to stop and warm up before turning around and skiing home. They didn't seem to mind being our makeshift ski lodge, always inviting us in for water or coffee, sometimes even rhubarb pie.

"Sure," Josh said.

We cut through the trees, sinking into the soft snow, and glided down the wide plowed driveway, the kind that's only possible if you have your own heavy equipment. I didn't even notice the bright yellow signs that had seemed so daunting on my first visit: Danger. Keep Out. Beware of Dog. The yard was speckled with tractors, loaders, generators, and other pieces of machinery that now looked so normal to me. Lorna's two mares, Dream and Princess, roamed freely among the horsepower. I unclicked my skis. Of all the things I loved about Colorado, I couldn't ski out the front door through a Disney-like forest to visit my neighborhood gold mine.

Clutch emerged from the garage in his trademark overalls, wiping his hands on a rag. He brightened up when he saw us, brimming with conversation topics like a freshly stocked vending machine. After commenting on the weather, he switched to one of his favorite subjects: hockey.

"You see the Nanooks game last night?" he asked Josh, a fellow hockey fan.

The University of Alaska Fairbanks had beaten Michigan State, claiming a spot in the NCAA playoffs. They talked hockey for a few minutes, catching up on goals and injuries and the latest alumni news, before Clutch led us into the garage to show us his new project.

Parked in one of the two bays was a red four-wheeler. At first it looked fairly standard, like the ones zipping all over Ester in the summer, except

I knew nothing in this garage was standard. I looked for something out of place, an after-market modification, and there it was—a blade attached to the front and a series of circular brushes under the frame.

"Wow," Josh said, leaning down to look under the carriage. "You made a Zamboni?"

Clutch rested a hand on the seat, looking pleased.

"Yep, got the cutting edge off a plow. Only thing I had to order were the electronic actuators to raise and lower it."

There were two 55-gallon drums on the back to resurface the ice and a towel on the underside to clear excess water off the rink.

Josh looked impressed.

"That sure beats the hell out of a hot mop," he said.

Tinkering with heavy equipment was one of Clutch's favorite past-times. He was pretty much born with a wrench in his hand, had started riding the Caterpillar with his dad when he was still in diapers and was rebuilding cars by high school. After he graduated, he got a job operating a coal shovel at a Healy mine and then fell into his full-time career—building roads all over Alaska for the Department of Transportation.

We walked back outside. In the corner of the yard was a rusty hunk of metal covered in snow.

"What's that?"

While my goal was to someday be able to identify the various pieces of machinery scattered around Clutch's property, I still had a long way to go.

"That's my dad's old compressor," Clutch said, brushing snow off the top with an ungloved hand. Steel guts hung out of a pig-shaped body, the words Ingersoll Rand welded on the side. "From '39. That's how he got into that hillside there." He nodded downvalley, past the horses and chickens and stand of spruce trees, where Lloyd's hard rock mine was located. Where a little red house sat in a clearing, with picture windows on every wall.

When Lloyd and Fay returned to Fairbanks, they started building this home on Eva Creek. But as they framed it up and closed it in, there was no way of knowing about the vein of quartz shooting right past the wall—the equivalent of a home office for a miner. After a bit more prospecting, Lloyd set a chisel in the rock and pounded it with a hammer, gouging out a hole about six inches deep. Liking what he saw, he made six more holes and loaded them up with sticks of dynamite, then went outside with Fay to watch the fireworks. But it wasn't until after the blast that Lloyd realized he'd forgotten to shut the back door of the house. By then the pressure of the explosion had blown out every window in their home.

Clutch looked down toward the cabin and chuckled as if he remembered the entire scene, even though it had happened before he was born.

"My mom was so mad she broke all the dishes," he said. "That's the only fight they ever had."

It took a while, but Lloyd eventually figured out a system for working the lode. Wearing blue overalls and a red hard hat, he blasted away at the walls, day after day.

"When my mom wanted to talk to him, she'd take a hammer and beat on the tracks and he'd show up in the living room," Clutch said.

After digging the first sixty feet by hand, Lloyd bought a diesel air compressor and a jackhammer, which saved a lot of time. Soon it started to feel normal living under the same roof as a gold mine. While Fay fixed up the house and planted flowers, Lloyd was hauling waste rock out of the tunnel in a hand-pushed cart. The ore he carried out in buckets that weighed as much as lead.

"Why did he stop mining it?" I asked.

After so much time and sweat, how could he give up on his own backyard creation? Clutch sighed. Like GL and Nellie, he said, it was due to forces beyond his control. And he didn't give it up easily. When Fay got pregnant with their first son, Lloyd continued chasing the vein. When he ran into an underground fault and the vein vanished in a puff of smoke, he kept searching for the other end. It wasn't until the War Department showed up in the late thirties and confiscated his equipment that Lloyd's hard rock adventure came to an end. Hitler was on the rise in Europe, sending terror through the rest of the world. The U.S. threw its entire weight behind World War II, building up its military and manufacturing muscle to support the Allied Powers. Fuel rations and blackouts went into effect around the nation, while the largest factories were commandeered to build weapons, tanks, and armor. Gold mining was designated "non-essential" to the war effort, and mines shut down around Alaska, as well as in the Lower 48. Lloyd's tractor was seized to build roads and runways. His dynamite was confiscated to make bombs. But unlike the automobile factories and power plants in the rest of the country, most mines in Alaska would never come back to life.

Five years later, peace had been restored. World War II had lifted the nation from the Great Depression, leading to a golden age for the economy: millions of new jobs, unprecedented consumer spending, and the birth of a novel middle class. As other nations attempted to rebuild, the dollar became the world's leading currency. But it wasn't so great for the gold industry. Inflation had taken hold as more cash flowed into the system, yet gold was stuck at $35 an ounce. And there it languished, for decades. At such a low value, mining eventually became uneconomical. Small-time mining shriveled up in Alaska, as dredges and draglines moved in to take its place—a classic story of corporations eating up the little guys. In 1971, President Nixon finally abandoned the gold standard. The next day gold prices soared to $120 an ounce.

Lloyd never restarted the mine on Eva Creek. He had carted $50,000 worth of gold past his living room in five years, sinking most of it back into the tunnel. Hard rock mining was not an easy way to make a living. He worked all alone, handling explosives and thousands of tons of ore. He spent all day underground without windows, heat, or fresh air. But it wasn't just about being a mole. You also had to be a geologist, a mechanic, and a businessman. To make a profit, Lloyd had to estimate how much gold he could recover per foot of excavation and what it would cost to process in his mill. Then decide if it was worth the trouble.

———————

Clutch leaned on the compressor, a last connection, perhaps, to his father. I thought about why Lloyd had come back to Alaska, why he had chosen this life. He had grown up on a farm, never knowing what the future would hold, his fate tied to the weather, the insects, and the market. He came of age during the Great Depression, as a dark cloud settled over his future.

Alaska was a bright spot, shining at the top of the world. That's why his parents had walked 350 miles to get here, why thousands of others had braved deadly glaciers and rapids with no promise of success. It was a land of immeasurable resources, where the people were as scarce as the rules. For Lloyd, it was a chance to make his own destiny, and maybe even make a fortune in the process. There was no guarantee of striking it rich, but there was always the possibility, shimmering brightly in the ore.

And what about me, I wondered, stomping my feet a few times to warm up. Why was I here? Was it just an adventure, an amazing story I would tell my grandchildren one day? Maybe I'd be better off at *High Country News*, writing stories for people who already cared about the environment, where we spoke the same language, and "climate change" and "sustainability" weren't considered dirty words.

Or had I found my place here, in a state where the motto seemed to be "Drill, Baby, Drill," and where there was still so much land, so much potential, so much left to lose?

5
Hot Rocks

ither the bugs or the heat was going to kill me, I was sure, before I found any gold. The sun pounded down on us and radiated up from the rocks under our feet. It had been shining twenty-four hours a day for two weeks straight, heating up the trees, rocks, and air to a temperature I never would have thought possible at seventy-five miles north of the Arctic Circle.

Clutch squatted in the creek and set a 45-inch sluice box in the current. It looked like a water trough for a pig pen, a skinny aluminum tray with high walls on the sides, except it was open on both ends so water could shoot right through.

"Let's dam up the mouth and get some more flow going through the box. You want about two inches runnin through there," Clutch said.

I ripped some moss from the tundra—soft and squishy, like a big organic sponge. As I stuffed it around the opening, I could already feel my toes going numb in the water. Above us glaciers clung to the walls of the canyon, shelves of dirty ice protected by caverns of shade. Even in the middle of June, winter never fully went away here at the top of the world.

From our little spot on the creek, the Brooks Range unfolded in every direction, a great wall across northern Alaska separating the Arctic coastal plain from the Yukon River valley. The mountains were wrapped in green vegetation, except at the top, where fins of schist jutted into the sky. Wildflowers lit up the meadow—purple lupines and fiery-red Indian paint brushes. In this collage of color, it was hard to believe that for most of the year the ground was frozen solid, the animals were sleeping, and this whole valley was blanketed in white. That the air was so cold it turned snow into dust and made ground squirrels freeze solid. It wasn't an easy place to live, and there were only a handful of villages scattered across an area larger than Colorado.

Ahh, Colorado. I hadn't taken the job at *High Country News*. It was hard to turn down, probably the hardest move I'd made in my relatively short career. In the end, it wasn't some lofty decision about saving the earth or falling in love or any one thing at all. I just couldn't bring myself to leave Alaska. It would have been like putting a book down before the ending, or leaving a soccer match when it was just getting good. I wasn't the first one to find myself in this predicament. I'd met plenty of people up here who concocted elaborate escape plans over the winter, vowing to head south at the first sign of spring. Then, when the sun came back and the world turned green, their resolve seemed to evaporate with the snow. They called it "seasonal amnesia," but it seemed more like an addiction to me. Either way, there was no known cure.

So here I was, standing with Clutch in a bone-chilling creek three hundred miles north of Fairbanks, learning how to sluice for gold. We were just outside of Wiseman, a tiny gold rush village where Clutch had been prospecting since before I was born. He laid a piece of black bristly turf in the bottom of the sluice box, then attached the riffle tray. The horizontal steel bars created eddies in the water, allowing gold to settle out onto the turf.

"Go ahead and start shovelin," he told me.

The sun bored down on my shoulders where I had rolled up the sleeves of my T-shirt. Had I known it would be this hot in the Arctic, I would have brought a tank top. I scooped some gravel from the creek and dumped it into the top of the box. It was wet and heavy, more work than I expected. But I was forty years younger than my companion, and I couldn't really complain. Clutch had brought me here to show me

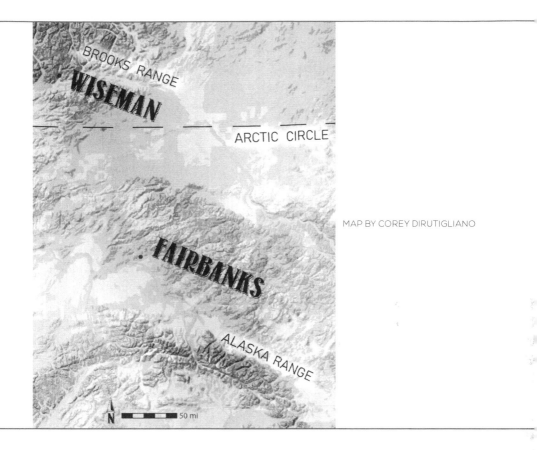

MAP BY COREY DIRUTIGLIANO

what prospecting was all about. I had learned a lot about the history of mining: how a single nugget had sparked a global stampede; how prospectors had filtered into every major river valley in Alaska, bouncing around the creeks like pinballs every time a new one was discovered; how the large dredges and drift mines had taken over, in typical capitalistic fashion; and how, ultimately, World War II had reshaped the entire economy, putting an end to the small-time miner.

I had hiked in the footsteps of GL and Nellie and explored the dark recesses of Lloyd's tunnel. I had accompanied Clutch to local miners' meetings and listened to them rant about environmentalists, Obama, and the EPA, silently biting my tongue among a roomful of hard-core miners. But I had never actually squatted in a creek, with my feet soaking in the icy water, and searched the gravel for gold. And really, that's what mining was all about—sifting through millions of ordinary pebbles in the hopes of finding a few precious flakes.

I brushed hair out of my face and squinted at Clutch.

"So how do you know where to look?" I said.

Surely there was a method to the madness. I couldn't possibly comb through every foot of gravel in this canyon.

"Oh, there's some tricks," Clutch said, with that hint of mystery I had come to expect. Clearly he wasn't going to share them with me. I'd have to figure it out for myself.

I watched a white rope of water gushing over some boulders, and I tried to imagine where I would be if I were a little particle of gold.

"I've been fooled," he continued. "I've seen places that looked like they had gold and didn't, and places that didn't look like they had gold and did. I'm just as miffed as the average guy."

At least I knew we were in the right neighborhood. Less than two miles away, in the same drainage, a palm-sized nugget was plucked from the water in 1901, creating the boom that gave birth to Wiseman. It weighed 34 ounces and 5 pennyweight, yielding $696.50 (or $42,000 today).

Clutch rattled off more local history as he cleared out the tray, working as deftly as a surgeon in an operating room or a bartender making drinks. It was easy to see he had spent a lifetime handling gravel.

"The next year they found a nugget twice that size, just three miles up the road from my place. They found a 60-ouncer and eventually a 150-ouncer. There was just huge nuggets lyin' all over this area."

"Do you think there's any—Oww!"

I dropped the shovel as something stabbed into the tender flesh above my elbow. The moose flies had found us. Super-sized horse flies with two pairs of scissors in their mouths, they could draw a pint of blood from a moose in a single day, making mosquitoes seem as friendly as butterflies. I dropped the shovel to put on a rain jacket and a head net, choosing sweat in a beekeeper outfit over bleeding in the breeze.

Clutch was still sluicing away, wearing only a T-shirt under his tan overalls. Apparently one could get used to the flies over time. Clutch watched me flail around, arms waving spastically over my head.

"So whaddaya think?" he said, sounding amused. "You wanna be a miner yet?"

I slapped another fly that was drilling into my back.

"Ha," I said. "We'll see how it goes."

Actually, I was surprised. So far, prospecting wasn't much different than how I usually spent my weekends, hiking up mountains or paddling down rivers. It was never glamorous, per se. Compared to the sunny skies and well-marked trails of Colorado, Alaska was a total wild card, a place where any outing was likely to include bushwhacking or mosquitoes or possibly even snow, registering somewhere on a sliding scale between suffering and fun. Like earlier this summer, when Josh and I were on the Chatanika River—one second we were paddling through some innocent-looking riffles and the next he was bobbing down the river trying to retrieve our capsized canoe. The X factor is big up here, but if you can handle it, the rewards are even bigger.

As we settled into a rhythm, Clutch told me how he got these gold claims in the first place. He began coming up to Wiseman back in the seventies with his older brother, George, who used to make deliveries in his Beechcraft Bonanza. One of his customers was an old miner named Harry Leonard. Like many of the sourdoughs who lived in the Bush, Harry wasn't known for his social graces. He had a crude metal shack on the north side of town, across the footbridge from everyone else (there were sixteen residents living in Wiseman at the time, about six more than today).

Though Harry didn't have many friends, he took a shine to the two young Lounsbury brothers. Clutch and George started visiting often to help with chores and hear his stories. Harry had been a cowboy in Texas before moving to Alaska in 1928. He got a job at the machine shop in Fairbanks. But his southern-belle wife didn't fall in love with the north like he did, and after a messy divorce, Harry needed a change of scenery. Hearing reports of giant nuggets in the Koyukuk region, he tracked down some mining supplies and a plane ride north. He staked some claims on Gold Creek and burrowed into the side of the mountain. For fourteen years, he lived there alone, miles away from the next human being. He worked the creek with a pick and a shovel, without a single piece of mechanical equipment. Over the years, he picked up more and more claims as other prospectors left, living on wild food and finding just enough gold to scrape by.

By the time the Lounsbury brothers came along, Harry was pushing eighty, and it was getting harder to work alone. So he asked Clutch if he wanted to join his venture. The younger miner didn't hesitate.

Though Clutch had spent his life working with coal, gravel, and oil, his first love had always been gold. In 1980, they started mining a small tributary of Hammond Creek. They set up camp on a grassy bench above the creek, just up from where we were sluicing. I could still see Clutch's old trailer parked there, plywood skirting around the edges and a piece of sheet metal slapped on the roof. The outhouse behind it was made entirely of Blazo boxes, crates used to deliver fuel in the old days. The squares of wood had been nailed to the frame like oversized shingles. To me it looked like a festering mosquito trap, but to Clutch it was something special.

"It's actually a historical monument," he said. "It was built in 1934 by, I believe it was Verne Watts."

For Harry and Clutch, this had been home away from home for the mining season: not much in terms of creature comforts, but surrounded by the quiet beauty of the Brooks Range. During the summer, they dug gravel from the streambed with a Caterpillar and a backhoe, and piled it on the banks. There it grew, day after day, like a squirrel's grand cache of acorns. In the fall, as the tundra burst into color, they shifted gears as well. Pumping water through a pipeline they'd built from the stream, they blasted paydirt into the sluice box to see what came out the other end.

Though they mined this site for three years, Harry and Clutch never got rich on Hammond Creek, nor any of their other creeks. In fact, that was the biggest thing I had learned from my jaunt through gold rush history. For many of the miners, it wasn't about money.

"My dad told me, 'Don't get gold fever,'" Clutch said.

"Meaning what, exactly?"

Clutch paused for a moment, something he rarely did, and I leaned in a little closer.

"Everybody thinks they're gonna get rich right away, but it's not gonna happen," he said. "Trust me."

Of course, all miners were obsessed with gold. They talked about it constantly, could quote the exact size, shape, and weight of a nugget, to the hundredth of an ounce. And in private, they all fantasized about stumbling upon a chunk of gold the size of a baseball, no doubt. But what were the odds of that happening? The main reason they were out here, shoveling gravel at sixty below zero, was because it beat working at a factory or living in a high rise, following the strict set of rules society required. The goal wasn't to have an easy life, but one where they lived on their own terms, at their own pace and by their own rules. They may have come to Alaska with the hopes of getting rich, but they stayed for some other reason, maybe the same thing that gripped us all, yet no one could fully define.

Now that I was up here, in Clutch's favorite place on earth, I felt like I finally understood my quirky neighbor. Certain things were obvious from the first day I met him, strumming the tub bass at the Golden Eagle; he was clearly proud of his family's history and eager to carry the torch. But standing in the creek, which he had probably invested more into over the years than he'd taken out of, I realized something else. Clutch was trying to hold onto something, to the joy of exploring a wild canyon, to a way of life that was disappearing. That's why he loved sharing his family's history, and why he cherished the old sourdough stories. That's why he still spent the summers in Wiseman, even though he hadn't actively mined here in years. He loved everything about it— the excitement, the grit, the raw outdoors.

"I never really cared about gettin' rich, ya know." He threw a fistful of gravel back in the water. "It was more of an adventure, like going over the Chilkoot Trail, lookin' at the next drainage."

Yet Clutch was born just as small-time mining was dying out: it was getting harder to compete with the big corporations, more expensive to comply with the rules. In a way he was born too late, and he was still living in the past. It made me sad to think of him grasping at something that was slowly slipping away. Perhaps this was the dark side of my environmentalism. I had always focused on protecting the land, on humans being good stewards of fish and animals, of putting trails and habitat before roads. But, like everything else, conservation had a cost. Not just jobs, but the identity wrapped up in those jobs. As a third-generation miner, gold was in Clutch's blood. Just like the coal miners in Pennsylvania, whose livelihoods had been lost to automation and the rise of cheaper forms of energy, prospectors seemed to be losing not just their jobs but something bigger. The world was moving on without them.

Clutch leaned down to examine the tray, almost dunking his hat in the creek.

"Well, that's probably good for one day," he determined.

I peeked into the five-gallon bucket, where we had been emptying the contents of the sluice box for the past hour. It was half full. Meanwhile, my shoulders were aching and I was getting hungry.

"Looks good to me," I agreed.

Clutch removed the turf from the sluice box and folded it neatly into the bucket. I grabbed the handle and carried it up the side of the creek, careful not to tip it as I picked my way through the willows. There was no way of knowing what was in there—a life-changing nugget or just a bunch of worthless muck.

6
Gold Fever

T he sun was still high in the sky when we fired up the barbecue later that night, bathing the mountains in tangerine light. It was June 22, summer solstice, the day when the earth bowed its deepest to the sun and we got twenty-four hours of daylight above the Arctic Circle. It wouldn't get dark for weeks up here. Until then, we were living in one perpetual day with no beginning or end, no signal from the sky about when to eat or when to sleep, no sense of closure that comes with the kiss of dusk. It was both exhilarating and confusing at the same time.

Clutch's B&B was sprawled in a grassy clearing on the banks of Koyukuk River. Surrounded by Arctic tundra, the lawn looked like a putting green. A sky-blue sign hung outside his cabin, which doubled as the front desk and the lobby, with curly yellow letters reading Wiseman Gold Camp B&B. As Clutch tossed a couple steaks on the grill, I grabbed two beers from a washtub full of ice he had harvested from the river. We sat at the patio table and popped off the caps, the sound of a satisfying day.

A hundred feet away, the turquoise waters of the Koyukuk's middle fork flowed through a wide gravel bar. Off to the right, a convoy of tractors, boilers, and winches was arranged in the lawn like a rusty old playground. Colorful daisies sprung from a tractor belt that hadn't spun since 1912. Clutch and his brother had salvaged the equipment from the surrounding gold claims, using a hoist to pull them out of deep mine shafts.

The canvas wall tent I was staying in had two fluffy beds and a small wood stove. Clutch had stocked it with bottled water and a four-pack of red wine, the airplane-sized bottles. The outhouse out back had two stalls, one labeled "Pointers" and the other "Setters," and a metal trough attached to the back of the building.

I had asked him about it during the initial tour.

"Funny story," he'd said, tapping it with his walking stick.

He had found the strip of metal resting against a tree at his grandparents' old homestead in Fox and brought it to the sheet metal shop in town.

"I said, 'Roy, what is this?' "

His friend leaned in close but wouldn't touch it.

"He said, 'It's a urinal.'" Clutch laughed out loud. "I almost threw it at him!"

But Clutch was too sentimental to get rid of a family heirloom, even a rusty old toilet, so he cleaned it up and recommissioned it.

Today Wiseman is a sleepy village with about ten year-round residents, members of a rare breed who can handle seventy below zero temperatures and long stretches of darkness without going crazy. Most homes are log, decorated with moose antlers and American flags, with old mining junk that's been refashioned into flower beds and lawn art. Many of the Gold Rush cabins have been dismantled for firewood, but a few remain, sinking into the permafrost like leaky boats. There's a chapel, an airstrip, two museums, and an old phone booth that still takes quarters. No restaurants or stores. The only jobs around are at Coldfoot, a truck stop twenty minutes down the highway.

Sitting in Clutch's yard, listening to the soft music of the river, it was hard to believe there used to be four hundred people living here—a real town with a school, a store, and even a U.S. marshal. They had dances and parties and dressed up in clean trousers, long silk dresses, and wide-brimmed hats for Sunday church. The roadhouse stayed open all night to feed weary travelers passing through by dog team.

Of course, there were certain luxuries they lived without. There were no roads—only dog trails and rivers. The sun went down December 5 and didn't come back up until January 9. News from the outside world arrived by boat, once a year. After the town doctor committed suicide in 1919, the graveyard swelled with the sick and the injured. But people came anyway, braving bitter cold and isolation to scratch a living from the gravel.

By 1950, the gold rush on the Koyukuk River had died down and most of the prospectors had left. But not Clutch's partner Harry. He didn't have anywhere to go, for one, and the solitude didn't bother him one bit. His house looked rather crude by normal standards—a one-room cabin made of sheet metal that was buried in snow for half the year—but it was a step up from the creek he had lived on. He shared it with his favorite white husky Blazo, who slept on the bunk below him at night.

Harry didn't have many friends, but there was one other fellow whose company he enjoyed, a Californian named Charlie Breck. One time Charlie came over for dinner. When he took off his coat to hang it on the chair, he saw three place settings laid out.

"Expecting someone else?" Charlie asked.

In reply, Blazo the dog jumped up on the chair and whined, ready for his dinner.

Clutch knew how much Harry loved his dog. He had seen it first-hand. One day, he and his brother George were helping the old miner with firewood. It was minus-fifty outside, and his ten-inch barrel stove could barely keep up. But Harry wouldn't let them buy him a new one. Clutch brought an armful of wood inside while George crouched on the floor splitting kindling. The old miner sat by the fire, his faithful dog at his feet. The dog went to stand up, then collapsed suddenly on the floor. Harry dropped down to see what was wrong, but it was too late. Without a moment's warning, he had lost his companion, his bear guard, his best friend. Though the ground was as hard as concrete and the cold cut like a razor blade, Harry insisted on a proper burial.

So George built a casket out of scrap wood while Clutch started digging a grave. He built a fire in a half oil drum to thaw the top layer of soil, then slowly shoveled out the muck, just as the early prospectors had done. It took three days to dig a six-foot hole. After Harry said goodbye to his beloved pet, they lowered the casket into the ground and started shoveling. They were almost done when Harry called out from his cabin.

"You buried him facing the river, right? He loved the river. It was his favorite place."

Neither Clutch nor his brother had any idea which way the dog was oriented, but they could tell it was important to their old friend, so they dug up the casket and turned it around.

"Now he can watch the river flowin' this spring," Clutch said.

When Harry passed away a few years later, he was laid to rest not far from his dog, in the town where he'd spent over half his life, digging for a fortune that never came.

The smell of steak and corn on the cob floated over the warm tundra, making my stomach growl. It had been a long day in the canyon. Clutch leaned back in his chair sipping a Summer Ale—a man one hundred percent in his element. When Harry passed away in 1989, he left his land and mining claims to Clutch and his brother. Soon after, Clutch and Lorna opened up this small inn by the river. Now he spends the summers up here, prospecting in the creek and visiting with the occasional tourist who makes it this far.

As we dug into our food, Clutch regaled me with stories about Wiseman, the same ones Harry had told him a few decades earlier. There was the twenty-ounce nugget on Nolan Creek and the time Magic Eightball rolled the Cat in a steep gulch. The time Harry held a murderer in his cabin for a week, tied to a chair, until authorities could come and arrest him.

There was one night Clutch will never forget. It was a cool spring day, about twenty years ago, and he had driven up from Fairbanks to visit Charlie Breck. Tall and lanky with closely cropped hair and a crooked smile, Charlie had grown up in Hollywood, and had some of the charisma to show for it. Locals called him the "common denominator" because he was the only one in town who got along with everyone.

Though he was heir to the Breck Shampoo empire his family had built, Charlie had taken a slightly different path in life. He was using his geology degree in a roundabout way, as he scoured the Arctic for gold deposits. And he had another important job, too. When a pilot landed on the airstrip one day and threw him a sack of mail, he became the unofficial postman of Wiseman. His one-room cabin was so full of newspapers and long-lost letters that there was barely room to sit down.

One thing he couldn't get by mail, however, were his favorite cigars. So whenever Clutch came to visit, he brought a few cases along. This time, Clutch had also brought a special treat to share. The large mason jar that he carried to Charlie's cabin contained a frothy white mixture that Clutch saved for special occasions, like a night full of libations and storytelling. "Moose milk," as Clutch liked to call it, was whole milk spiked with whiskey.

"Everybody would drink it and nobody would ever get drunk because the milk would coat your stomach."

As they sat by the stove sipping creamy cocktails, the whiskey awakened the memories. Charlie told him about an evening many years ago, before oil was discovered in the Arctic and a road was built to Wiseman, back when the valley was so quiet he could hear his own heartbeat. Charlie was prospecting in the creek when he discovered some interesting colors in his pan. He leaned down to get a closer look and saw another face staring back at him. When he turned around, a six-hundred-pound grizzly was reared up on its hindquarters, not 20 feet away. "He looked at the bear, looked at the pan, looked at the bear, looked at the pan," Clutch said, quickening his pace for dramatic effect. "And he let out this great big holler and startled the bear." The grizzly took off down the creek, running straight for Charlie's partner. Charlie hollered again. This time, the animal made a ninety-degree turn and disappeared in the woods. The two miners waded to shore, then back to their cabins in a mild daze. It wasn't their first close call with the king of the food chain and certainly wouldn't be their last.

Though Clutch knew he couldn't top Charlie's story, there was no harm in trying.

"Did I tell you the one about the horse and the black bear?" he'd said, reaching outside for the jar of moose milk.

Their stories ran late into the night. By 5 a.m., the jar was almost empty and Clutch needed some fresh air. He decided to go grab the belts he had brought for Charlie's Jeep from his truck. The ground was squishy with freshly melted snow as he walked a mile back to the road. Spring was a lively time in the Arctic, and Clutch made plenty of noise so as not to spook any wildlife. He hummed to himself, every few minutes calling out the standard warning in grizzly country: "Hey Bear!"

As he crossed the beaver slough and approached the road, something came crashing out of the bushes. Clutch squinted at a large brown shape: maybe it was just the moose milk. The shape stopped between him and the truck and squared up. Nope, definitely a grizzly.

"Looked like the hide was fallin' off and he hadn't eaten anything all winter, and I looked like his first meal."

While grizzlies enjoy a spot at the top of the food chain, they won't attack just anyone. Rather, they choose their battles carefully and always like to know what they're up against. The bear sniffed in Clutch's direction, trying to identify the respectably sized figure in its path. But Clutch was downwind, and it couldn't get a good whiff.

Of course, grizzlies are also known for their individual personalities. There's no telling how one will react in a given situation, depending on its appetite, mood, and a hundred other factors. While they typically try to avoid conflict, you never know when they might be having a bad day. Unfortunately for Clutch, this one decided to charge, barreling toward him like an angry bull. Clutch froze. It was surprisingly fast for such a large animal. There was no point in running (it would only get the bear more excited), and the scrawny willows surrounding him provided little protection.

He pulled out his .357 revolver and pointed it at his adversary. He could feel the adrenaline surging through his entire body, gathering in the tip of his index finger. Facing one of the world's most fearsome predators, the small piece of steel in his hand felt ridiculously inadequate.

"The closer it got, the smaller that chamber looked."

A dramatic pause.

"I thought to myself, 'This could be it.'"

Experts say to hold your ground in this kind of situation. Speak loudly and raise your arms to make yourself big—the conventional wisdom in bear country. Instead, Clutch thought about Charlie's story, how his friend's primal reaction had saved his life. He let out a bloodcurdling scream that pierced the dawn like a shot.

"The thing went from thirty-five miles an hour to a dead stop, just like that. It jumped up, was lookin at me, poppin his teeth, and I slowly backed away until I couldn't see him anymore."

He lowered his gun, took a deep breath, and walked back to the cabin.

"I said, 'Charlie, I think I need another moose milk.'"

Sitting across from me, Clutch threw back his head and howled in laughter.

"I didn't go back outside until noon, and not without my twelve gauge."

I joined in with him, thinking about how unfunny it would have been at the time. Though I never got tired of bear stories, each one sent a shiver down my spine. I glanced at the canvas tent where I would soon be sleeping. It didn't look very bear-proof.

"Have you seen many grizzlies around this summer?" I said, trying not to sound too nervous.

"Oh, don't worry, they don't like comin into town."

"Town" was a strong word for Wiseman, I thought. But I tried to push it to the back of my mind.

My eyes fell on the bowl of mountains around us, where so many of Clutch's favorite memories had originated. Ever since he was young, he had loved hanging out with the old-timers, learning their secrets and reliving their adventures. Now the tables had turned. He was the sourdough and I was the student, hungry for stories of the past.

Through these stories, I had felt the thrill of the gold rush, the hope and fear of traveling across the world on a whim, facing everything the wilderness could throw at you. Not just through caricatures but through real people. Knowing the stories of GL and Nellie, of Lloyd and Fay, had forced me to confront my own stereotypes. I could no longer pretend that mining was categorically bad, or that all mining was done by greedy corporations, polluting the earth for their own profit.

On the contrary, in many ways those early prospectors weren't so different from me. They had come to Alaska to get away from the grind. To live close to the land, with their hands in the dirt and their boots sinking into the tundra, deeply in tune with the resources and rhythms of the earth. I thought about Clutch's friend Charlie, panning in the creek at sunset, and felt a twinge of romance.

Yet I could almost hear the little conservationist on my shoulder, crying out in protest. The rose-tinted image of the prospector had died long ago, around the time the bulldozer came along. As technology advanced over the past century, the footprint of mining grew bigger and bigger. Panning turned to drifting, drifting turned to surface mining, and surface mining to dredging. At each stage, the environmental impacts magnified exponentially.

Today, most of the world's gold comes not from mom-and-pop prospectors like Harry and Clutch but from massive open-pit mines, where huge volumes of rock are churned up to extract tiny flecks of gold. Fort Knox, just north of Fairbanks, is one of the largest gold mines in the United States. Nearly a mile wide and a half mile deep, the gaping pit can be seen from space. Two hundred thousand tons of rock are extracted each day, hauled from the bottom of the pit in dump trucks and pulverized in a ball mill. Producing more in a day than GL's drift mine had in a whole season. The low-grade ore is stacked in a leach pile and sprayed with a cyanide solution to dissolve any remaining bits of gold. The tailings are impounded behind a huge earthen dam, the only barrier between millions of tons of mining waste and our own surrounding watershed.

Regulation had come on the heels of technology. Rules didn't even exist until 1872, when Congress passed the first mining law. And of course, that law didn't look anything like the regulations of today. The goal wasn't to protect the environment—why would the Wild West need protection? But to create enough industry to drive people west. When GL and his crew sluiced their giant piles of pay dirt, they didn't worry about capturing the wastewater. When Lloyd's coworkers blasted the hillsides with hydraulic jets of water, spraying gravel and muck a hundred feet in the air, they weren't breaking any rules. And when

Dredge #10 plowed through Ester, literally turning the valley inside out, the people of Fairbanks cheered about the new job prospects.

The law had succeeded in settling the frontier. By the time it was amended in 1976, America was a far different place. A century of mining had taken its toll on the countryside. Especially out west, where half a million abandoned mines could be found littering the mountains, and nearly half the watersheds had been contaminated by acid mine drainage. As power plants and factories spread across the nation like a rash, wilderness seemed like an increasingly precious resource. Faced with rising public outcry, Congress finally updated the law to protect the scenic, recreational, and ecological values of land as well. The government finally started making miners clean up after themselves.

It had happened not to punish miners, or to attack the gold industry in general, but because of the environmental devastation of the past. Driven not by fear, but by lessons learned. People like Clutch were paying the price for what their parents and grandparents had done, for the free-for-all spirit that had flourished on the frontier.

Of course, nobody likes new restrictions, and the changes caused a lot of friction between miners and regulatory agencies. As the price of gold has risen over the past two decades, the chafing has only gotten worse. The government has stepped up its enforcement—requiring baseline water testing and scrutinizing the roads and trails that miners use to access their claims. For many of the old sourdoughs, it seems like an act of war.

Just recently, Clutch received a letter in the mail stating the shed on Hammond Creek was in disrepair. If it wasn't fixed, he would have to pay a fine.

"You know what they were talkin' about? The outhouse!" he said, his voice pitching in disbelief. The one that had been built eighty years ago out of old Blazo boxes, the one he liked to call a "historical monument." The part that really fired him up was the satellite image included in the letter.

"They spy on you with satellites and then charge you for gas to drive out and deliver the fine by hand."

He shook his head in exasperation. I had to agree—it did seem ridiculous. Sometimes regulations were. Though well-intentioned, they only worked when properly applied, accounting for the nuance and context of every situation. Which was virtually impossible for blanket rules enforced by Washington bureaucracies. What works in Montana's drift mines or Arizona's copper mines wouldn't necessarily work for the six miners living in Wiseman, Alaska. I knew the agony of being caught in red tape; just think of the long lines at airport security, the flabbergasting process of trying to get a hunting permit in one of Alaska's twenty-six game management units. We had all run into it, one way or another. Sometimes it felt like the government was a giant wall, trying to shut you down at every turn. Just imagine trying to dig a hole in a national park. And we needed resources, after all. I wouldn't have my car, my phone, or my grandmother's fancy silverware without them. As the classic Fairbanks bumper sticker proudly proclaimed, "This truck is a product of mining." And yet my bumper was much more likely to say "No Pebble Mine."

I set down my corn cob, totally cleaned of its golden flesh, and searched for a blade of grass to floss my teeth. There was nothing on earth better than sweet corn on the grill. I couldn't eat it without thinking of home, of the corn fields that surrounded my parents' old farmhouse in rural Pennsylvania, built in 1860, of the lush canopy of oaks and maples that gave us shade and quiet. While strip malls had overtaken much of the countryside, our property felt like a vestige of another time, our own little buffer against development.

I guess there were some things we just couldn't change. After meeting Clutch, spending time in his home and his gold camp and hiking his beloved canyon, my views on mining had widened. I had seen the other side of regulation, the real damage it had done to the industry. I had felt the pain of lost traditions, of losing your place in the world. I didn't want miners to go away. Ester wouldn't be half as interesting without people like Clutch and Lorna. But environmental regulations shouldn't bear all the blame, either. Technology and globalization had transformed the economy in ways that weren't so friendly to the backyard miner.

And I kept returning to the belief that had been stamped somewhere deep inside me: we only had one planet. Clutch and I would probably never agree on how much regulation was the right amount, or on the true impacts of mining. Our values were just too different, too deeply ingrained.

He leaned on the arm of his chair and stood up, snapping me out of my reflection.

"Well, ready to get paid?" he said.

The glint was back in his eye.

"Oh yeah!"

I had almost forgotten about the bucket of paydirt we had collected from the stream. Clutch led me over to a little shack stuffed with rocks, crystals, and old photographs—a museum he had put together honoring Harry and Charlie and the other Wiseman sourdoughs. Behind it was a water tank the size of a small hot tub. He scooped some gravel into a gold pan. I wasn't expecting much, as we hadn't sluiced very long before succumbing to the flies. Clutch showed me how to swish water around the pan to bring the fine particles to the surface, then release them with a gentle dunk. I tried a few times (it was harder than it looked). As the silt and rocks washed away, I felt my hope going with it. There was only a tablespoon of shimmery black sand left in the bottom. Then Clutch stopped the pan with a thick index finger.

"Wait. What's that?"

A tiny speck, the size of raw sugar crystal, was stuck to the edge of the pan. With my heart fluttering, I pressed my index finger to the sparkle and brought it closer to my face, thinking how far I had come to find this precious little particle of gold.

PART TWO
AIR

"There are old pilots and bold pilots,
but there are no old, bold pilots."

—E. Hamilton Lee, 1949

7
The Bush

I forced myself to breathe as the canyon closed around us like a tightening fist. At first the wings of the airplane were level with the top of the mountains, as if gliding on invisible strings, then all of a sudden we were inside them, surrounded by walls of limestone. An invisible bump knocked us up and down, side to side. I glanced at the pilot, but his stony face provided little comfort. "It's okay," I told myself. "He does this every day."

A strange tingling spread through my limbs, settling in the pit of my stomach. I took another deep breath. Then the clenched rock opened up to a clearing.

This was my first time in a bush plane and, since taking off ninety minutes ago, it was like seeing the world for the first time. The Cessna 206 was light and nimble, like a bird. As we sped down the runway and jumped into the sky, I'd pressed my nose to the glass and looked down at Fairbanks: the homely little downtown, straddling the Chena River; the university perched on the ridge, its towers and satellite dishes outstretched to the sky; a few roads looping it all together. The second largest city in Alaska, but just a small town by most standards. Houses were scattered in the hills like pieces on a board game, growing sparser and sparser, smaller and smaller, until all signs of civilization disappeared.

Then it was tundra, as far as the eye could see. There's no way to comprehend the scale of Alaska until you fly over it in a bush plane: rivers that curl like ribbons through valleys large enough to fit entire cities; spruce forests that build slowly into foothills and finally crescendo into rough granite peaks. Only a thousand feet from the ground, the world spread out in high definition. As we flew north, the sharp jags of the White Mountains gave way to one of the world's great swamps. The Yukon Flats covered 11,000 square miles, so low and so wet it was hard to imagine how anyone ever made it across before the airplane. Finally, we reached the next, and last, set of giants: the Brooks Range, some of the farthest north mountains in the world. The pilot pointed to some white specks on a ridge. A handful of Dall sheep scrambled uphill, safely above their predators.

We were headed to Anaktuvuk Pass, a small Inupiaq village deep in the Arctic. I would finally get to see "the Bush," the ninety percent of Alaska not on the road system. Not connected to Walmarts or gas stations or grocery stores—the lifelines that keep most of us going these days.

I had seen what life was like on the Alaska frontier, how pioneers had carved a life from the woods a hundred years ago. But what was left of it today? Outside of a handful of small cities, Alaska was still in many ways a blank map, a chunk of land that could swallow any other state whole. Strewn across it were more than two hundred villages, ranging in population from ten to a few hundred, where people still spoke their Indigenous languages and scratched a living from the land. Where they lived in tune with nature, not in control of it.

At least, this was the picture I had in my mind. It was the main reason I opposed mining and drilling in many cases. This was the whole point of conservation, right? To protect places like the Alaska bush—not just the wildlife but the subsistence life that still thrived there, which had been extinguished in so much of the world.

And that's why I was going to Anaktuvuk Pass, in a way. I was writing a story about a new house, a design that was based on the age-old art of sod igloos people had lived in for hundreds of years. Except this house had a modern twist. It was super-insulated and designed by researchers, using the most advanced building technologies of today. According to them, it would make life easier for people in the bush, providing a way to live a traditional lifestyle without giving up modern comforts.

As we flew north, I found the hum of the propeller oddly comforting, especially when I was so far out of my comfort zone. It wasn't the flying that made me nervous, so much as the idea of what awaited me on the ground. I knew almost nothing about construction, Native culture, or the Arctic. Yet here I was, four hundred miles from Fairbanks, about to land somewhere that meant "place of caribou droppings" in Inupiaq.

The nerves had kicked in earlier that morning, when I'd walked into Wright Air Service with a blue backpack and large camera hanging around my neck. There were no kiosks or security agents or body-scanning machines, just a young guy at a counter who asked my name and how much I weighed.

"First time to Anaktuvuk?" he said.

"Yep."

Was it that obvious?

I removed the bear spray from my pack, a canister of highly concentrated pepper spray that can supposedly deter an attacking bear, and handed it to him. If it detonated in the airplane during flight, it could blind the pilot and kill us all, so it would have to go in the wing with the other weapons and hazardous materials.

"Got a gun?" he said, sizing me up with a quick glance.

"No, just the bear spray."

He laughed.

"We call that 'seasoning.'"

It wasn't the first time I'd heard the joke. Alaskans loved to scare newbies like me—suggesting bear spray, for instance, only made you tastier for bears. I smiled nervously and took a seat in a row of orange vinyl chairs to wait for my flight. Next to me, two Elders chatted in a language I didn't recognize. Across the room, a teenager in a pink hoodie tapped on her phone. A smiling toddler jetted from one row of chairs to the next, clutching any grownup leg he could find for balance. Almost everyone here was Alaska Native, and most of them seemed to know each other. I fidgeted in my seat, trying to look nonchalant, like I did this sort of thing all the time. But this was my first trip to the bush, and I had no idea what to expect.

The pilot's voice snapped me back to the present, reporting our location and airspeed. Judith, the only other passenger, looked out the window in front of me. She wore a headset over her long, fiery red hair. She was also going to Anaktuvuk Pass to see the new house—in fact, she had helped design it. She worked for the Cold Climate Housing Research Center, a Fairbanks organization that built sustainable homes across Alaska. When I had first seen her in the hangar, I was slightly awestruck. Dressed in Carhartt work pants and XtraTuf boots and sporting a small nose ring, she looked glamorous as she hauled heavy totes up to the counter one by one. Hardly sparing a look at anyone else, she exuded total confidence. Clearly this wasn't her first trip to the bush. Originally from Virginia, Judith had been an architect in India before moving to Alaska a couple of years ago. She and her husband embraced the lifestyle right away, renting a dry cabin in the woods and buying a small plane. She had asked to sit up front since she was learning to fly.

The pilot followed the twisty line of the John River north. Dressed in a fishing T-shirt and baseball hat, he was a far cry from the brass-buttoned airline captains I was accustomed to. Up ahead, some dots of color appeared on the tundra, the first sign of human civilization since leaving Fairbanks.

Anaktuvuk Pass was swimming in mountains, completely surrounded on every side. It sat right on the Continental Divide, the invisible line that separated two of the earth's major watersheds; everything north flowed into the Arctic Ocean, everything south into the Pacific. The wide valley was like a superhighway across the Brooks Range. Each spring, hundreds of thousands of caribou used it to cross to their calving grounds on the coast.

In fact, that's why the village was here. For thousands of years, Arctic people had relied on these animals for food, clothing, tools, thread, and art. For life. That was the reason I wanted to write this story. I had seen what life was like in Fairbanks and Anchorage and some of the roadside villages, but that wasn't the "real Alaska" I had in my mind—just the westernized version that had arrived within the last century or so. Now

I would get to see a traditional Native community firsthand, to see how they lived in such a harsh environment, how they had survived since prehistoric times. Maybe, from them, I would finally learn what it meant to live sustainably.

The pilot fiddled with an instrument, somehow finding the appropriate one among a dizzying array of dials and levers. As I watched the village go by, for a moment I thought we'd missed it. Then we made a wide arc over the valley. As the airplane banked left, a full view opened up outside my window, fifty colorful homes dotted the tundra like rainbow sprinkles. The John River flowed out of a U-shaped valley and split the town in half. A little neighborhood outlined by electrical poles, untethered from the rest of the world. Suddenly Fairbanks didn't seem so remote.

I could barely feel the fat tundra wheels touch down on the gravel, and just like that we were back on solid land. The pilot helped us off the plane and unloaded our bags, then sprinted down the strip and took off. As the plane disappeared through a different mountain pass, the hum lingered in the quiet sky.

Well, here I was.

I had seen Indian reservations before, as we drove to Cape Cod every summer, the highway exits with flashing billboards for bingo halls and casinos. This was a different story. In Alaska, Native villages are scattered across an area more than twice as big as Texas. For most of them, the only way in and out is by airplane. They retain Indigenous languages and practice subsistence lifestyles.

I was still getting used to that word—"subsistence." Aside from the occasional show on Nature, I had never actually heard anyone use it before. But in Alaska, it was part of everyday conversation. Fishing, hunting, and harvesting firewood all fell under the heading of "subsistence activities." Even in more developed areas like Fairbanks, subsistence was an integral part of the lifestyle. Last fall, I had squatted on the tundra for hours picking blueberries, long after Josh had fallen asleep in the sunshine, until the bushes were scoured clean and my hands and knees were dyed bright purple. I filled as many empty yogurt containers as I could find, then cleaned and sorted them in the kitchen, carefully handling the delicate fruit to avoid crushing the flesh. I didn't stop until there were six gallons of the little blue beads stashed in the freezer, a sense of accomplishment I savored with my oatmeal every morning.

So I suppose I had gotten a taste of subsistence, if only a small one. It had a whole different meaning out here in the Bush, where life revolved around nearby plants and animals. In Anaktuvuk Pass, they picked berries not by the gallon but by the garbage container. Instead of working at an office all day to pay for groceries, people spent much of their time outside, growing and gathering food. Subsistence wasn't just a fun weekend hobby. It was their economy, their identity.

While preparing for this trip, I'd stumbled upon a fascinating old video of the Nunamiut people of Anaktuvuk Pass. They used to live in skin tents at a lake about fifty miles west of here. The men were hunters, and the women picked berries and greens, sewed parkas, mukluks, fur hats, and mittens, while also taking care of the children. In the spring, they went to fish camp and spent the entire summer catching whitefish, char, and lake trout. Moving around was the only way to survive, to find enough food for everyone. The best thing about the video was that it was filmed in 1954—which meant some of those people were still alive.

That's why I had been so eager to come here. To see an ancient culture preserved in the Arctic, a living link to the past. At a time when NASA was getting ready to send the first humans into space, and most Americans were buying dishwashers and lawn mowers, the people of Anaktuvuk Pass were still living in skin tents and commuting by dog team. Certainly, they could teach us something about what it meant to live sustainably, about how to get by with fewer resources.

Of course, I wasn't expecting to walk into a time capsule. I knew the village had changed over the past half century. Now they had a school and a post office, and food and technology that had come in on the airplanes. But surely, underneath all that was knowledge that could guide us forward.

———————

Fortunately, Judith had a ride waiting for her at the airstrip. Not a dog team, but a six wheeled vehicle called an Argo, which could drive on water, tundra, ice, mud—pretty much anything the Arctic could throw at you. The driver was a tall, quiet guy named Ben, one of the carpenters who was building the cold climate house. His friendly, soft-spoken manner made me trust him right away, and I hopped on the back of the ATV and tucked my legs up as it roared to life.

The moving air felt good, and it knocked down the mosquitoes that had already started accumulating. As we drove down a long dirt road away from the airstrip, I saw a clean-cut grid of homes, laid out just like a city block in Hershey, PA. Of course, the houses looked nothing like the ones I grew up with. They weren't brick and mortar. There were no porches or bay windows or grassy lawns. Just rows and rows of rectangular boxes, painted in bright candy colors that reminded me of a Greenlandic village. The yards were cluttered with broken furniture and engine parts, outdoor freezers and satellite TV dishes. A little shabby, but surprisingly modern.

Ben turned right down another unnamed gravel road, slowing down so I didn't go sailing off the back. An Argo passed in the other direction with a driver who couldn't have been older than ten, holding an even younger kid in his lap. I felt a prickle of worry—should they be riding alone? It's not like there was anyone out here to stop them. Outside one of the homes, a dog that looked like a wolf ran to the end of its chain and barked, sounding the alarm there were strangers in town. A few other dogs sat up to look, but most didn't seem to care. They curled up by the stoop or napped on top of their plywood houses, unemployed now that machines had taken their job.

We stopped in front of a grassy lump next to the road. Moss crawled across the weathered logs and clumps of grass sprouted from the roof like tufts of wild hair.

"An old igloo," Ben said.

This is what the Nunamiut people had built when they first settled here some sixty years ago. They carved holes into the hillsides and built willow frames, covering them with thick slabs of sod for insulation. They sealed the gaps with spruce pitch to keep dirt from leaking inside, and draped a caribou skin over the door. The houses were small and dark, but they were warm. It was a design that had lasted for countless generations in one of the harshest climates on earth.

"Look, they chinked it with sod," Judith said, admiring the traditional method of weatherizing the cracks between logs.

I looked at the house across the street, a plywood shoebox with peeling red paint. People moved into these tract-style homes in the sixties, when government agencies showed up from the Lower 48 with the intention of modernizing the villages. The prefab designs were fast and cheap, produced by the lowest bidder. They weren't nestled into the ground like the sod house, but stood on wooden legs high up in the air. As I looked at the red house, I could almost feel the Arctic winds blowing through the scrawny walls, howling under the exposed floor. The fuel tank against the wall was the same one I had in Fairbanks, but I knew it would cost at least twice as much to fill up here, since oil had to be flown in by plane. *Strange*, I thought. *In some ways, I'd rather live in an igloo.*

Ben gripped the throttle and we surged forward, toward an imposing gray peak called Soakpak, or "Big Mountain." It looked like a deadly arrowhead stabbing the sky, a visual reminder of the harshness of this country. We were in the tallest mountains in the Arctic Circle, a land too cold for trees or grass, and for most living things as well. Where shelter was the difference between life and death. And yet most of the homes zooming past appeared to be unfit for a New England winter.

Ben made another right turn, and there was the new house. Impossible to miss, even if it hadn't been swarming with construction workers. The locals had nicknamed it "Spongebob," because of the odd-looking spray-foam insulation that covered the entire structure. But to me it was a cross between an adobe house and something from the future. It was banked into the soil, like the old sod igloos, to take advantage of the natural insulation of the earth. But it also had super thick walls and a steel frame foundation that floated on the permafrost, and was much warmer than an elevated floor. The research center had designed these technologies specifically for this windy mountain pass, and was now testing them for the very first time.

We climbed down to meet the crew. There were eight workers, all local, ranging from a girl in high school to a thirty-something guy with a few years of construction experience. The hodgepodge group of caribou hunters could have been any building crew in Fairbanks, dressed in Carhartts and sweatshirts, with tool belts dangling from their waists.

Takpaan Weber, the pretty 17-year-old in a green California hoody, was cutting strips of wood for the door jamb. It was her first time building a house, and she was excited about the unique design. While her grandmother was raised in a skin tent, she had grown up with vinyl siding and indoor plumbing.

"It's pretty cool to have something close to what we used to have," she said, looking up from the table saw.

Tak was still deciding what to do after high school, whether she wanted to stay in the village or move to Utah and go to school for radiology. I grabbed a hard hat from the shipping container toolshed and followed Judith toward the house, where the crew was unloading fresh sod from the back of a pickup. Three men threw slabs of earth on top of the roof while two others laid them down like bathroom tiles, batting away the mosquitoes that swarmed their heads. They worked in sync, talking and joking in a cloud of earthy-smelling sod. Soon the roof looked like a miniature soccer field.

The next task: solar panels. The first ones ever in Anaktuvuk Pass, possibly the farthest north system in Alaska. Between the panels, the sod roof, and the twelve-inch walls, the house was definitely one of a kind. And that was the whole point.

Like other things about village life, housing in the Bush had become largely *un*sustainable. The cookie cutter homes propped up on the tundra had clearly been intended to make life better for the Nunamiut, to provide plumbing and electricity and other first-world amenities. But they had actually become a tremendous burden. They guzzled heat. Water and electricity were exorbitant too, because everything relied on flown-in diesel. Meanwhile there were few jobs in the village to support these new expenses, and the local people had quickly become depen-dent on outside funding to survive.

The Cold Climate Housing Research Center was attempting some-thing different, to combine the knowledge of the Indigenous people with the best science and technology of today.

"They've gotten so far away from their traditional housing," Judith said, slashing open a box with a utility knife. She worked with purpose, less like an architect than like a member of the crew. "We want this house to perform like a twenty-first century house, but also resonate with the history and culture of this place."

This was the only way to make the bush more sustainable, she pointed out. Housing and energy had become so costly that it was killing the little villages. Even with millions of dollars in subsidies from state and federal programs, people still couldn't afford to heat their homes. That's why many villagers were moving to the city in search of jobs and housing, leaving their families and traditions behind. And it was happening fast. After surviving up here for thousands of years without any help at all, now, within a single generation of modernizing, this lifestyle was on the verge of dying out.

As I walked around the village taking pictures for my story, I tried to process this new view of rural Alaska. Anaktuvuk Pass was not the place I'd expected, an idyllic village in the wilderness, nor an ancient culture preserved in amber. Rather, it was more like a microcosm of the outside world, where people had the same clothing and gadgets I did. I shuffled to the edge of the road as a massive truck drove by and sprayed a mist of water on the swirling dust. This was not a paradigm for sustainability, after all. It was far from sustainable.

Suddenly, the things I'd been covering for the *News-Miner* made more sense. The struggle to hold onto Native culture, the need for cheaper forms of energy. How else could you live a modern life out here, stranded on the tundra? This also raised more questions. What was the bush like before prefab homes and diesel tanks and subsidized mail planes showed up, before you could import just about anything you desired? As I watched Tak attach the door frame with a pneumatic nail gun, I wondered what had precipitated all these changes, and whether any of them had actually made life better.

That night, the Nunamiut people gathered at the base of the mountains. The Elders were dressed in traditional clothing, while the kids wore Nike shoes and sweatshirts. It was the Fourth of July games, the biggest night of the summer. Ladies walked around the tundra modeling bright flowery tunics they had stitched by hand, laughing and cheering for one another in Inupiaq as they strutted past the judges. Next to the fashion show, two kids were throwing "horseshoes" back and forth, two bullets spliced together by electrical tape, trying to hit sticks spaced ten feet apart. Another group was flinging darts off various body parts onto a chopping board. It was called "napatchuk," they told me, an ancient game that tests poise and precision.

I had never seen so many mosquitoes in my life. They surged up from the tundra, every footstep releasing a new cloud of vicious little vampires. I zipped up a full mesh jacket that covered my head, arms, and hands like a Hazmat suit, swatting at my face continuously just so I could see.

While Judith and I huddled inside our bug jackets and head nets, the locals didn't seem to notice. Ladies stood in the billowing smoke while kids cinched up their hoods and continued playing. Later, as I headed back to the bunkhouse to go to sleep, I heard engines firing up—Argo races were about to start.

As the rest of the country barbecued and watched fireworks light up the night sky, the Nunamiut people frolicked under the midnight sun, playing their ancient games on the tundra.

Anaktuvuk Pass was not the village I had expected. And yet, underneath the din of the Argos and generators and chirping cell phones, I could see their culture was still alive.

———

It wasn't until a little later that I learned how the Nunamiut had given up their nomadic way of life. In the 1940s, Sig Wien, a famous pilot from Fairbanks, used to deliver mail to the group of families living at a nearby lake. He began trading with them—swapping rifles and axes for wolf hides and crafts. But he wasn't fond of landing on the lake. He had to climb over a big hill to get there, and he never knew what the weather would be like on the other side.

There was a spot nearby that was totally open, a break in the mountains with clear access on both sides. So he encouraged the group of families to move east, promising more reliable mail service and a school for the children. In 1949, the Nunamiut Eskimo packed up their tents and belongings and moved to a windy plateau at the headwaters of the John River. They were soon joined by more families from around the region, and within a couple of decades there was a school, a church, a post office, and a few rows of tract housing.

There was nothing wrong with their earlier site. They weren't driven away by flood, famine, or fire—but by technology. Airplanes were the reason Anaktuvuk Pass existed. They were the next big boom to shake Alaska.

8
The Dream

Minto, Alaska • 1931

A young boy stands on a gravel bar and looks up at the sky. There's a faint buzzing in the air, almost like the sound of mosquitoes on the moist tundra. It grows louder and louder. He can't see it yet but he already knows what it is. The sound is unmistakable, completely unlike any other in this valley. To him, it screams adventure. A speck appears over the river, off in the distance, getting bigger every second.

He takes off, running down the trail as fast as he can. Clear Lake is a couple of miles away, and he can't afford to waste any time. A skin boot slips on the snow as he takes a corner too fast, but he manages to stay upright. The thud of his footfalls drown out his pounding heart. A few minutes later, he comes to the lake and stops to catch his breath. The pilot is just finishing unloading packages on the shore. He wears a large beaver coat, which isn't unusual in these parts. But with his leather helmet and goggles, the pilot might as well be from outer space.

The boy walks over to get a closer look at the airplane. It sits on two wooden skis, not much larger than the pair his dad straps on to go hunting. The pilot is just latching up the door of the airplane. He winks

Al Wright as a young man growing up in the village of Nenana. PHOTO FROM WRIGHT FAMILY COLLECTION.

at the boy as he climbs into the cockpit. It's not the first wide-eyed kid he's seen on the mail route. He shows up once a week to drop off mail, stopping in all the tiny Native villages scattered up and down the river. He usually lands right in front of town and makes a big scene. The kids come out in hoards to see the plane, to touch it, to look inside. They all want to be pilots. To a kid in the Bush, it's the equivalent of being Superman. Not that they've ever heard of superheroes.

The short visit is almost over. The boy can feel the draft from the propeller as the plane taxis away, etching fresh lines in the snow. Here comes the best part. The boy holds his breath as the pilot guns the engine, and the air around him explodes with energy. The plane skims across the lake and jumps into the sky, on to the next village. Free as a bird.

Standing on shore, the boy watches the speck fade out of the valley.

He would give anything to be in that plane. But he knows it will never happen. It's expensive to learn, and his family is poor.

Plus, who ever heard of a kid from the bush becoming a pilot?

Alaska Range • December, 1948

Alfred Wright remembered that feeling nearly twenty years later as he flew his Taylorcraft over the Tanana River. He could have played a pilot on TV by now, tall and handsome with deep brown eyes and ears that stuck out a little. The light hair of his youth had darkened, but still had a bit of the curl. As he flew toward the Alaska Range on a clear day in December, Denali filled the windshield in front of him, the south peak soaring above the ridge like the tower of a cathedral. "The Great One," as his Athabascan ancestors had named it, before they had any way of knowing it was the highest peak on the continent.

Al had put a lot of miles on the little T-Craft in the past two years. The single-engine propeller plane had a 65-horsepower engine and two seats, not much bigger than the old lifeboat he used to take fishing. Except it could take him to places he had never imagined—to sheep-covered valleys, hanging lakes, and glaciers dangling from the tops of mountains.

Today he was on his way to Bearpaw, a tributary of the Kantishna River that flowed out of a large glacier in the Alaska Range, to drop off supplies for a trapper camped at the mouth of the creek. Fur trappers were his main clientele at the moment. They were returning from the war in large numbers and needed a ride back out to their traplines. Dogs had been their main mode of travel in the past, but airplanes were faster, saving precious time during a short trapping season. After growing up in the area, Al knew most of the trappers scattered up and down the Tanana River. But he was hoping to expand his market at some point, because they weren't the most reliable customers.

"It was a tough operation because you had to haul 'em on credit 'til they caught something," he said.

And he had to keep a low profile as he flew in and out of the airfield in Fairbanks. The authorities wouldn't be happy if they knew he was flying without a license. He had only taken a few lessons before buying his first airplane. But he was learning a lot from the seat of his T-Craft—figuring out how to read the weather and the terrain, as well as the sounds, smells, and sensations of his airplane.

Today the airplane smelled faintly of salmon. Dog salmon, to be more precise. When he'd dropped the trapper off about a month ago, he'd promised to come back with a bunch of dog food. At the time, the plane had been filled to the brim with steel traps and snares, snowshoes and canned goods. He had managed to pack six dogs into the small space behind the seats—squeezed so tight he didn't have to worry about them causing any trouble. The sled wouldn't fit in the plane, so Al had tied it to the wing strut. Though many trappers were flying out to their camps these days, they still needed dogs to run their traplines all season.

Al felt bad it had taken him so long to return. He'd been planning the trip for nearly two weeks, but the temperature had been stuck at fifty-below zero, too cold to start his little engine. When the cold snap broke, he loaded the plane with boxes of frozen fish and took off from Nenana.

"I figured that guy's dogs'd be starving," he said.

He was about halfway through the one-hour flight, and had been following dog trails most of the way. He passed the Tanana River and flew into the foothills of the Alaska Range. It had been a high snow year, and the rugged country was smoothed over in white. About twenty minutes in, Al heard the rhythm of the engine change ever so subtly, as if it were skipping a beat. He didn't know what was wrong, but there was no way he could keep the plane in the air if he lost a cylinder. There was a lake about twenty miles away, so he turned toward it. If the engine could hold on for a few more minutes, he could set it down on the lake rather than crash-landing in the trees. When he got close, he killed the engine and glided onto the ice.

Bullet dodged, Al thought, hopping down from his seat.

He lifted the cowling and looked at the engine. Hmm, nothing seemed amiss at first glance. It must be something internal. His mind turned to the last trip he'd made near Beaver, a village on the Yukon. Running low on fuel, he'd stopped to fill up at one of the coal mines scattered around the area. They didn't have aviation gas, so he bought the closest thing: Blazo stove fuel. It wasn't ideal because there was no lead to slow down the combustion, but it had always gotten him home in the past.

Maybe the Blazo had overheated his engine. In any case, there was no way to fix it out here on the lake, with no heat and no tools. The more pressing question was, how was he going to get out of here? He had not filed a flight plan. Nobody knew where he was. He didn't have skis or dogs. It was going to be a long walk.

Al opened the compartment behind his seat where he always kept his emergency gear.

"Shit."

The food was gone. So were his extra clothes and heavy sleeping bag. In fact, the compartment was empty. During the cold weather, some-body must have broken in and stolen everything.

The only items left were the snowshoes (which he'd tied to the wing struts) and the sleeping bag liner he'd been using as a seat cushion. This was going to be worse than he thought.

It was too dark to start hiking, one of those painfully short December days where the sun barely breaches the horizon. Al made a fire and huddled into the skimpy bag, bracing himself for a cold night. He woke up early and started walking, long before the sun came up. Punching through knee-deep snow was exhausting, and he was barely making one mile an hour. He needed to find a trail as soon as possible.

He knew of an old one nearby that had been established by the postal service. Until recently, mail had been shuttled around Alaska by dog team, ten or twelve huskies driven by an intrepid mailman. These dog sleds covered hundreds of miles on their routes, crossing steep summits and icy overflow, with their drivers losing fingers and toes, sometimes even their lives, just to deliver the post. Mail carriers slept in cabins spaced every twenty miles or so, and Al was pretty sure there was one nearby. The trail was still used regularly by trappers, so it should be nice and packed down—a highway back to civilization. He just had to find it.

He cut through the woods, willows scratching his face and clawing at his parka. He continued hiking long after dark, long after his muscles ached from fighting the soft powder. It was fairly warm, just below zero, and the moon reflected off the snow to light his way. Just before midnight, after what felt like a year of walking, his boot landed on a firm surface. The trail.

Al almost laughed out loud.

Now if he could just make it to the cabin, he would be pretty much home free. As he started down the trail, the adrenaline wore off and he realized how tired he was. When he couldn't take another step, he stomped a flat spot on the snow and threw his sleeping bag down.

He was only planning to rest for an hour or so and then keep walking. He crawled into the bag, just to hold his heat, and passed out immediately. When he woke up a few hours later, he realized his mistake. While drifting off to sleep, he had left his hands outside of the sleeping bag. He was wearing thick gloves, but they were drenched from hours of vigorous hiking.

"So I got up and I was gonna build a fire, but I couldn't move my hands. And I couldn't get these gloves off because they were froze to my fingers."

When he tried to wiggle his hands, there was no response, almost as if they belonged to someone else. He had no choice but to start moving again. He slipped into his snowshoes (luckily he had the strapless kind) and started down the trail, his fingers throbbing as the blood flow returned. About a mile and a half later, he came to the log cabin, barely big enough for a bed, stove, and a small table in the corner. The door was open and the stove was loaded with wood.

"In those days they left shavings and kindling and a box of matches, everything you needed to get a fire going in the stove. So all you did was light a match," Al said.

He held his hands close to the iron as it got hotter and hotter, feeling the pain of circulation returning. Finally, when his whole body had thawed out and his cheeks were flushed, he curled up next to the stove and passed out. It was after noon the next day when he woke up. The fire had gone cold, though the cabin still held a trace of heat. He hadn't eaten for two and a half days. He found a can of Campbell's chicken noodle soup on a shelf and sawed it open with his knife. He guzzled down the cold gloopy meal, using his fingers to scoop out every last chunk. He cut some firewood to replace what he had used, then went back to sleep. The next day, he set up the stove exactly as he had found it and took off before daylight. By two in the afternoon, three days after he had left, he was back in Nenana.

Fairbanks · 2014

Al leaned back in his suede easy chair, feet propped up on the leg rest. He was dressed in brown slacks and a plaid button-down, thick silver hair combed neatly to one side. It was a few months before his ninetieth birthday.

"Did you ever figure out what happened to the airplane?" I asked, sitting across from him on a chair I'd pulled over from the dining room table.

"Burned the piston out," he said.

Just as he'd suspected. When he'd arrived in Nenana, he talked another pilot into retrieving the engine from the far-flung lake and bringing it to the shop in Fairbanks, where it was confirmed that the Blazo fuel had been a bad idea. It had burned so hot and fast it had scorched a hole in the metal.

"I'd always made it home so I thought it was alright to do. But I found out later that was not the thing to do," Al said. His lips twitched as they tended to do when he was recounting a funny story or a silly mistake that had nearly gotten him killed.

And, as I was starting to discover, Al had no shortage of stories like that. Not because he was reckless or cavalier, but because he had basically taught himself to fly. Hundreds of hours of flight time weren't required back then, and nobody was really checking. Plus, these were the days before instruments or weather data or fancy navigation systems. Al learned to fly with a map and compass, with no reference point but the mountains, valleys, and creeks he could see from above. Each flight took a little dash of luck, and Al was the first to admit it.

"I guess I got someone watchin over me somewhere," he said.

He chuckled softly. It was as close as he would get to sounding sentimental. Over the next few years, as he steadily transformed from my interview subject to my friend, I learned that Al was a man whose feet were firmly planted in the physical world. It's not that he was remote or cold. In fact, as I got to know him better, I found he was incredibly big-hearted, always greeting me with a warm hug and sending me home with tomatoes from the greenhouse or a giant King salmon fillet. It's just that he had stared death in the face so many times—he'd fought in a war, lost a child tragically, and watched so many friends die in plane crashes over the years—that it must have lost some of its emotional charge.

I looked out the living room window. The Chena River was freezing, ice slowly crystallizing from the surface down, until it would be strong enough to support skiers, snowmachines, even airplanes. A bright orange ski plane sat in the driveway like a tropical bird resting on the beach. The 1946 Aeronca Chief was the last of Al's fleet. A paved ramp led down to the water so he could take off right from his backdoor.

Al built this home with his third wife, Jeannie, five years ago, as a place to grow old together. It was one floor with a roomy kitchen and a heated garage, and a big garden where they could work side by side. But she passed away shortly after they moved in, leaving a void that was still palpable today.

"She was a good woman," he said, nodding slightly to himself. "We got along real good."

Al shifted in his recliner, uncrossed and recrossed his feet. He wasn't what I had expected when I knocked on his door that afternoon. I had flown on Wright Air Service before, like anyone who traveled to the bush regularly, so I definitely knew the name Al Wright. And I had heard stories about the early aviators like him, the ones who pried open Alaska's skies with their small planes and big dreams. I suppose that's why I had expected a cowboy of the sky, a death-defying personality who looked down on mere mortals. But with his soft-spoken manner and wire-rim glasses, he seemed more like a professor than a bush pilot, throwing around numbers for payloads and air speeds in the same tone you might use for a lecture on thermodynamics.

Behind him, a host of flying awards stared down from the wall, in gold lettering and official stamps: FAA master pilot, a certificate of honor from the Alaska Legislature, Alaska Aviation Legend. The poor Native kid who had become a famous bush pilot, the dream that had somehow come true. That little boy racing through the woods had no reason to believe he would ever set foot in an airplane. Al had grown up in the bush with no money or connections. He dropped out of school in fifth grade to help take care of his family. He barely knew how to read or write.

But then things happened that no one could have anticipated, things that nearly ripped the world apart but also created unthinkable opportunities. That's why I was sitting in Al's living room on a frosty day in November, sipping a cup of green tea. I wanted to know what life was like before the airplane, when the fastest mode of travel was on the back of a dogsled. How had airplanes changed the trajectory of Alaska, and at the same time, the fate of one village boy? Al had catapulted himself from one world to another, had taught himself to fly and then soared to the top, starting one of the most successful air services in Alaska, the same one that had flown me to Anaktuvuk Pass. Clearly airplanes had been a major turning point for Alaska, a groundswell on par with the Gold Rush.

Having seen it from both sides, maybe Al could answer my question about airplanes, and all the modern things they brought with them: Had it really made life any better?

9
Beaver Creek

The float trip was my idea. It was Labor Day weekend, one of the last chances to go camping before winter, and I wanted to see fall colors in the high country. The White Mountains wrap around the northeast rim of Fairbanks, a four-thousand-foot wall of limestone chiseled with sharp cliffs and rounded valleys. Each one holds a creek, some fast, some dry, some silty, some clear, rushing down from the mountains like a liquid orchestra toward the enormous basin of the Yukon.

I had heard Beaver Creek was especially beautiful. It flows around the southern end of the mountains, before veering north and draining into the Yukon River. We were planning to launch our boats where Nome Creek came in and float about forty miles to Fossil Creek, then hike through the hills back to the car. This wasn't new territory for me or Josh—we'd done lots of winter trips in the White Mountains, armed with skis and snowmachines and sleds full of gear. But we had never been hiking there. It wasn't a very popular destination in the summer, and we were about to find out why.

We packed everything we'd need for four days of hiking and paddling in the backcountry: bug spray, bear spray, camping gear, food, and pack rafts—amazing little inflatable kayaks that weighed less than five pounds and slid easily into our backpacks. We launched from the Nome Creek campground, about an hour drive from town. On the way to the trail-head, Josh called his mom to share our plans, always a good idea when heading into the Land Without Cell Service. He told her if we were not back by Monday night to call for help. It was more a formality than anything—we weren't expecting any trouble in the White Mountains, one of the more modest ranges in Alaska.

If anything, I expected the hiking might be a little sloppy. Interior Alaska is famous for tussocks, shin-high mounds of grass that grow on top of permafrost. They can't spread out like normal vegetation because the ground is too cold, so they grow in wild tufts surrounded by fields of moss or water. Aside from fire or live snakes, I couldn't think of anything worse to walk on. But after studying the map, we found a route that looked pretty safe—we would hike up Fossil Creek, over Cache Mountain into the next drainage, and then follow Beaver Creek back to the car. If we were lucky, we'd have nice ridge hiking most of the way. At worst, a few miles of slogging and really wet feet, pretty standard for a weekend in Alaska.

I was also looking forward to seeing the country where Al Wright had grown up, in this waterlogged land of Alaska's interior. He had told me so many stories of his life out here, of traveling and hunting and flying these mountains. Now I would see it for myself.

Our dog, Atigun, jumped in my boat as I pushed off with my paddle. At thirty-five pounds, she fit perfectly in my lap with her paws resting on the bow. While Australian shepherds weren't exactly bred for water, she loved river trips because they promised lots of squirrels. Beaver Creek was a really nice float—brisk water with some fun riffles and channels to navigate. And the colors were fantastic. We paddled through paper birch the color of sunshine and thick patches of willows. There were Merganser ducks diving for fish and muddy chutes where river otters had slid into the water. Every once in a while, a falcon or kestrel would swoop down from the treetops, warning us away from their nests. After a half day of paddling, we found a sunny gravel bar and set up camp.

As we sat by the fire in the crisp night air, I realized this was probably our last camping trip of the year.

"It's been a good summer," Josh said.

If one metric was spending more weekends in a tent than in your bed, he was right. We'd floated creeks, hiked mountains, and camped on lots of gravel bars. Every night outside felt like a night well-spent, leaving me smiling and refreshed when I got back to work on Monday.

I scanned our campsite, amazed at how much gear I'd accumulated over the past few years. The bright yellow tent from REI filled with foam pads and feathery sleeping bags, our backpacks tucked under the vestibule. Two bubbly rafts propped upside down on the gravel, drying out, and a row of willows decorated with spray skirts, dry bags, neoprene gloves and booties.

I thought of the Indigenous people who had lived in skin tents and paddled down these same creeks and rivers in birch bark canoes. They didn't have life vests or dry suits or GPS apps on their phone, telling them where the next creek came in. In those days, camping wasn't a hobby but a means of survival. Especially here in the Interior, home of the Athabascans. It was the most extreme climate in Alaska, holding titles for the coldest winters, hottest summers, and most mosquitoes. As a result, food was scarce, and people had to travel great distances to survive.

"If a family found a moose and killed it, they didn't take it to their camp. They moved their camp to the moose," Al had told me.

There were no villages in those days, not in the way we think of them today. Native people lived in small bands of four or five families, following food with the seasons and building temporary shelters from wood and animal skins. It was a tenuous existence, a constant battle against cold and predators. Some years there wasn't enough food to go around, and the weakest members of the group were left behind.

A harsh life, I thought, as the creek flowed peacefully by. The fading light danced on the surface, reminding me of a kaleidoscope. It was one thing to do this on the weekends, when I had a shower and fresh sheets waiting for me at home, but full time? I sipped my hot chocolate. I couldn't even imagine.

The next day we got on the water early. It was mid-morning when we made it to Big Bend, a rugged pyramid of limestone where the river made a hard right turn and flowed north, toward the Yukon.

Al had told me about this spot just the week before, how it had taught him one of the most important lessons of his career.

Today the sky was a cerulean shade of blue, but the great mass of rock we were floating past happened to be a magnet for storms. Parked at the intersection of the mountains and the flats, it's where cold mountain air meets with moisture from the Yukon River and makes clouds froth up like foam. As the current carried me around the bend, I wondered what it was like a few thousand feet higher. There was no telling from down here.

"That's the first time I figured out where weather came from," he'd said.

The lesson happened about sixty years ago, as Al was flying to the village of Fort Yukon. It was a snowy winter day, and the village clinic had called him in a panic—they had a patient who was very sick. If he didn't get to Fairbanks immediately, the health aide said, he wouldn't make it through the night. Al knew it was snowing in Fort Yukon, but he decided to give it a shot. He left Fairbanks in his Cessna 180 and crossed the White Mountains without any problem, but as soon as he got to the north side, he saw that the entire Yukon valley was fogged in. He flew just above the fog, cruising at about 3,000 feet, looking for a place to poke through. But as he got closer to the village there was no sign of the ground.

He decided to abort the mission and turn around. He wouldn't be paid for the trip, of course, but at least it wouldn't cost him his life. As he climbed out of the valley, the plane started icing up. This was a common risk of changing elevation quickly: the moisture picked up at lower elevations could freeze when you hit colder air up high. Al felt his wings grow heavy with ice. He could tell he was losing power and didn't want the airplane to stall, so he dropped down to pick up a little more speed. By now the fog had folded around him. Outside the world was white.

He maneuvered calmly, trying to find the sweet spot between speed and altitude—though keenly aware that he didn't have much time. The White Mountains were approaching fast, and he needed to climb higher to clear them. The wheel skis weren't helping. They were handy for bush travel, allowing him to land on either gravel or snow, but added about a hundred extra pounds to the airplane. Al inched up a couple hundred more feet. He could tell he was picking up ice again, because he had to keep increasing power to maintain his speed. The propeller was shedding most of the ice, but the rattling was unnerving.

Only ten miles to the mountains, and he still needed five hundred more feet of altitude. His Cessna felt maxed out, like a waterlogged ship that wanted to nose into the sea. It was all he could do to hold steady.

"So I just held that altitude and stayed right on the stalling point."

Finally he saw some darkness through the fog.

A hole in the layers?

He crept a little higher.

"Then the sky opened up to bright moonlight and I just followed Beaver Creek around the Big Bend."

When he landed in Fairbanks, he was relieved the harrowing trip was over. He called Fort Yukon to tell them what happened.

No problem, they said. Their patient was feeling better. No need to make the trip after all. Al could only shake his head; he had risked his neck to save another, and fortunately, this time had made it back alive.

The cold air wafted off the river like air conditioning. I paddled a little harder, trying to warm up my hands, as we headed into the massive shadow of the mountain. Fossil Creek was just a few miles ahead, where the hiking portion of our trip would begin. We had floated forty miles into the wilderness; now we had to get out. There were no good sandbars to pull up to, so we had to jump out of our rafts awkwardly, while still in the water, and wade to shore. The current didn't look that strong, but it managed to flip Josh's boat as he slogged over to the muddy bank.

"That was smooth," he said, emptying river water from the cockpit.

But he was laughing. It was a beautiful day, and we were in a beautiful place. No reason to fret over a little water.

Once on shore, the transformation from paddlers to backpackers began. This part always made me feel like an action hero. I swapped my rain jacket for a T-shirt, neoprene booties for wool socks, a winter hat for a brimmed one. After letting our gear dry out in the sun, we broke down our paddles, rolled up our boats, and jammed all the various pieces and parts into our backpacks. Time to hike.

That's when it all went to hell.

The first two miles led us through an old burn, a battlefield of dead trees lying at horizontal, vertical, and diagonal angles. You couldn't take two steps without having to climb over a trunk or shimmy between branches. I felt like someone in a spy movie, trying to crawl through laser beams to break into some secret government facility.

I tried to walk across a tree like a balance beam, but with a forty-pound pack it seemed like a recipe for disaster. Josh started angling left, toward the other side of the valley.

"Maybe there's a game trail over there," he said.

I managed a grunt of acknowledgement.

Please, God. Let there be a trail!

Within another twenty minutes we ran into Fossil Creek. Oops, that's where we were supposed to take out. I guess we'd misread the map.

"Let's cross here. The trail's probably on the other side," Josh said.

I eyed the water. There was no telling how deep it was, but it looked pretty swift, like it could sweep me downriver with one false step.

Atigun had already scampered across and was looking at us, tail wagging, wondering what the holdup was.

Josh went next. With his strong legs and sturdy frame, he wasn't easily pushed around. He gave me a thumbs up from the other side. Wading into my shins, I crossed quickly, managing to avoid any slippery rocks. Josh pointed to the top of the cut bank, where I spotted a lovely little trail.

It's amazing what a mile of pleasant walking can do for the spirits. The birds were chirping, and my feet were drying out. But my smile disappeared as we walked through Fossil Gap and into the next valley. The creek bed we were planning to coast up was covered in thick, head-high brush. Bashing through dwarf birch for miles did not sound appealing, so we decided to shoot for the hills. There's a general rule in the boreal forest that the higher you go, the better the ground.

I guess that doesn't apply in the White Mountains. The hillside was covered in swampy tundra, each step like sinking into memory foam. I kept my eye on the ridge ahead of us, envisioning nice firm ground.

After six hours at an excruciatingly slow pace, we realized we weren't going to find anywhere better before dark. So we pitched our tent on the flattest spot we could see and cooked up some dehydrated noodles.

As I laid in my sleeping bag, I thought of Al's reaction when I told him we were floating Beaver Creek.

"How you gettin out?"

"Walking," I'd said, with the chirpy confidence of someone who has no idea what they're getting into.

He looked at me and shook his head.

"That ground's no good for walking."

Al grew up among the meandering rivers and vast swamplands of the Interior. He knew it was a land for dog sleds or boats, or better yet—airplanes.

"There's a nice airstrip right at the mouth of Fossil Creek. I used to land there all the time," he said.

A private flight was way out of our price range. Plus, we were young and tough.

"It's okay, we don't mind walking," I said.

Josh had spent years trudging through tussocks as a firefighter, and I was no stranger to bushwhacking either. It's not like we were the first ones to ever attempt such a thing. After all, how else would Al's grandfather ever have made it here?

In the late 1880s, a young prospector named Henry Wright was working his way down the Yukon River. Originally from Montana, he had been in the North for a few years looking for gold, bouncing around the mining camps and Native settlements that dotted the river. While they shared many of the same creeks and trails as the Indigenous people, the prospectors easily stood out in their heavy wool trousers and floppy felt hats. Henry traveled light, carrying only the essentials on his long journeys: a rifle and camping gear, and some gold mining equipment. You didn't need much in those days—a gold pan and a shovel were enough to get you started. The rest could be bought, bargained for, or built.

Al didn't know much about his grandfather, only bits and pieces he'd picked up along the river over the years. But he knew Henry had owned a bar in Montana before being swept up in the gold rush. When he didn't strike it rich in the Klondike, he joined the flow of prospectors heading down the Yukon River into Alaska, filtering into all the little creeks and valleys, looking for gold. He stopped in many of the gold rush towns to restock on supplies and socialize, encountering many of the same faces as he worked his way from Circle all the way down to Ruby. In fact, Henry was pretty well-known among the footloose miners, having organized a few parties with local Alaska Native people that were well attended. Those dances used to last all night, a distinctive blend of square dancing and two-step with native drums and singing. Perhaps it was at one of these parties where Henry met Al's grandmother, Annie Glass, an Athabascan woman with long dark hair and regal cheekbones. They had their first son Joe in 1888. Al's dad, Arthur Wright, was born two years later.

Grandfather Henry continued prospecting with his young family for a couple years before he got itchy feet. Alaska hadn't coughed up the riches he'd hoped for, and he was getting restless with village life. While many prospectors brought their Native wives and children back home, others left without a trace, leaving only their surname behind. Al's dad was two years old when Henry disappeared from his life.

Nobody knows what happened to him. By one account, he went back to visit his former business partner in Montana and was met with a bullet in the chest. Apparently, Henry had cleaned out the bar's cash register to pay his way to Alaska, and his partner was still bitter about it.

"That's one way I heard it," Al told me.

He knows a little more about his grandmother, Annie. She was still around when Al was little, though she was very old by then. He remembers chasing her around and getting whacked with her walking stick. Though she didn't speak much English, his grandmother would tell stories in her native language. And, wow, did she have stories to tell. Annie Glass was born in Nulato, a Native settlement on the west bank of the Yukon River. The Russians had established a trading post there in the early 1800s, where they bought fur from local trappers and lived relatively peacefully with the local people. Until a dark winter night in

1851, when the neighboring Koyukon Athabascans stormed the camp-site and slaughtered everyone in sight.

"They stuffed up the chimneys, smoked em out, and killed em," Al said.

While raids were fairly common in those days, this kind of all-out massacre was rare. No one knew what had provoked it: perhaps the Koyukons had been insulted by the Russians, or they were envious of their trading relationship with Nulato. Whatever the reason, most of the band was killed that night. Annie was just a young girl. She and her sister escaped and walked more than two hundred miles upriver, where they found a small group of families camped by the Chatanika River. The young girls were accepted into the band and lived there, near an open hole of water where they could fish all year long.

It got cold overnight. In the morning, a hard frost crusted the tundra. Maybe it would make for better walking, I hoped, as we ate oatmeal spiked with coconut oil and packed up camp. But as we started hiking uphill, my calf muscles cried out in protest. It was like trying to walk on crème brûlée. As we worked our way toward the highest mountain in sight, we kept getting stuck in saddles, making it to the top of one ridge only to discover we had to drop down again.

Al's words replayed in my head as I trudged along miserably.

"That ground's no good for walkin," he'd said.

Why hadn't I listened?

Sensing my gloom, Josh kept up a steady stream of chitchat, telling me about some of the worst terrain he had encountered back in his firefighting days. The steep Idaho mountainsides, the horrible swamps outside Nenana where he "cold-trailed" fires for miles and miles, drag-ging his hand through the ashes to check for live embers. And the unfor-gettable bushwhacking he had faced on his very first fire.

"We had to cross three sloughs to get to the fire line, then three sloughs to get back to our camp. I got swamp foot so bad I couldn't wear shoes for a week."

Though I had never experienced swamp foot, I could indeed feel blisters tearing at the balls of my feet. By lunchtime, we made it to the ridge. Finally, solid ground! And a 360-degree view of the surrounding country. The tundra blushed a deep red, almost burgundy, streaked with golden stands of birch and cottonwood. To the south, I saw the twisty line of the river we had floated, wishing I was still in my boat. We celebrated our progress by soaking our bare feet in the sun. There was nothing better than fall in Alaska. If you could figure out how to bottle it up, surely it would be worth more than gold.

From here, the hiking was bound to be much better. And for the next eight hours, it was. Ati the pup was having a blast, racing up and down the hillside poking her head into ground squirrel holes. I was more conservative with my energy, knowing how far we still had to go, but the gravel under my feet had never felt so good. There were some challenging spots on the ridge. We had to sidehill across a steep face and descend a boulder field so dicey I had to crab walk down it. But compared to what we'd been through, it was heaven.

Meanwhile, in the back of my mind, I was getting a little worried about time. The ridge walking was great, but it was basically taking us in a huge circle around the valley we needed to cross, sacrificing speed in exchange for decent ground. We couldn't stay up high forever. Eventually, if we ever wanted to get back to the car, we'd have to drop down and face the tussocks again. According to the GPS app on Josh's phone, we still had a long way to go.

We camped in a nice bowl that night. The sunset torched the sky in reds and oranges, like a private show that had been staged especially for us. Off in the distance, Beaver Creek curled through the valley. I looked at the wide green gap between us and the creek, and between the creek and Josh's truck. It looked so lovely from here. But I knew better.

Drifting off to sleep, I imagined the worst-case scenario. We wouldn't make it out in time to check in with Josh's mom. She'd call the Troopers and they'd send in a search party. I'd never recover from the shame of having to get rescued in the White Mountains, and would have to leave Alaska forever as a result of sheer embarrassment. Just as I was getting comfortable here.

Al Wright with
his first airplane.
PHOTO FROM
WRIGHT FAMILY
COLLECTION.

The next day we dropped down from the ridge and faced our fate. The tussocks were the worst I'd ever seen, mounds of spiky grass spaced every couple of feet, like giant pimples, far worse than anything we'd been through. Creeks trickled down the hillside and collected on the valley floor. We had the option of walking on top of the tussocks, which was like trying to balance on a soccer ball, or stepping between them into an ice bath. Each step seemed to drain all my effort, and then somehow I'd take another. Did this even qualify as solid land, I wondered, or were we in some whole new category? We drifted up the hillside looking for better footing, but were shut down by a wall of willows. I could see why the beavers liked it here, but with two long legs it was almost impossible.

Even Atigun was tired. There was no more sniffing, no whimsical squirrel chasing. She was all business—keeping her head down and charging through water that came up to her belly. When we stopped for a break, she immediately found a big tussock and curled up on top of it, shooting me a look that said, "This is your fault." To take my mind off the present conditions, I focused on the flip flops waiting for me in Josh's truck, and the juicy burgers we were planning to get at the Chatanika roadhouse on the way home.

Just keep going.

We have to get out.

We never have to come back.

That was the mantra that got me through two more miles of burned-out tussocks and a handful of creek crossings. As I bashed through willows along Beaver Creek, I heard a hum overhead. Up in the sky, high above the tussocks and brush and stagnant brown water, a little airplane buzzed cheerfully over our heads.

As I traced it through the sky with longing, I finally understood the strength of Al's dream.

10
Life on the River

Nenana • 1959

I was getting dark as Al approached Nenana. It was shortly before Thanksgiving, and the ground beneath him was frozen solid. The Tanana River cut through the valley like spilled paint, long white cords flowing over a dark canvas, weaving and winding, splitting and joining back together, as if time and space were no object at all. Al grew up on the Tanana, and knew its many moods. He knew that a strong current ran just below the ice, that the glacial water gushed and churned and roiled toward the sea. But from way up here, it looked as peaceful as a painting on the wall.

Al traced the contour of the river in his small airplane, as if he were following a trail. It made a big bend to the right and opened up to a small village on the bank. The Athabascans had called it Nenana—"a good place to camp between rivers." He looked down at the little boxes of fuzzy light, glowing in the wilderness. He would be home just in time for dinner.

At thirty-four years old, Al was already on his fourth airplane. The Gullwing Stinson was the nicest one yet—a single-engine, propeller-driven plane with a stubby nose and humped wings, like a seagull.

He had worked hard to get it, had flown trappers and fur buyers and trophy hunters around the backcountry; had shuttled whale and seal and moose meat between villages; had helped biologists count sheep and surveyors measure mountains, all from the worn leather seat of his T-Craft. With double the horsepower and three extra seats, the Stinson was his ticket to the next level.

Al had just finished fixing it up, tuning the engine, replacing fittings, installing an extra heater to get ready for winter. The only thing left was the fuel selector valve, a tiny piece of metal between the pilot and copilot seats that switched from one fuel tank to the other. He knew it had a slow leak, but the replacement part hadn't arrived in the mail yet. He figured it would hold out for another week or so.

Al's elbow nudged a two-by-four as he reached across the control panel to flip a switch. He had just picked up lumber in Fairbanks for a house he was building over the summer. Al and his wife Shirley had been living with his mother for the past year, but with a toddler in the house, it was starting to get crowded. And so a stack of two-by-fours stretched the full length of the cabin, short edges resting on the floor next to Al. He had removed the passenger seat and loaded them through the cockpit window, a trick he had learned from one of his mentors many years ago.

Al's friend Hank was squeezed in the backseat, behind a wall of wood. Hank managed the airport in Nenana, and they'd been friends since they were kids.

From a thousand feet up, Al could barely make out the bell tower of St. Mark's church. Made from milled logs with arched, stained glass windows, the church had been built by Episcopal missionaries around 1907. How strange to think such a modest little building had wielded so much influence over his life. It's where his dad had worked as a kid, where he had met Al's mom as a young man, and where they had both decided to dedicate their lives to the church.

Arthur Wright was a priest, but one who believed in science and medicine as much as the power of prayer. He was a master mechanic who could fix anything, a loving father who taught his kids how to survive in the woods. He was a man who had overcome his circumstances to accomplish a great deal in life, especially for an orphaned "half-breed" who was never expected to amount to much.

Arthur was only two when his father dropped him off at the mission in Tanana and continued downriver. Arthur never saw him again. Though he had inherited his mother's thick black hair and intense gaze, he had never really known her as a child. Instead, he was raised by the missionaries of the Episcopalian church. Though they accepted the orphans left at their doors, it wasn't an easy life.

"They made slaves out of those kids when they got old enough to do anything," Al said.

Arthur chopped wood and worked in the garden, while his younger sister Celia cooked and cleaned. Domestic life was quite a change from the subsistence culture he had come from. Arthur's older brother, Joe, detested the chores. When he was nine, he ran away and moved in with another family downriver.

But Arthur had thrived within the structure of the church, and he impressed the missionaries who ran it. Reverend Jules Prevost and his wife, Louise, had moved up from Philadelphia to live with the Athabascan people and teach them about Christianity. When they noticed Arthur's quick wit and desire to learn, they took the young boy under their wing. He spent mornings studying English and violin and afternoons playing with their son, Horace, who happened to be the same age. Within a couple of years, Arthur could play just about any hymn by ear, and he could read and write just as well as he could hunt and fish. He'd become best friends with Horace, and practically part of the family.

Of course, the missionaries couldn't erase his roots completely. When Arthur was 16, Mrs. Prevost remarked in a letter to her mother: "We want to give him every chance in life, but we wish he showed less of the Indian and more of the white ambition."

As a teenager, Arthur yearned to go to school, to study engineering or blacksmithing, things he would never have a chance to learn in the bush. Though it was a privilege typically reserved for white children, Arthur saved up his money from the sawmill and soon found himself traveling four thousand miles across the country, to a private boarding school in Massachusetts. At the Mount Hermon School for Boys, he learned about agriculture, carpentry, and religion, as well as subjects he'd never even heard of. Though he had finally gained entry to the modern economy, his heart was still in Alaska. In a letter to Mrs. Prevost, he talked about coming home.

"I hope I shall some day be of some use in this world for my people. How often I think of my people, my poor people and wish I could help them in some way."

His concern was well-rooted. It was a time of upheaval for Alaska Native people, whose land and way of life were under assault. First the gold rush had swept through, bringing white prospectors into every region of Alaska, staking claims and building cabins on lands where Natives had hunted and fished for thousands of years. While the pioneers took their land, the churches came after their culture.

Without an organized religion or even a written language to fall back on, Indigenous people were an easy target for the missionaries. Given the harsh environment they lived in, Alaskans had been too busy trying to survive to write books of philosophy or build elaborate cities. Instead, their history and values had been passed down through stories, sitting around a campfire or inside a dark tent. And this type of oral culture was very susceptible to the tactics used by missionaries. Churches pushed into every region of the state—the Episcopalians in Tanana, the Presbyterians in Barrow, the Moravians in Bethel—opening schools and churches and hospitals. They ordered people to stop singing their traditional songs and dancing their traditional dances, teaching them to dress and talk like westerners instead.

Al's father had been caught up in this wave, as an orphan looking for his place in life. After finishing his studies in Massachusetts, Arthur rode a train to California to learn about agriculture, seeing how people lived on both coasts of this foreign land. When he came back to Alaska a few years later, he resumed his work for the church. The Episcopalians were expanding throughout the territory, and needed locals who knew the language and the country. Arthur worked as a guide, ferrying clergymen around Alaska to visit remote villages and preach at tiny parishes, from Canada all the way to the Bering Sea. He fixed boat motors and dog sleds, found the best camping spots, and communicated with Indigenous people they met along the way.

"My dad could talk any dialect all the way down the river. He could interpret for all the church people who went on these tourist trips," Al said.

Arthur was eventually picked up by Hudson Stuck, Archdeacon of the entire Yukon. Originally from England, Stuck was loved throughout Alaska for his kindness and respect for Native traditions—not such a common trait among the early missionaries. Al's dad accompanied him all over the Interior as he gave sermons and performed baptisms. Stuck talked about Arthur often in his diary, calling him "the best English-speaking boy in the whole Yukon, putting many a white boy to shame."

The ridge smudged against the darkening sky as Al looked down at the land he called home.

Al had been born in Tanacross, a tiny Athabascan village far upriver. When his mother went into labor in the spring of 1925, a mission nurse had traveled two hundred miles by dogsled for the delivery. Al was nine when his family moved to Nenana. By then it was a whole different place than his parents remembered, with roads and a school, and even a small movie theater.

Al spotted his house in the center of town. The lights were on, and he could picture Shirley making dinner while their two-year-old daughter Kathleen toddled around the wooden floors. His mother would be seated in her favorite chair, knitting, perhaps, as she kept an eye on her grandchild. His mom was barely more than a kid herself when she had first traveled to Alaska. It was where she had met Al's father and raised seven children, where she was now watching her grandchildren grow up. But it was very far from where she had come.

Myrtle Rose was a child of a different frontier. Her parents ran a store in Idaho, where they sold everything from fuel to tobacco to crop seeds to pioneers migrating west to start a new life. And she would start a new life for herself, too, far away from everything she knew. After finishing nursing school in Philadelphia, she found a job as a mission nurse half a world away. In 1919, she took the train across the country, boarded a ferry, and rode another train north. She chatted and played cards with her sister, who had come along to keep her company. After a weeklong tour of the settling country, the two young women stepped off their steel passenger car in the middle of the Alaska Range.

The train tracks ended one hundred miles from Nenana, on the opposite side of Hurricane Gulch. Myrtle and her sister had to climb down the plunging ravine in their traveling dresses and cross a frothy stream to reach the wagon road on the other side. From there they followed the road north, hitching rides with passing wagons whenever they could. It was just before winter when they made it to the mission, which consisted of a school, a dormitory, and a small hospital, where Myrtle worked.

She was just getting oriented when the Spanish flu epidemic hit, with a ferocity the world had never seen. It had already ripped through most of Alaska, decimating nearly half the Alaska Native population, who had no resistance to the virus. The young nurse was inundated with patients as the whole village caught a fever. It was the middle of winter, a difficult time to be laid up for weeks.

"She says half of them died from pneumonia instead of the flu because they'd be out trying to cut wood too soon and get cold," Al said.

Across the state, thousands of people froze to death or starved, too weak to manage the daily work of survival. Children lost parents; entire villages disappeared.

"There was one village that used to be in Minchumina, it was probably about thirty people living there. The whole village died," Al said.

As the Elders passed away in staggering numbers, taking many of their traditions with them, Myrtle and the other health workers could only watch in despair. Despite their efforts to fight the virus, it wiped out a quarter of Nenana. Somehow, Myrtle never got sick. After the pandemic passed, she met a handsome young missionary named Arthur Wright. Their backgrounds were as different as their looks: Myrtle with fair skin and chestnut hair, Arthur tall, dark, and strong. Though interracial relationships were frowned upon by the church, especially when they involved white women, Al's parents fell in love. They got married in 1922, the same year Arthur was ordained. Then they were sent deeper into the woods.

Looking down at the shingled roof of St. Mark's, Al thought about how much his parents had given to the church. They had traveled across the country to follow their faith, had moved to some of the wildest places on earth to minister to people who still worshipped animal spirits. For ten years, they had bounced around the bush with a herd of small children, all in service to the church. If only the church had been so loyal in return.

Al came to a fork where the Nenana River flowed into the Tanana just south of the village, and two bold white lines became one.

"Set any lines out for blackfish?" Hank said from the backseat.

"Yep, gotta check em tomorrow."

Though Al's career as a pilot meant he could afford to buy groceries these days, he still lived a largely subsistence lifestyle. It was the only way he knew. His family had never had the option of picking up meat or vegetables in town. The closest store was fifty miles away, and they didn't have enough money to shop there, anyway. So the Wright family had lived like everyone else in the region, hunting and foraging from the vast grocery store around them.

He saw the island on the north side of the river, where he'd spent so many days of his youth. The strip of gravel had been sliced away from the bank, just barely attached like a hangnail. One of the best fishing spots on earth. When the salmon started running in June, the Tanana River turned into a fast-flowing food court. As thousands of fish swam upstream, fighting the current with every bone in their body, they paused in eddies along the banks to rest. That's where Al's family had put their fish wheel. The large wooden wheel looked something like a turbine, sitting on a floating dock and rotating in the current. Except instead of blades, it had two giant baskets that scooped fish out of the water and dumped them into a holding tank, far more efficient than a line or a net.

As boys, Al and his brother Gene had paddled out in an old alumi-num-bottomed boat every morning to check their haul. They grabbed cold slippery fish from the basket, one by one, and flung them in the boat. When the fish were really running, they could barely keep up. Salmon flopped out of the wheel, wriggling and thrashing like slimy demons, some almost too big for Al to hold. Once he was able to grip the tail, he silenced them with a swift club to the head.

His brother Gareth was too young to collect fish, so he set up a table on the beach to process them. Working swiftly with an ulu, he slit the salmon lengthwise, removed the backbone, scored the flesh into one-inch sections, and hung them on racks in the sun to dry. After a few days, their wooden fish house would be overflowing with salmon, bright pink strips dangling from the spruce poles like tinsel. These fish camps lined the river, spaced every twenty miles or so, with families working side by side to pull protein from the water. Al and his brothers cut fish from morning until night for six weeks straight, enough to feed nine mouths for the whole year, plus the dogs.

It was the only reliable food source, after all. Caribou were unpre-dictable, their migration always in flux, but the salmon surged up the river every summer like clockwork. Once the strips had dried, the boys packed them into bales the size of small suitcases to store for the winter.

That was the center of life in the Bush. Everything revolved around winter. Summer was more of a mobilization period, a chance to put away enough calories and firewood for the whole year. Because soon the cold would drop like a hammer, and most of the food would vanish— migrating south or crawling deep into the ground. The Wrights planted a huge garden in the backyard and preserved as many vegetables as they could in the root cellar under the house.

"We always had cabbages til Christmas," Al said.

Keeping things frozen was easy enough. They built a wooden shack behind the house and sawed hundred-pound blocks of ice from the river, covering them in sawdust so they wouldn't melt. Temperatures started dropping in August—the berries plumped up and the aspen glowed yellow. Then one day, when kids in the Lower 48 were still swimming in the ponds and playing baseball late into the evening, Al would wake up and see fresh snow in the mountains. Hunting season had arrived. Fall was the last chance to load up on game until spring. For two weeks, the valley surged like a brown tide as thousands of caribou migrated down from the White Mountains. The McKinley herd spent the winter on the north side of the Alaska Range, feeding on tundra that was blown clear by the wind. It was one of the freshest meat markets on earth. In an average year, Al and his dad got about twenty caribou, shooting the fattest animals they could find. They piled the carcasses on the ground and waited until Freeze-up to come back for the meat.

While automobiles were taking over in the Lower 48, and a highway system sprouted across the nation like a spiderweb, the main form of transportation in Alaska still had four legs. The Wrights had six Mackenzie River huskies that were one-quarter wolf, like many village dogs back then. Built like the freight trains that sometimes whizzed through Nenana, the large furry dogs could haul heavy loads of ice or meat or firewood for miles on end. But they were work animals, not pets, with a very different personality than the family retrievers down south.

"They were always itchin for a fight. Man, they'd tear each other to pieces. You'd have to get a club and club em before you could get em to stop fighting," Al said.

He remembered the time his little brother Jules came running outside when the dogs were loose. Al had just returned from a hunting trip and hadn't chained them up yet. Jules was wearing a parka and skin boots. Smelling the fur, one of the dogs started chasing him. Jules's screams only made it worse.

"The dog grabbed him and knocked him down, and the other two dogs came running over and chewed the heck out of his one leg."

Al and Gene dove in with sticks, beating the dogs until they finally retreated. He lost some blood, but fortunately Jules kept his leg.

Though they weren't the cuddliest of creatures, huskies were absolutely indispensable to living in the bush. One year, when Al's family ran out of potatoes toward winter's end, he accompanied his dad to Totchakat Slough to restock. A farmer had settled there and carved long rows of potato patches into the side of a riverbank, using six bloodhounds to pull his plow. Al hooked up the dog team in two strings of three. He rode in the sled while his dad stood on the runners, calling out occasional commands as they loped through the woods. They didn't need much direction though; navigation was in their bones. The dogs knew how to handle the thick trees and soft spots of ice, knew which path to take when the trail forked. When they got to the farm, they purchased a few sacks of potatoes and laid them inside a wolf hide in the sled.

When it started getting dark about halfway home, Al's dad found a clearing where they could camp for the night. They never brought tents or sleeping bags, just made do with the resources around them. Arthur cooked dinner while Al tied the dogs off to trees and tossed them some frozen fish chunks.

While his dad kept the fire going, Al sawed branches from the standing dead trees and built a second fire on the snow. By the time they finished eating, it had melted all the way down to the ground, creating a pit large enough to park a car. Arthur cleared out the coals and laid fresh spruce boughs over the heated ground, a homemade radiant mattress. Over the bed he laid a large wolf robe lined with wool.

"We got in there, man, we were nice and warm all night," Al said.

He had learned so many tricks like that from his dad, survival skills that had been passed down since ancient times. Ways of tracking animals, reading rivers, and finding his way through country that could kill you a hundred different ways. But times were changing. The new world was pushing in, with its strange people and rules and technologies, and there was nothing any of them could do about it.

Al flew over the river just south of the railroad bridge. Nothing embodied change more vividly than the seven-hundred-foot span of webbed steel stretching across the Tanana River, connecting the southern peninsula of Alaska all the way to Fairbanks. The bridge between the past and the future. President Warren G. Harding had even come up to drive the final golden spike in the ground in 1923. After nearly twenty years and millions of dollars, he was hoping the Alaska Railroad would pay off, attracting mining companies and businesses just as the railroad had done in the west a generation before.

When Al's family moved back to Nenana in 1934, after a decade of bouncing around the bush, they found a whole different place than the one they had left. The railroad had brought thousands of newcomers to the old fish camp, transportation officials and engineers, merchants and missionaries, creating a newfangled class system in a clan-based society. The groups didn't exactly meld.

"The whites lived on one end of town and the Indians down at the other. The half breeds were in between. I was three-quarters white—that wasn't quite as bad as being half," Al said.

The racism didn't end at the door of the church. While Al's dad had spent his entire life serving the Episcopal church—had escorted clergymen all over Alaska, had built farms and schools and missions—he was never fully accepted.

"They'd invite my mother to parties when all the bigwigs of the church would show up and they wouldn't invite my dad, and that made her mad," Al said.

Myrtle complained to the leadership, but nothing ever seemed to change. Finally his parents had enough and left the one community they had always known. Arthur moved on to other odd jobs, while Myrtle continued caring for people who couldn't afford to pay.

It's hard to overstate the impact that missionaries had on Alaska, or to imagine how history would have unfolded without them. During the gold rush days, whites and Natives had gotten along pretty well, the Natives helping miners hunt and fish, while miners hired them as their boat captains and guides. White men had married Alaska Native women and lived in relative harmony, with a prevailing philosophy to "live and let live." But that was not the motto of the churches that were pouring into Alaska, looking to spread their influence and gain more converts.

"There was tons of them churches moved into the country tryin to take it over," Al said, his voice tinged with anger. "The Catholics, Protestants, Old Seventh Day Adventists, Presbyterians, a bunch of those holy roller churches. Probably a dozen total."

In the eyes of the church, the Alaska Native lifestyle wasn't just primitive but tainted with sin. That was the reason bad things were happening, the missionaries told them. Why they were losing the land and animals they depended on, why they were dying by the thousands from hunger and disease. It was because of how they lived and what they believed.

They needed to settle down and stay in one place to be closer to God, to abandon their feasts and ceremonies, their dances and language, and live like good Christians. And perhaps because of all the suffering they had already endured, many of the Natives actually listened.

The churches weren't the only ones forcing them to change. The federal government was part of it, too, launching a massive assimilation campaign through a vehicle that had proven so effective in the past: schools. Ever since the United States had "purchased" Alaska from Russia in 1867, at least in the legal sense of the term, the government had been pretty lax about education. But as more and more non-Natives flowed north—miners, merchants, and men of business—lawmakers decided it was time to step up their authority. They realized education was their greatest weapon when it came to "civilizing" Indigenous people: while they believed that most of the adults were a lost cause, the children could still be saved.

In 1905, Congress passed a law creating schools throughout Alaska, not just in the mining towns and Native villages but all across the bush. A few years later, the territorial legislature declared all children must attend. Some schools were operated by missionaries, some by the territorial government, and some by the federal government through the Bureau of Indian Affairs (BIA). But they all had one thing in common, the same policy that had been applied to Native American communities across the country—to erase Indigenous culture and replace it with western values.

Al saw it happen before his eyes. At the mission school in Nenana, his Alaska Native peers were forbidden from speaking their language, even though most of them didn't understand English. They would hide in secret spots to communicate, and stayed quiet the rest of the time.

"They'd give em a good whaling if they heard em talk Indian. They didn't want em to have nothin to do with any of the customs of the Indians, or their language, or anything. They were trying to turn em into white people," he said.

When Alaska Native families refused to settle down, the BIA took a more aggressive approach. In some regions, they made a registry of local residents and started tracking down school-aged children—rounding them up from hunting and fishing camps and sending them to school, often hundreds of miles from home. Parents who resisted were threatened with jail. Thousands of children were sent to boarding schools, where it was easier to cleanse them of their language and culture. Physical and sexual abuse were rampant in these schools, not to mention the emotional toll of being ripped away from their homes and their families, from everything they knew. It was a trauma that had reverberated through the generations, and that many Alaska Native families are still struggling with today.

Al, for his part, hated school. While his dad had seen education as a path to freedom, to him it felt more like prison. He attended public school with most of the white kids, where he was lumped into a class with fourth, fifth, and sixth graders, with a white teacher from the States.

"She was just an itty-bitty thing. This one gal in my class beat her up one day so she was scared all the while she was there," Al said.

They studied math and grammar, the Civil War and the Constitution, the same curriculum as kids in Boise or Philadelphia. When it came to Alaska history and culture, it was as if they didn't exist. When Al's teacher left class to go to the bathroom, he used to climb out the window and run away. He knew she would never turn him into the principal and besides, he had better things to do. The real excitement wasn't happening in the classroom or in the busy shipyard on the edge of the river; but on a straight section of ice just below the bridge.

The aircraft mechanics were used to seeing the curious ten-year-old wander into the hangar. Al usually showed up in the afternoon, when the pilots were returning from their trips. Pacific Alaska Airways had set up a base in Nenana to haul mail and mining equipment out to the Alaska Range. The pilots landed on skis and steered their planes into large tents propped up on the ice.

Al shadowed the mechanics as they checked engines and oiled parts, rattling off questions about the airplanes. But his real attention was focused on the cockpit. He watched in awe as pilots hopped down from their planes, picturing himself in their balloon-shaped flight pants, their heavy coats and insulated mitts. One of the regulars, Frank Pollock, would often stop and chat with him, telling him stories about his adventures or showing him little tricks about how to load the plane.

That's how Al knew how to fit those extra-long two-by-fours into the Stinson, stretched from the tail to the nose. He would start building the interior walls this weekend. He was looking forward to moving into their own house. One bedroom for little Kathy, and another for the future children that were sure to follow. Unlike the room Al had shared with his six brothers, lined up on the floor like rows of potatoes, his children would actually have some space to themselves.

Al carved a wide circle over town, signaling his wife to head to the airstrip to pick them up. He was the only pilot who lived in Nenana, so there wouldn't be any confusion. Then he heard a shout from the back of the airplane, and three little words shattered his thoughts like thin ice.

"We're on fire!"

Al twisted around. The whole bottom was burning out of the airplane. Hank had already opened the door behind the pilot seat and was looking down at the ground. Al yelled over his shoulder.

"Don't jump!"

But at second glance, he saw his friend was just trying to get a better angle with the fire extinguisher, spraying the flames that had engulfed the engine. The cotton fabric that covered the plane ignited like tissue paper. In those days, the fabric was treated with nitrate dope to tighten it to the frame, which also happened to be highly flammable. Hank attacked it with the white spray, but it was no use. With an endless supply of fuel and oxygen, the fire inhaled the skin of the plane, burning rapidly toward them.

Al spun back around, mind racing. He had never covered this scenario in flight school. He tightened his turn and headed for the runway. If he could make it to the ground in one piece, they could jump out the door and run. A long shot, but possible. And his life had been full of long shots.

He tried to concentrate on the landing as the cockpit filled with smoke. Black, acrid smoke that flooded his nostrils and stung his eyes. He could barely see the altimeter as he dove toward the airstrip. They were six hundred feet in the air when Al was distracted by a deafening boom.

"The whole airplane belly exploded. The fuel tanks were in the wings, and why they never went, to this day I don't know," Al said.

It was getting harder to shield themselves from the heat. Hank huddled into the wool sleeping bag he'd been sitting on, wrapping it around himself like a cocoon.

Flames closed in on the cockpit, licking Al's boots, crawling up his legs. He pulled up the hood of his parka, covering his face with the wolf ruff. The fur burned off. His cheeks flared. But his hands stayed on the controls, protected by heavy fur mitts.

"These flames were just all around us, and I look at the instrument panel. The last thing I saw we were going one-hundred-thirty miles per hour and we were down to three hundred feet off the ground, and I could feel the airplane quit flying. The wings had burned off."

They went into freefall, dropping through the sky like a rock. Al had been in a stall before. Typically he would push the nose down, forcing air over the wings to produce lift. But the maneuver wouldn't work without wings.

"I thought, 'Well this is it. We're gonna die for sure on this.' I wasn't scared or nothin. I just figured, 'I wonder what it's gonna feel like to die.'"

Down on the ground, the residents of Nenana were just finishing up the workday, heading home from the shipyard and trickling out of the forest with loads of firewood. They looked up and thought they were seeing a comet—a fireball plummeting through the night sky, leaving chunks of burning fabric in its wake.

"They could see all the ribs of the airplane because there was no fabric left on it. We were just falling."

Al's mother watched in horror, praying for a miracle.

His younger brother, Punk, heard a neighbor yelling and raced outside.

His wife steered the truck toward the airstrip, with no idea what was happening in the sky.

Al caught one last glimpse of the river through the black smoke. Then everything went dark.

11
Kaboom

Al felt the crash vibrate through every bone in his body. He closed his eyes. But instead of blowing up, they continued falling. They hadn't made contact with the ground after all. Instead, the frame of the wing had caught a large spruce tree and swung the plane sideways. Now they were careening down the spine of the tree, slowing down with every branch they hit.

But there was only so much impact the tree could absorb. When the plane slammed into the ground, it sheared the wheels clean off the bottom, tossing Al forward like a rag doll.

The ball of burning metal came to rest a few hundred yards from the end of the airstrip, not far from the mangled tree that had saved their lives. Al opened his eyes. He didn't know how he was still alive, but every nerve in his body was firing the same instructions: run. He squeezed around the console and fumbled for the exit, leaning his shoulder into the door.

"Well, I went right out on the ground because the door was gone."

He took a big gulp of oxygen and called for his friend.

"Hank!"

No reply. Back into the fire. Al groped around in the smoke until he felt a hand, and pulled with all his strength. Hank snapped to and they started running, with no sense of direction except away from the heat.

Within thirty feet, Al's lungs filled with smoke and he passed out. When he came to, he was sitting by the road with Hank, barely able to hold up his head. His younger brother stood above them, and the three men watched in silence. The plane's fuel line had snapped, spewing gas onto the fire like a fountain from hell. The aircraft that had shuttled them safely over the mountains minutes ago was now a pile of rubble, blazing in the night sky.

It wasn't until the fire department arrived that Al realized he was hurt. When they hit the ground, he'd been slammed forward, tracing the shape of the instrument panel onto his face. It had sliced the skin away from the bottom of his nose around the outside of his eye and halfway up his head.

"Just about scalped me," Al said, running a hand over his forehead. "Just shaved the hair off."

His left eye felt weird, like it was glued shut, and for a moment he thought he might be blind. But it was just his eyelid hanging over it.

As the adrenaline wore off, his head started aching with a pain he had never experienced. Luckily a doctor was in town giving annual check-ups to kids along the river, and he sewed Al back together. Al was so sore from the impact he couldn't move for a week.

"It felt like somebody just worked you over with a sledgehammer from head to toe. Why we didn't break any bones or get burned is just a miracle."

Federal investigators never could determine the source of the fire. But Al has his own theory regarding the fuel selector valve, the one with a small leak. It must have gotten worse, soaking the airplane fabric in fuel during the flight. When Al started circling town and goosed the engine, it would have caused extra gas to build up in the exhaust. When he opened the throttle again, flames must have shot out of the exhaust pipe at the perfect angle to hit the belly of the plane and ignite. By that point the fitting had snapped and gas was squirting onto the fire, creating an unforgettable pyrotechnics display above the town of Nenana.

———————

Al touched the small scar on his hairline, a daily reminder of that long-ago night, where fate went in his favor. He remembered it like it was yesterday, but I guess that's not the kind of thing you forget. We sat in silence for a few moments.

I asked if he ever thought about quitting flying after the accident.

"No," he said, without hesitating. "It never crossed my mind."

12
Drafted

Al waited in line for lamb stew, the same thing he'd eaten for eight days straight. If he ever made it back from this mission alive, he would never touch lamb again. Or spam with reconstituted eggs, the only other meal served on this ship. He would trade his entire GI salary, in fact, for a bite of his mom's moose steak.

He was somewhere in the Pacific Ocean, with 1,600 other men—an assortment of husbands, sons, and fathers from all over the United States. They had no idea where they were going, except they knew it would be hot. They had been training in Fort Ord, California, for the past two weeks, ripping off rounds at the firing range and crawling across the terrain on their elbows, as live ammunition whizzed overhead, reminding them to keep their butts low. Then they were outfitted with tropical gear and loaded onto this ship.

Al steadied himself as the floor tilted. Growing up in Alaska's landlocked Interior, he was still adjusting to the constant motion of the sea. The long white vessel he was riding on was called a "Liberty ship," and they were being churned out in American factories by the thousands, to replace the ones being torpedoed by the Germans. It was a workhorse, an ugly freight vessel designed to hold nine thousand tons worth of tanks, airplanes, and Jeeps. But this wasn't a cargo run, and they weren't crossing the Atlantic. For the past week they had been getting pummeled by strong currents and powerful waves that could only be the Gulf of Alaska. Al knew they were going to Asia.

It had been a rough ride down in the cargo holds, where the troops were squeezed into the tiniest bunks Al had ever seen. They were piled ten men high, from floor to ceiling, stacked on top of one another like cordwood. If someone got sick, everyone below him did too. That's why Al had ditched his bunk and moved to the top deck, outside, in a quiet little corner nobody seemed to know about. While it rocked and rolled with the ocean, at least it didn't smell like puke.

The cook dumped a spoonful of stew in Al's bowl. Though it was gray and lumpy, he started eating immediately, shoveling it down with the insatiable hunger of a twenty-year-old who was only fed twice a day. They ate standing up, moving down a bar like a line of Jeeps getting refueled. Al heard the soldier in front of him curse as his tray was snatched away by the mess boy. It was a challenge to finish your food in just twenty feet, no matter how hungry you were. Al took one last bite and grabbed his dinner roll before his own tray disappeared in the garbage.

With his stomach still growling, he left the mess hall and headed onto the deck, where the wind changed direction with the capriciousness of a toddler. It certainly wasn't the interior Alaska weather that Al was used to, with stable temperatures and desert-like calm. Out here it could change in a flash, with blue skies erupting into sideways rain. As he curled up in the warm space next to the smokestack, he thought of the *S.S. Nenana* riverboat he had worked on as a kid. It had been his first real job, making three dollars a week. After twelve-hour shifts washing dishes, he used to sleep in the loft above the kitchen, where the ship's smokestack ran right past his head. It was hotter than hell in that little nook, thanks to the massive wood boilers down below. This ship ran on oil, not wood, and didn't kick out half as much heat. And out here on the frigid gulf waters, every bit of it felt good.

Looking out at the blue chop, Al wondered what was lurking under the surface. The Japanese had the fastest submarine torpedoes on earth; they could slice enemy vessels in half before you even saw them coming. Now that Al was finally headed to combat, it was strange to think how badly he had wanted this. Not just to join the Army, but to see a piece of the action. It seemed like all the guys his age were doing it, even from backwoods Alaska. When the military had shown up in 1942, they scooped up all the young men—the city guys from Anchorage and Fairbanks, as well as the trappers and miners and Alaska Natives from the farthest corners of the bush. You had to be eighteen to fight, but only sixteen to work for the Defense Department. Thousands of young guys like Al were swept up in the wave, assigned to build airports and docks and roads, while the older ones were trained to fight.

Al was nineteen when his wish came true. He'd been trying to enlist for months, but he kept getting deferments to work on other projects. When the draft orders finally arrived, Al's mother accompanied him to catch the train in Nenana, the same one that had brought her to Alaska two decades before. She held back tears as he gave one last wave through the window, the excitement plastered on his face.

After basic training in Anchorage, Al was stationed in Whittier, the main supply port for all of Alaska, where he'd spent ten hours a day loading and unloading boats. It was hard work, carrying hundred-pound bags of cement up creaky ladders, but they managed to have a little fun too. Al smiled thinking back to last Christmas, his first one away from home, when he and a few buddies nearly ended up in the brig after a seal hunting trip gone wrong. After getting stranded on an island in a nasty snowstorm, they were rescued by a military landing ship. How could they have known the boat they had borrowed without permission actually belonged to a VIP, the company commander who ran the entire base?

Al tucked his knees to his chest and looked out at the Pacific. He wondered where his friends were now, and whether they were still alive. It was hard to keep up with everyone at this point. So many had been killed the summer before, in the bloodbath they were calling D-Day. In early June 1944, sensing that Germany was beginning to weaken, the Allied Forces had launched the greatest invasion ever seen, flooding the beaches of northern France by ground, sea, and air.

The first ones sent in were the paratroopers. It was still the middle of the night when hundreds of C-47s took off from England, each carrying more than a dozen men in parachutes, moved into a V-formation over France, and carpeted the sky in big, white canopies.

"They just threw em out of the airplanes with a parachute, no training or anything. They knew they'd never make it, and fifty percent never even got to the ground before they got shot," Al said.

The parachute rip cords were hooked to a static line attached to a cable inside the plane. If a soldier got cold feet, the commander just pushed him out of the plane and the chute would open automatically.

"I had a buddy that went on that and he was killed before he even hit the ground," Al said.

Thousands of GIs were loaded onto gliders, silent aircraft with no engines or weapons, towed behind enemy lines by C-47s and cut loose. If they made it past the German anti-aircraft gunners, their job was to take out key targets on the ground.

"About half of them would crash because they didn't know how to fly em, and they'd stall out. The ones who did make it, most of em got killed shortly after they were on the ground," Al said.

By the time the flotilla landed on shore—five thousand vessels spread across five beaches—many of the airborne troops were dead. And that was only the beginning of the body count. More than 400,000 men were killed or wounded or disappeared during the Battle of Normandy, including many guys Al had trained with. It was a pivotal victory for the Allied Forces, and D-Day ended up turning the tide of the war in their favor. By the end of the summer, they had pushed the Nazis out of Western Europe and were getting ready to invade Germany. The next spring, just a few months before Al boarded the Liberty ship, Hitler's Army surrendered.

But even as the Nazis signed a treaty laying down all German forces, the eastern side of the planet was still raging with war. Though Japanese leaders knew they couldn't defeat Britain and the U.S. on their own, they had embraced the kamikaze code to fight to the bitter end. As parties broke out in the streets of Britain, the Japanese Army was still fortifying coasts and mountains to prepare for the inevitable coup de grace.

Al knew he was lucky to have made it this far. A few months earlier, his name had been on a list of paratroopers headed for Germany. But

Hitler's Army had crumbled faster than anyone had thought possible. So instead he was going south into the jungle, to a land he couldn't even imagine.

Then, on the tenth day, the ship turned around. There was no announcement from the officers' quarters—in fact, no information at all. Life at sea continued in a droll cycle of eating and sleeping. A few days later the ship landed on a speck of volcanic rock in the middle of the Pacific. The GIs didn't even know where they were as they walked off the ramp into a cold bank of clouds, but it clearly wasn't Asia. Most of them had never heard of Adak, a small island on the tail end of the Aleutians, home to just a few hundred Indigenous people. As Al carried his green rucksack across the rocky beach, he wondered what was going on. There was no way of knowing an attack was unfolding across the ocean at that moment, an attack that had changed their orders and would forever change life on earth.

"They dropped the atomic bomb just about the time we got to the Aleutians," Al said.

He leaned back in his chair and took a sip of water, having delivered this line about nuclear war in the same matter-of-fact tone he used for all his near-death experiences.

"Wow," I said.

Al's story, which already seemed apt for a Hollywood screenplay, had finally merged with my own version of high school-level history. I looked at my ninety-three-year-old friend, a war veteran and decorated pilot, and searched for that young man in uniform, walking across the Aleutian beach with no idea of what the future would hold, or whether he would even have one. Al had joined the military as a teenager, going from fish camp to boot camp overnight, called upon to defend a nation he had never even seen. World War II took the lives of sixty million people across the planet, shattering nations and shifting the center of world power. He had narrowly escaped a mission to Normandy and then another to the Eastern Front, battles that he likely wouldn't have come home from. But he had survived the war, and then so much more.

When I showed up on Al's porch three years ago, I had wanted to know how a boy from the bush had become a famous pilot, had overcome barriers of economics and education and geography to start a successful business that would become part of reshaping Alaska. Now that I had heard about the war, the picture was finally coming together. But just to confirm my theory, I wanted to hear it straight from him.

"So, was the war the biggest thing in your life, would you say? The thing that had the greatest impact?"

Al started nodding before I even finished my question.

"Yes," he said. "Definitely."

My original focus was airplanes, on how they had transformed Alaska, had brought the modern world into the farthest corners of the bush and turned life upside down for people like Al. But really, airplanes were just the byproduct. If it weren't for World War II, we never would have had the technology, the infrastructure, or even the pilots themselves. Someone like Al likely never would have set foot in an airplane.

Al had just been discharged when the U.S. government rolled out the GI bill, thanking veterans for their service with free tuition to the school of their choice. Across the nation, millions of young men started training to be doctors, electricians, teachers, and mechanics. But there was only one thing Al wanted to do. The thing he had wanted to do since he was six years old—to fly.

As soon as he heard about the program, Al hustled over to the small airfield in Fairbanks and signed up for flight lessons. He wasn't the only one who wanted to learn how to fly. Many Alaska kids had grown up worshipping pilots. Others had come up during the war and fallen in love with the Last Frontier. Being a bush pilot was pretty much the epitome of the Alaskan dream. Young guys swarmed the flying school in Fairbanks, waiting for hours to get access to an airplane. Soon a second school opened up just to handle the demand.

Of course, it wasn't a viable profession at first, without a license or an airplane. So Al made his living digging basements for new homes. A construction boom was rippling across the nation, from the east coast clear to Alaska, as the government scrambled to provide housing for all the returning veterans and their families. In between shifts on the bulldozer, Al ran over to Weeks Field to jump in an airplane, trying to squeeze in as many flight hours as he could. Two weeks in, he received some bad news. His teacher, Al Lorenzo, had been killed during a lesson, when the airplane lost a wing and crashed into the trees. After that, there weren't enough instructors to go around, and Al's formal training was over, almost as soon as it began.

But that didn't stop him when he saw a Taylorcraft for sale a few months later, for just $3,500. With a bold red stripe racing across white canvas, the little bush plane seemed to scream adventure. It had a 65-horsepower engine, two seats, and high wings that could land pretty much anywhere without getting hung up. Al was working at a coal mine at the time, busy supplying fuel for the rapidly growing railroad. This airplane would take him out of the mines and god only knew where else. So he counted his savings, borrowed a little money from his brother, and became the proud new owner of his first airplane. Of course, he would have to keep a low profile at first. You were supposed to have at least two hundred flight hours to get a commercial license. Al only had six.

Flying in the early days of aviation was a high-stakes game of trial and error. Aircraft had few navigation aids, and pilots literally flew "by the seat of their pants," relying largely on their gut to stay aloft. Crashes were more the rule than the exception, and he lost many friends over the years.

"Out of ten friends I had that were learning to fly the same time I did, all of them were killed in an airplane accident within ten or fifteen years," Al said.

Al's own younger brother "Punk" was killed when he was thrown from his cockpit during a snowstorm when he was only nineteen. Al searched for six months before he recovered the body. Another family he knew lost all four sons in plane crashes.

There were just so many things that could go wrong. You could fly into fog, lose contact with the ground, and not know which way was up. Or you could hit freezing drizzle, ice up the propeller, and stall the engine. When trying to cross the mountains, you could fly up the wrong draw, run out of power, and "auger in"—boring into the ground like a lawn dart. And those were just a few of the most common mistakes.

So why was Al different, I wondered, why was he still sitting here today? Was it natural-born talent? Superior judgment? Dumb luck?

Pilots just call it "instinct"—the ability to feel their way through a whiteout, to read the ice from a thousand feet away, to know what to do if an engine dies in mid-air. Maybe it came from growing up in the Bush—an innate understanding of the land and the weather. Before instruments, Al had to calculate wind speed by looking at leaves on the trees, waves in the water, or drifts in the snow. If he needed to know which way a river was flowing, he studied the trees along the banks.

"The stumps are always upstream, and the tree part is downstream," he said.

And if he ever got disoriented, there was always a fallback.

"If you follow a creek, it doesn't matter where you are. It will always bring you to some kind of village or town," he said.

It was this deeply ingrained knowledge of the land, of the country, that had kept him alive. The bush wasn't just a place he had come from, a place he'd escaped—it was the place that had made him a survivor.

I looked outside as a plane landed on the Chena River behind Al's house, floats skimming the dark water like the expert feet of a goose. Al had flown every inch of Alaska over the past seventy years—had landed between calving icebergs, swooped over valleys teeming with caribou, and nearly been clawed from the sky by an angry bear. He had seen sights that didn't seem possible—trappers pulling mink from under the sea ice and a grizzly hunting seals with the polar bears.

These were things most of us could only dream of, the type of natural phenomena that brought millions of tourists to Alaska each year, fueling a billion-dollar industry of cruises and helicopter tours and guided wilderness trips. The things that had brought me to Alaska. And Al had seen them all, not from a roped boardwalk or behind the window of a stuffy tour bus, but from the private gallery of his cockpit. He knew firsthand how amazing Alaska was. He must have felt passionate about keeping it that way, I thought.

Al Wright works
on his airplane in
his hangar on the
Chena River

Inside the living room, a news story flashed on TV with the words
"Arctic National Wildlife Refuge" crawling across the screen. The refuge
covered the whole northeast chunk of Alaska—twenty million acres of
mountains, rivers, and wild coastline. It was the largest refuge in the
United States, home to grizzlies and muskox and caribou, and considered one of the most pristine areas on earth. It was also a political lightning rod that, for whatever reason, had divided the rest of the country.
While most of the land was set aside as a wildlife refuge, where animals
were allowed to roam freely, one spot had been left open for potential
drilling. Oil companies had been trying to pry it open for decades.

Now President Obama was announcing plans to protect it. As I felt a
small flutter of victory, Al grumbled beside me.

"Environmentalists won't let us develop Alaska," he said, flicking off
the TV. "They're killing us."

He sounded eerily like Clutch, except Clutch was a miner whose
entire livelihood depended on resources, and Al had grown up in the
bush. He had lived off the land, had depended on the same fish and

game that would be impacted by this kind of development. He still did, for that matter. For some reason I expected his views to be different.

"So you think we should drill in the refuge?" I asked, trying my best to sound neutral.

"Sure," he said, as if I were asking an obvious question, like whether I could fish in the river outside his house. "We gotta develop our resources. It's the only way we'll survive."

I shouldn't have been so surprised, I suppose. After a few years of armchair conversation, I knew Al leaned to the political right, especially when it came to environmental issues. But I had also heard him complain about aspects of resource development: how gold mining had destroyed the fisheries where he grew up, how he had watched glaciers disappear before his eyes. Was he truly willing to risk the natural resources that had supported his family, and his ancestors, for so long? Or did he actually see conservation as the bigger risk? As I spun it around in my head, my eyes settled on the picture next to the front door. Inside a heart-shaped frame, an Athabascan woman stared solemnly at the camera. Al's grandmother, Annie Glass, stood in front of a canvas tent, her face seeming to bear the story of a hard life.

How different her life had been from Al's, I thought, and just two generations apart. Could she even have imagined this lovely house on the Chena River, with heated floors and a two-car garage, and a hangar full of airplanes and river boats and bulldozers? Or the second home he had owned in Hawaii, surrounded by banana and macadamia nut trees?

There had been no fresh fruit on his family's table in Minto, no airplane in the driveway. I guess that was the difference between the two of us. While I saw the past through a rose-tinted lens, admiring the adventure and self-sufficiency of the frontier days, Al didn't have to. He came from that world. He had never wondered what it would be like to live in the woods. He had experienced the hard edge of cold and hunger, and knew what it took to survive. He had climbed his way into the modern world, and the modern world was built on resource development.

That's why he wanted to drill in the Arctic Refuge, I realized. That's why he supported new roads and mines in Alaska, and maybe even why he believed that climate change was a liberal hoax. We had come from two different realities. While I had grown up dreaming about things like college soccer and world travel, Al was focused on whether he had enough fish and meat to get through the winter. My life had been a steady detour away from the hustle and bustle of urban life, and closer to the wilderness; his was a slow escape from it. He may have missed the adventure of the frontier days, he may have grumbled about the growing crowds and regulations of today, but he had no desire to go back in time.

I thought about the question that had led me here in the first place, to this cozy seat next to Al's stove. Were we better off today because of airplanes, and all the development that came with them? For Al, the answer was clear.

PART THREE
OIL

13
The Proposal

When Josh dropped down on one knee, I started laughing. I didn't mean to, it just came out. He was kneeling on the side of a mountain holding up a ring made out of candy. I honestly thought he was joking. It wasn't a diamond, or a gem of any kind, but a plastic band with a bright blue bauble of molded sugar on top.

We were hiking in the Wrangell Mountains over Summer Solstice. I had driven down from Fairbanks with three other friends to meet up with Josh, who was working down there for the summer, to do a four-day backpacking trip. As we started up the drainage of Lost Creek, we entered a kingdom of sculpted rock where thoughts of work and school evaporated into thin mountain air.

On the first day, we climbed up a high ridge to get a view of the surrounding peaks. Josh had been going his own pace for most of the afternoon, hiking ahead of the rest of us. Every time we caught up with him, he started charging uphill again.

"Wow, somebody put a quarter in him today," said my friend Kristin, a bubbly mid-westerner who had an expression for everything.

Two thirds of the way up, we sat down on the fluffy tundra to rest. Kristin pointed out the glacier on the opposite side of the valley, a long tongue of ice shooting down from the mountains. Suddenly Josh was kneeling in front of me.

"Molly Donovan Rettig, will you marry me?"

Apparently, everyone else knew it was coming. Josh had called Jake (Kristin's husband) and asked him to pick up a couple extra "rings" at the gas station on the way down. Backups, I guess, in the event the first one broke. Or a bear stole it or something.

It was one of the few weekends of the summer we would actually get to see each other. Josh was working six days a week, twelve hours a day, rebuilding the highway between Tok and Glennallen (a highway only by Alaska standards—it was really just a two-lane road through the wilderness that was slowly being dismantled by frost heaves). After finishing his civil engineering degree, Josh had gotten a job with the Alaska Department of Transportation, or as the insiders called it, D-O-T. Considering what the roads had to endure up here, it was a good line of work to be in. But it also meant that his summers were no longer spent floating rivers or barbecuing under the midnight sun with the rest of us, but living in a man camp on the side of the road—a cluster of campers and tents with two portapotties propped up in the middle, five hours away from Fairbanks.

I must say, he caught me by surprise. It wasn't the setting, so much. The white domes of Mounts Blackburn and Wrangell offered a dramatic backdrop for the big moment. And since we spent a lot of time in the mountains, it was a natural place for him to propose. The timing wasn't too shocking either—we'd been living together for a few years, and marriage seemed like the natural next step. Honestly, even the giant blue Ring-Pop didn't throw me off. Josh knew I loved candy and wouldn't be able to resist it. But I had never pictured having an audience when presented with the big question.

When Josh unsheathed the ring from his pocket, our friends Jake, Kristin, and Anna were sitting off to my side, just a few feet uphill, possibly more agog than me.

"Seriously?" I said.

Josh just stood there with a goofy smile on his face. I must have repeated myself three times before Kristin jumped in.

"Molly, answer him!"

I took a deep breath and let it sink in. It wasn't such a hard question, after all.

"Yes!" I said finally, practically yelling.

He slipped the plastic band on my finger. Blue raspberry—my favorite. The rest of the weekend was a bit of a daze, as we hiked up miles of gravel bars, climbed a six-thousand-foot pass, and scrambled up the side of a waterfall, as we played cards by the campfire drinking apple cider and whiskey. I thought about what a huge step we were taking, to commit to being together forever, or at least to try.

And when Josh walked through a wasps' nest on the last day of the hike, I worried that we might not even make it to the wedding. The last encounter with a yellow jacket had landed him in the ER. After some ibuprofen, he was fine, but I had a glimpse of life without him. Though in the back of my mind I wondered—did this mean I was here in Alaska forever?

That's what Josh's mom had been wondering, too, when she followed the man she loved to the place that was calling him. Patty Allan and Mike Kunz met at a ski club event their freshman year at Eastern New Mexico University. Though they were both dating other people at the time, soon they had rearranged themselves into a couple, and by their junior year they were married. Mike had always talked about going to Alaska, ever since he was a kid tromping in the woods and trapping small game in upstate New York. He loved the Adirondacks, but he craved more space, and fewer people—all arrows pointed north.

When Mike found a summer job in Fairbanks after they graduated, Patty agreed to meet him there in the fall. She was twenty-seven, tall and willowy with strawberry blond hair that she wore in long tresses that were in style in the sixties. She and Mike had been living like hippies since college. They spent the whole summer in a tent one year, hauling logs and picking berries to save up money for grad school.

Patty was always up for an adventure, but she wasn't planning to spend the rest of her life in Alaska in 1970, when she loaded her worldly belongings into a '49 Dodge pickup with chipped black paint that said "Alaska or Bust" on the tailgate. With one last hug for her best friends, she left behind a life she loved in the high desert. Not knowing when she and Mike would be back, she had found a new home for their pet owl, but the cats were coming along. Her Siamese cat Naiobi was curled up on the seat beside her, and Saki was in a cage in the bed of the truck, draped under a tarp. Patty felt bad sticking her outside, but thought it was best in case she got pulled over. Saki wasn't an ordinary cat. Twice the size of Naiobi, with dark spots and a striped neck, it didn't take an expert to tell she was a wild bobcat. Mike had found her in a culvert when she was just a kit, and she'd become a loved, though very large, house pet. And having a bobcat as a pet wasn't exactly legal, even in 1970.

Sharing the front seat with Naiobi was a box of potato chips, Patty's favorite snack, with a .32 revolver hidden inside.

"You might need it on the road," her old professor had said when he tucked it in her purse.

A map lay on the floor beside her, her route highlighted in yellow. With a hundred dollars tucked in her purse, she was ready for the 3,500-mile drive to Fairbanks. But she had only made it twenty-five miles before she popped a freeze plug and had to be towed back to Portales. The next day, she set off again, this time driving two hundred miles before the heater core failed and hot water started spewing all over the cab. While the cat recoiled in horror, Patty calmly disconnected the heater and plugged off the tube. The water pump went out near Tucson, just as the mechanic had warned. But he'd given her a spare and shown her how to replace it. She had already unbolted the part and removed it when a car pulled up behind her and a friendly man strolled up with a toolbox.

"Looks like you could use some help," he said.

While he disappeared under the hood, a pair of hitchhikers emerged from his car and wandered over.

"Wanna joint?" they asked Patty.

"No thanks," she said.

Perhaps something else?

"I'm fine," she said, turning her back to them.

It wasn't rare to get this kind of offer on the side of the road, but she didn't do drugs, and she really just wanted to get back on the road. While her helper searched his toolbox, Patty dug through the truck bed for her spare pump. When she came back, he was wiping his hands on a rag and looking satisfied. Patty glanced under the hood, then back at him, and paused. She didn't want to sound ungrateful.

"You just put my old one back on," she said.

Once they had straightened everything out, she was back on the road to Arizona. Her next stop was Scottsdale. Mike had had a gun stolen from his car when he passed through there in the spring, and the police had called to say they recovered it. But when Patty pulled up to the station, it was closed for the day. She sighed. She hadn't budgeted for lodging, as she was just planning to sleep in the truck. But the cats were wilting in the heat, so she dipped into her gas fund for a motel, waiting until dark to smuggle in the bobcat.

With two guns, two cats, and a full tank of gas, she was back on the road the next day. So far, so good, she thought, though she still had two thousand miles to go. Her next stop was Seattle, where she was planning to stay with some friends before driving the rest of the way to Fairbanks. Hours and hours of red rock passed by as she followed the highway north, snacking on potato chips to help stay awake. The sun was setting as she drove through northern Utah, painting the ridged sky in pinks and purples before draining away like bathwater. Then it was black— totally, impossibly black. She could feel her eyelids growing heavy, and she wasn't sure how much longer she could last. Finally she stopped at a pull-off to nap.

"I just did not like the look of it, and I was real nervous about stopping there, so I decided I'd wait til the next town."

As she merged back on the highway, a massive shape appeared from the corner of her eye and lunged in front of the truck. Was it a deer? She'd never seen one so large. But there was no time to tell for sure before she hit it dead on. She barely glimpsed her spare tire flying through the air as she spun off the road and landed in the ditch. When she opened her eyes, the animal was nowhere to be seen. And the truck was unresponsive. She sat there clutching the wheel in darkness, her heart pounding in her ears, not sure what to do next.

Half an hour later, a semi pulled up behind her.

Thank goodness, she thought.

The trucker pulled her out and towed her to the next service station.

"Thank you so much," she said, standing beside her vehicle in the empty parking lot.

But he wasn't ready to say goodbye to the beautiful young woman he'd saved from the ditch.

"Not so fast," he said, putting an arm on either side and trapping her against the car.

She opened the door and slipped inside.

"I need to check on my cat," she said, shutting the door tightly behind her. She rolled down the window, just an inch or two, but he didn't seem to get the message.

"It's not safe out here for a pretty girl like you. Sure you don't want to stay in my cab tonight?"

"I think I'm okay," she told him, patting the seat beside her. "I've got my gun right here."

At that, he finally left. She watched him climb back in the truck and drive away before she tipped her head back and fell asleep. The next day was spent sitting outside the gas station writing a letter to her dad as the mechanic worked on her truck. He managed to weld the radiator back together, but it was leaking like a sieve.

"Make sure to keep it filled up," he warned, as she steered back onto the road.

It was hard to get very far when she had to stop every half hour to refill the tank, and when her engine started overheating on the ridiculously steep hills of Idaho, she nearly gave up. "I had to stop every ten minutes to put water in, let it cool down, and put more water in."

But she made it to Seattle, just two days behind schedule. In the comfort of her friend's house, she took stock of the situation: the decrepit radiator, the two travel-weary cats, and still over a thousand miles left to go, on the rough Alaska-Canada Highway no less. Could she really make it all the way to Fairbanks like this? Her friends urged her to take the ferry instead, and she agreed.

The night before her ship sailed, Patty stopped at a park outside Seattle. Naiobi purred in her lap as she admired the magnificent Douglas firs, giants compared to the yuccas and junipers she was used to. A handsome young guy with a camera approached and asked about the "Alaska or Bust" truck.

Yes, she said, it was hers.

"I'm meeting my husband in Alaska," she told him. "He's working up there for a while."

He was charming and easy to talk to. She told him about her trip so far, including all of the car troubles. He couldn't believe she had a pet bobcat. Then he asked if he could take a picture of her with the truck.

Why not? she said.

She perched on the tailgate with the cat in her lap. When he invited her back to his house for the night, she declined, but he politely led her to the campground where she was staying and waved out the window. It was a pleasant interaction, and Patty didn't think about it again until five years later when a news story caught her eye on TV. Ted Bundy had been arrested in Utah for a massive killing spree across the west, including a number of victims in Seattle. She peered at the mug shot on the screen. Though a few years had passed, she was pretty sure she knew that face. It was the handsome stranger from the park, the same guy who had taken her picture by the truck.

Bundy ultimately confessed to thirty murders before his execution by electric chair. One of his tactics, police said, was to approach women in public places, take their picture, then lure them back to his car, where he murdered them in horribly gruesome ways.

I looked at Patty and felt my jaw drop.

"I'm pretty sure he was Ted Bundy," she said. "I suspect the only reason he let me go was because I told him I had this bobcat who couldn't live without me."

"Oh my god!" I squeezed her shoulder. "That's crazy!"

Patty just nodded in her matter-of-fact way. "I know it. The police said they had a lot of pictures of young girls they never found the bodies of. I've always wondered if there's one of me sitting on the tailgate of my truck."

The next morning, with no idea of the fate she may have escaped, Patty caught the ferry at daybreak. She couldn't afford a cabin, so she hung out on the top deck of the boat, where many young travelers were camped. They chatted and played cards as mountains and waterfalls paraded by. It was beautiful, but Patty felt guilty about the cats holed up in the truck. She went down a few times a day to feed them, but the conditions in the parking garage weren't ideal. Saki only ate raw meat, for one thing, and she liked to roam around. But every time Patty considered opening the cage, she pictured a bobcat running loose on the ferry and decided against it.

Two days later, the boat docked in Ketchikan on Alaska's southern coast. Patty walked down the ramp with a few ferry friends to explore the quaint buildings and fudge shops of the small fishing village. Standing on the footbridge in the center of town, they looked down between the slats and saw salmon swimming up Ketchikan Creek. Then she sat in the grass with another friend and soaked in the warm sunshine, which they hadn't seen much of the past few days. Closing her eyes, she thought of New Mexico, which felt farther and farther away with each stop.

"We should probably head back," she said, not opening her eyes.

"Don't worry, they never leave on time."

Just a few more minutes of this precious sun. By the time she got to Fairbanks, winter would be well on its way. She wondered what was in store for her, and whether she was prepared. Growing up in northern Wisconsin, she was no stranger to the cold. But she had gotten used to the Southwest over the years, to the dry heat and seemingly endless supply of sunshine. And she was planning to return soon. Though she had agreed to move north with Mike, hopefully one winter in Alaska would be enough to scratch his itch.

Suddenly a whistle shrilled from the water. Patty felt her heart stop beating. They ran to the dock just in time to see the ferry pulling away.

She rushed over to the tender and begged him to call the ship back. She had a vehicle on board, and two cats, she pleaded. He radioed the crew, and a minute later the ferry drifted back toward them.

Thank god, Patty thought, feeling herself relax. Of all the things that could happen.

Then she saw a rope ladder being lowered down the side of the boat. That couldn't seriously be for her? Below, waves slapped the harbor wall, and a knot twisted her stomach. Okay, she thought, I guess this is it. Gripping the rope with white knuckles, she willed herself not to look down as she climbed a distance that felt like Mount Everest, trying to ignore the tourists snapping pictures from the top deck. She had never been so embarrassed in her life.

As she swung one leg over the railing, she landed on the deck with a new realization. She had no idea what was coming next, and the adventure had still just begun.

It was a huge relief to see Mike waiting at the harbor in Haines, a familiar face at the end of a long journey. The small village looked like something from a fairy tale, the lights of the wharf twinkling against the white cones of the Chilkat Mountains. Mike seemed to fit right into the rugged backdrop. His sandy hair had grown long over the summer, and he was lean and tan from months of working outside. His summer had been spent on an archaeology dig at Healy Lake, south of Fairbanks, working with a crew from the University of Alaska. It was an old village site that had been occupied for almost 13,000 years, a montage of the cultures that had lived there since the glacial age. They were finding all kinds of cool artifacts—bone tools, hide scrapers, projectile points— buried at different depths within the soil based on how old they were.

As an archaeologist, Mike was in heaven. He loved piecing together the story of those who came before him. It was a little like being a forensic policeman, uncovering a bunch of clues to help solve a mystery. Except instead of being on the scene immediately, archaeologists only showed up a few millennia later, when the witnesses and DNA samples were long gone. Which meant they had to dig a lot deeper.

In addition to the work, living in the bush was just as exhilarating as he'd imagined. As he ate breakfast at the altar of the Alaska Range, Mike thought about his great grandfather, Charles Miller, a lighthouse keeper from New York, who had come to Alaska during the Klondike Gold Rush. Like so many others with gilded dreams, his trip didn't pan out exactly as planned. It was a long and arduous journey from the east coast to the mouth of the Yukon River, where Charles and his partner had purchased fares on a riverboat that would take them to Dawson City. They arrived late, and only made it about halfway to their destination before the river froze up. With no other option, they stopped to overwinter at the Dall River, tucked into Alaska's frigid interior. Still hundreds of miles from Dawson City, they knew they'd never make it in time to catch the rush, but couldn't bear to go home without seeing any gold. They hired an Indigenous guide to take them to the Kanuti River, a tributary of Bonanza Creek, a bitter overland voyage in the dead of winter. While Mike's great grandfather would never stake a claim, at least he found the flakes he had dreamed of.

The story had always excited young Mike, and now he had a chance to stake his own future in Alaska. He wasn't sure what that would be, exactly. He was still in the middle of graduate school down south, and he knew Patty wasn't thrilled about leaving New Mexico. But as he looked around at the mountains and thought of the ancient history locked inside, it was clear he was where he was supposed to be.

And things were falling into place. About halfway through the summer, he'd gotten a promotion, of sorts. He'd been knee-deep in a pit when his boss, John Cook, got a message on Tundra Topics, the local radio program that connected people in the bush with the rest of the world. It was from the TransAlaska Pipeline System, the company that was gearing up to build a massive pipeline across the state. They needed to speak with him right away.

John jumped in the riverboat and drove across the lake. The University of Alaska had landed the contract to do the cultural resources assessment for the entire pipeline route, an eight-hundred-mile stretch from the Pacific Ocean to the Arctic coast. It was an enormous project, and incredibly technical—carrying millions of barrels of hot oil over frozen ground. This kind of thing had never been attempted before, not at such a massive scale, and the excitement surrounding it was equally grand: Alaskans were hungry for another boom. The unions, the oil companies, the lawmakers—everyone was practically giddy to start pumping money from the ground. Even the archaeology community saw the shine of opportunity. Finally, a chance to explore a place that was virtually untouched, to write a foundational chapter in the story of how the western hemisphere was settled.

Mike's boss turned onto the Tanana River and skimmed down the wide brown thoroughfare to the sawmill, where his work truck was parked. After driving another three hours back to his office in Fairbanks, he was finally able to get in touch with his contact at the pipeline, and hear the urgent news. The group that was supposed to be surveying the southern portion of the pipeline route hadn't even started yet, and the execs were starting to sweat. There was a tremendous number of tasks that had to be accomplished before construction could begin. Could John help them out?

"Let me check with my team."

He made his way back to Healy Lake. He knew the man for the job. Though Mike was new to Alaska, he had some solid field experience from his time in New Mexico. And John knew firsthand that he could handle the elements.

"Would you be willing to go out on the right of way and take care of this?" he asked.

It was quite an opportunity, one that Mike never saw coming when he moved to Alaska. Plus, the whole point of coming here was to see new country. It was pretty much a no-brainer.

A few days later he was on his way to Delta Junction, to spend the rest of the summer exploring the heaving hills and valleys of the eastern Alaska Range. At this stage, the pipeline was nothing more than a three-foot-wide corridor brushed out through the trees. The project had caught a legal snag, as it became clear how much was at stake. The Alaska Native community had filed a lawsuit to halt construction of the pipeline, claiming it was going to cross land that was rightfully theirs. The U.S. Secretary of Interior happened to agree with them, and had placed an injunction on the pipeline until the dispute was settled. In other words, the project was as frozen as the ground underneath it.

In the meantime, the pipeline builders were moving ahead, ticking off all the environmental hurdles that would eventually need to be cleared. That's where Mike came in. His job was to see if the proposed route crossed any important archaeological sites along the way. When they saw an area that had potential—for example, a high dome or a nicely exposed riverbank that may have appealed to prehistoric people—they excavated some test pits to see what turned up.

Not much, from an archaeological standpoint. But it was Mike's ticket to what would become the biggest construction project on the planet— in fact, one of the greatest of all time. The pipeline drew workers from all over the world and transformed Alaska, and the nation, on an epic scale. It would launch his prolific archaeology career and change the trajectory of his life, and of so many others as well.

He laughed thinking back to his very first summer in Alaska, almost fifty years ago.

"That didn't really dawn on me at the time."

14
Boom Time

osh stopped at the top of the pass. Ten sheep the color of snow stood in the middle of the road like a welcoming committee, having scampered down the steep scree field to our left. I admired their long agile legs, essential for living up here in the mountains. Three had horns, not thick curls but slender arches.

"Lambs and ewes," Josh said.

As a hunter, his first instinct was always to look for a legal ram. There were none in this group.

We sat there a few minutes, in Josh's gold Tacoma truck on the summit of Atigun Pass. Just staring at each other. Then one of the ewes broke the impasse and lunged past us off the other side of the road, which banked steeply down to the right. The other nine followed, as if controlled by a single mind. Within seconds, they were climbing up the neighboring mountain, moving vertically the way most of us go horizontally. I looked back at the giant slope we'd just driven up, a strip of gravel winding almost a mile up to the pass, the one and only road through Alaska's most rugged mountains.

I thought of the craziest drives I'd done in the past—the winding road hanging off the edge of the Swiss Alps, the four-wheeler trails zigzagging through New Zealand, the tire-chewing lava leading to my favorite beach in Hawaii. They all paled in comparison to this one.

The Dalton Highway, known colloquially as the "Haul Road," ran like a squiggly vein up the forehead of Alaska, a four-hundred-mile jaunt through the wilderness, riddled with active fault zones, frozen landslides, and hundreds of miles of unstable permafrost. Oversized trucks roared right down the center, sling-shotting themselves over hills that could give you vertigo. The road switched from pavement to gravel without warning, just the sudden punch of potholes and spray of rocks. There were two gas stations spread across an area longer than Pennsylvania, and no other services to speak of. Not a place you wanted to break down. It terminated ten miles from the Arctic Ocean, at the richest oil deposit in North America.

Only an incredible amount of resources could justify building this road in the first place. When oil companies started exploring the North Slope in the sixties, Alaska's leaders were desperate to find something. Alaska had just become a state, and it needed some kind of industry to hang its hat on. As part of the statehood deal, Alaska was allowed to select one hundred million acres of its own land to develop however it pleased. A state geologist was the first to notice the ragged swatch of coast along the Arctic Ocean. Prudhoe Bay reminded him of the great oil basins he had seen in Wyoming, and he convinced the state to claim it as their own.

But as drills bored into the tundra across the North Slope, every test well was coming up dry. By 1967, most exploration companies had given up and pulled out of Alaska, focusing on more profitable areas elsewhere in the world. The new state's prospects seemed to dim. The final drill rig was moved to Prudhoe Bay. While the feverish optimism had died down, Alaska's leaders held out hope. If they didn't develop an industry soon, the state might not be able to support itself.

It took several weeks to drill the well. When workers opened the valve to test the pressure, gas shot out of the pipe like an invisible geyser, shaking the rig as if in celebration. When workers ignited the stream, it sparked a fifty-foot flare that flashed in the sky for more than eight hours. Hoots and hollers rang alongside it. Suddenly the future for the forty-ninth state didn't look so grim.

Governor Bill Egan summed up the sentiment in a 1970 speech.

"Alaska has become established as America's greatest oil province," he said. "Ponder for a moment the promise, the dream, and the touch of destiny."

Prudhoe Bay was estimated to hold ten billion barrels of oil, enough to meet the needs of the entire country for one year. It turned out to be much bigger. Of course, it wasn't exactly on tap to the masses. Stranded on the Arctic coastal plain, it was hundreds of miles from the nearest road, and ten miles from an ocean that was locked in ice for most of the year. But the appetite for petroleum was powerful. Domestic production was declining, and the U.S. was becoming increasingly dependent on oil suppliers from the Arab world. Alaska was seen as an answer—a way to free the country from the unstable politics of the Middle East, and to move toward energy independence. It didn't take long to decide how to liberate this precious pocket of oil. A long pipe made of steel would be built from the source all the way down to the sea, where it could be loaded onto tankers and shipped all over the world. But the closest ice-free port was eight hundred miles south, in the small fishing town of Valdez.

That's why this road was here, slicing through rock and water and ice, in one of the most unlikely places on earth. It was also handy if you wanted to drive up to the Arctic for the Fourth of July. We had left Fairbanks right after work and camped just past Wiseman, where Clutch Lounsbury had taken me gold panning the summer before. The next morning, we woke up early to a sunny day in the Brooks Range. As we continued north, I gazed out the window at the fingers of limestone jutting from green mountains, and the fields of pink fireweed reclaiming forests blackened by wildfire, like a beautiful entwinement of life and death. We saw a black wolf striding across the road and a great horned owl swooping low for prey. And just off the side of the highway, as if Photoshopped onto the natural landscape, was the oil pipeline. Not buried in the ground like most pipelines, but slithering over the earth like a giant steel snake. It was quite a sight to behold. Shiny and silver, forty-eight inches in diameter, elevated on vertical H-shaped supports that actively refrigerated the ground to keep the permafrost from thawing.

Once the sheep disappeared from view, Josh shifted into first gear and rumbled forward. We were heading to Galbraith Lake for a long weekend of hiking and camping in the midnight sun. As we descended the north side of the pass, I saw a giant plume of dust in the distance, almost like a mirage.

"Here comes another one," I said, stiffening in my seat.

There was a reason the History channel had filmed two seasons of Ice Road Truckers out here. These tractor trailers were like nothing I'd ever seen before. It wasn't their numbers but their sheer size and stature. Unlike the standard eighteen-wheelers I'd grown up with on Highway 81, these semis seemed more suited for space travel. Extra wide and extra long, some carried dual trailers that had a life of their own, while others dragged eighty-foot lengths of pipe and drill bits that looked like small rockets. As we got closer, Josh scooted off to the side and slowed down almost to a stop, as if genuflecting to higher powers. It was the best strategy, we had learned, as truckers were much less likely to run you off the road if you at least made an effort to yield. Which meant your windshield was much less likely to be shattered by rocks. The glass in front of me was already spiderwebbed from the ding last night, received shortly after crossing the Yukon.

These trucks were big, they were fast, and they were more than a little intimidating. And they were all going to one place: the oil fields. The North Slope received more than two hundred deliveries a day, hauling drills, backhoes, loaders, snow blowers, portable buildings, steak, toilet paper, and all the other equipment needed to keep oil production running. When oil was struck at Prudhoe Bay, the infrastructure had materialized almost overnight: a whole complex of multi-story offices, airstrips, dorms, and drilling rigs sprawling across the frozen tundra, resting on oversized gravel pads linked together by boardwalks. It was a little city in the middle of the Arctic, with more than two thousand residents at any given time—engineers and drillers, cooks and clerical workers. And a wealthy little city at that. The average oil worker made six figures a year, no college degree required. I guess it was the only way to get people to leave their families and live in an Arctic mancamp for two weeks at a time.

The world went brown as the truck passed. I coiled up in my seat, bracing for impact. But there were no sharp pops or loud cracks. Just a harmless cloud of dust. I let out all my breath as the dust cleared.

Less than an hour later, we turned left toward the mountains. Galbraith Lake sat at the foot of the Brooks Range, where hulking piles of rock faded into the vast coastal plain to the north. As we turned off the Haul Road, it felt as desolate as the Sahara, if you didn't count the caribou and musk ox and other four-legged creatures that lived here. A dirt road led us back toward the lake, the pipeline running alongside it like a guardrail. After four hundred miles, it almost seemed like another cool geologic feature that belonged to the natural landscape. But before 1974, none of it was here. No road. No pump stations. No dust-whirling trucks. Just pristine country, practically as untouched as it had been at the end of the last Ice Age, when humans set eyes on it for the first time. I thought about how much the pipeline had changed Alaska, not just the eight-hundred-mile corridor we were driving on, but the economy and culture of the entire state. It was like a new paradigm or a new language, redefining everything in terms of oil. Roads, teachers, firefighters, and parks weren't just considered basic public services anymore. They were directly contingent on how many barrels of oil flowed through the pipe each day. Could we afford music and art classes for our kids, or a university hockey team? That depended on the price of crude. It had changed the political stakes forever, getting rid of the state income tax and putting cash in the pocket of every Alaskan. Free money just for living here.

We came to the long skinny lake where 737s and C-130 Hercules had landed during the pipeline days, carrying thousands of tons of construction equipment. Galbraith Lake was one of the main construction camps that had sprung up back then. It was the hub for the entire Brooks Range, the most extreme section on the route. And it was where Josh's dad had spent four years of his life, including most of the year Josh was born. It's where he had unearthed ancient cultures and fallen in love with Alaska. From this frozen patch of tundra, he had watched Alaska transform from a poor bush state to one of the world's oil kings.

"The beginning of the oil era for Alaska was on par with the gold rush or World War II or any of those things," Mike had said.

But this time the gold was black. And the prospectors were not young men with wool trousers and gold pans but the most powerful corporations in the world.

Mike wasn't one to mince words or sugarcoat things. He didn't bother with political correctness or false modesty, and he had been working with big egos too long to care what people thought. He spoke with purpose, and sometimes with his mouth full, as if what he had to say was too important to wait until he finished chewing. He also happened to have a phenomenal memory. And when he flashed back to the seventies, whether recalling a mammoth tusk he plucked from a stream or a fabulous piece of cheesecake, he could still describe the details as if he were holding it in his hand.

That made him the perfect person to ask about the oil boom, and how it had created the Alaska I knew today. By 1974, Mike had been in Alaska for five years, working archaeology projects and other odd jobs, when the pipeline really got going. He was summoned back to work and stationed at the most remote spot of the whole route. There was no road or train or even airstrip at Galbraith Lake when he first landed on the ice in a Fokker F-27 turboprop airliner. In other words, there was no infrastructure by which to stage a project of this scale.

"We were at the end of the Galactic Arm is what it amounted to."

And it wasn't like they were building on normal ground. Depending on the season, the tundra could be as hard as volcanic rock or as soft as cottage cheese. How would they ever transport the bulldozers and drills and cargo needed to assemble a massive Arctic pipeline? First they needed a road, and with the deep pockets of Big Oil, it didn't take long to come together. Tractors were ferried across the Yukon River on hovercraft—enormous floating barges that could carry eight eighteen-wheelers in one load—and soon the road was ready, and the true undertaking would begin. As pipeline construction broke ground, Galbraith Lake swelled from two hundred to twelve hundred workers, men from Louisiana and Lebanon and South Africa, the type of mixed bag that only a multibillion-dollar construction project could create. There were surveyors and operators and laborers; cooks and chambermaids and mechanics; helicopter pilots and truck drivers. And the

largest group, the welders, who were as famous for their hot-shot atti-
tude as their strong and steady hands.

Stirred into the blue-collar stew were Mike and the other archaeologists, mostly grad students working on their second or third degrees.
Mike was in charge of all the cultural assessments from Linda Creek
to Prudhoe Bay, along with another young archaeologist named Dale
Slaughter. At barely thirty years old, they were running a project with an
almost bottomless budget, overseeing up to seventy employees at once.
They lived in a cluster of steel trailers perched up on concrete blocks.
Each trailer had ten rooms, two beds in each, with shared bathrooms
and showers in the middle. Their dorm, called D Barracks, was identical
to every other in camp except for one thing: it had women.

It was something of a scandal at first. There weren't supposed to be
any women working in the backcountry camps—in other words, north
of the Yukon River, where the pipeline route dissolved into total wilderness. It was an unwritten rule that came straight from the top. Co-ed
camps were bound to create drama, and managers didn't want any
unnecessary distractions slowing down the project. But the University
of Alaska had won the archaeology contract, and half its employees were
female. Mike's boss, John Cook, laid it out for pipeline executives in no
uncertain terms.

"Sorry boys, half the people on our crews are going to be women."

As they were well aware, there would be no pipeline until the archaeology surveys were complete. And that's how the first females broke
into the Arctic camps. It didn't take long for the Teamsters and culinary
union to find out there were women working at Galbraith Lake and take
it up with management. Soon the door was wide open for both sexes.

When all the grad students headed back to school at the end of
summer, Mike's dorm got very quiet. He and Dale practically had it to
themselves. But new roommates soon started to trickle in, milling in the
halls at all hours of day and night. They worked in different departments
and had different schedules, but they did have one thing in common:
they were all women. Since D Barracks had already been designated
the "co-ed dorm," it was just easier to put them there. And that's how
Mike and Dale found themselves living in the equivalent of a sorority

Dale Slaughter (left) and Mike Kunz (right) at the Chandalar Lake camp during the pipeline construction. PHOTO FROM KUNZ FAMILY COLLECTION.

house. In a mancamp oozing testosterone, it made them kind of famous. Mike remembers guys would sometimes sit next to him at lunch to hit him up for details.

"So, what's it like in there?" they would ask, in between bites of chicken casserole.

"We started off telling them it's just like living in any other barracks, you go to sleep. But they wanted to hear about all these rowdy things going on. They all thought there was a big orgy."

In reality, it was more like having a bunch of sisters. He remembers his female coworkers walking by on their way to the showers in the morning.

"Some women thought it was really funny if Dale or I were standing there taking a leak, they'd walk through and slap us on the ass."

He tilted his head back to release a hearty laugh.

Despite the rumors, there were no juicy scandals taking place at D Barracks, at least not that Mike was aware of. There was barely time to sleep, after all, with the intensity of the schedule. They worked twelve hours a day, seven days a week for eleven weeks straight, before getting two weeks off to go home and rest. Construction ran around the clock. There were two shifts—6 a.m. to 6 p.m. and 6 p.m. to 6 a.m. Every morning, Mike and his crew boarded the Bel-205 Huey helicopter at 5:45 a.m. to fly out to their survey area. They spent the next twelve hours either excavating or hiking around, looking for new sites. It was tiring work, but it beat mopping floors or sitting in a bulldozer all day like most of the other workers. By the time he got shuttled back to camp at night, there was barely time to wash up for dinner.

Dinner was the highlight of the day, an event to truly look forward to. The management understood that good food was key to morale. The happier the employees, they reasoned, the faster the oil would be flowing. That's why they had recruited one of the top chefs in the country to come out to Galbraith Lake. Charlie Van Dyke had been at the Four Seasons in New York City when he was offered a salary he couldn't refuse. Though he was stuck in a place where only a few small tundra plants could grow, his menus incorporated fresh ingredients from around the world.

"We had frog legs for dinner. We had lobster. We had four or five different kinds of salad every night. You name it," Mike said.

Mike has always been a big dessert guy. When Patty makes rhubarb pie or cranberry pudding, he shovels it down like a little kid, before rushing back for seconds. He looked nostalgic as he recalled the platters of homemade cookies, chocolate eclairs, and cream puffs that were available around the clock. Luckily, he was born with the metabolism of a sled dog, and never seemed to put on a pound.

Between the food and the paychecks, life was pretty good at Galbraith Lake. Each morning, as Mike stepped out of his trailer into the chaos of construction, the helicopters buzzing through the sky and the bulldozers chewing up the tundra, he felt the weight of responsibility on his shoulders. Only a few years out of school, he was on a multibillion-dollar construction project, not just as a worker bee but as a supervisor. He had to deal with engineers and surveyors and foremen, deciding which sites to excavate and which ones to leave in the ground, figuring out how to survey the entire pipeline route and all the material sites without slowing down the project. He had to order equipment, draw up schedules, and even entertain the media and film crews who flew in from all over the country, to document the massive pipeline being built at the end of the earth.

"There I was, basically still a kid, on the biggest construction project in the world, with guys who had been on projects like the St. Lawrence Seaway."

It was a glimpse of Mike I rarely saw, of an inexperienced guy who didn't have all the answers, maybe even a little daunted by the task before him. I suddenly understood certain things about him, the confidence he seemed to wear like a Kevlar suit, shielding him from the scrutiny and judgement of the outside world. He had cut his teeth on the construction project of his generation, had been thrown into a pressure cooker and come out even tougher.

The pipeline was making front pages of newspapers across the nation, not only for its dazzling engineering but because its contents had become even more important since the project had broken ground. The nation, by now, was engulfed in a full-blown oil crisis. Americans were consuming more than ever before, most of it imported from the Middle East. But when the U.S. got sucked into conflict in the region, backing Israel during the Yom Kippur War, OPEC wasn't too happy, and the resulting oil embargo created a shortage that rippled across the United States, causing a run on heating oil and hour-long lines at the pump. Thus, it was an understatement to say that domestic oil production was a priority, and that all eyes were on Alaska.

For that reason, the pipeline builders didn't want to cut any corners. And since it was being built on federal land, they needed to comply with every rule in the book, including the Clean Water and Clean Air acts that had just been created by the newly formed Environmental Protection Agency. The mission of the new agency was right there in the title: no more free-for-all development. Before digging up public land, developers must first create a baseline picture of what the environment looked like and make a plan to ensure it stayed that way. This meant measuring rivers, counting birds and plants, testing soil, and more.

The archaeology piece was a bit more complicated, as it centered on ancient bits of stone and bone that were mostly buried underground. Mike and Dale worked on the front lines, right along with the surveyors.

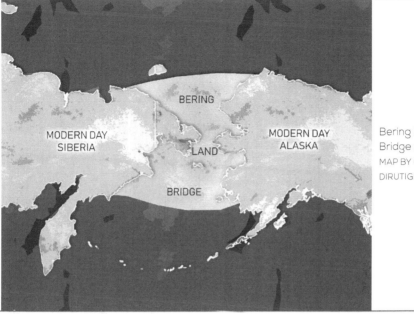

MODERN DAY SIBERIA

BERING

LAND

BRIDGE

MODERN DAY ALASKA

Bering Land Bridge map.
MAP BY COREY DIRUTIGLIANO

When they found something of interest, it had to be dealt with quickly, so it wouldn't hold up construction.

And they were finding lots of stuff. Unlike the earlier area Mike had worked on in Delta, the Brooks Range was an archaeological gold mine. By the end, they had recorded roughly three hundred sites, more than the rest of the whole route put together. One site, in the Atigun Valley, was so big it took an entire summer to excavate. There was a pretty simple explanation: They were at a transitional zone in the landscape, where the mountains met the foothills and formed a type of oasis. The fertile ground produced sprawling blueberry bushes, scraggly willows, and endless sprigs of Labrador tea, food for ground squirrels and birds and hares and voles, which drew in the fox and lynx and caribou and sheep. It was a smorgasbord for a huge community of wildlife. And humans, as we know, tend to stick close to our food sources.

"Prehistoric people lived where the groceries were," Mike said.

―――――――――

For Mike, the daily discoveries were laying brush strokes on a canvas that was mostly blank, revealing a world that came long before any record of modern civilization. Yet it was still called "the New World" because it was the last place on the planet to be settled. Humans didn't arrive on the western hemisphere until 14,000 years ago, after most of the earth was already populated. Originating in Africa some 70,000 years ago, our predecessors had long ago ventured to Europe, Asia, and Australia. They pushed all the way up to the east Asian Arctic, the place we call Siberia today.

But how did they cross west, into the Americas, and move down the entire continent? By land, or perhaps boat?

Archaeologists weren't sure. But they knew Alaska was an important part of the story. That's because it was connected to Siberia a long time ago by a massive landmass stretching across the Pacific Ocean called the Bering Land Bridge. With most of the earth's moisture locked up in ice in those days, the seas were about three hundred feet lower than today. That left far more land exposed, including this critical path between Asia and the Americas. The Bering Land Bridge measured a thousand miles from north to south, which is longer than the entire state of Alaska is now. Geologically, it was less a "bridge" than a shared basement between the two continents. But practically speaking, it was absolutely a bridge, creating a wide open passageway from west to east. By all indications, this was the link between the old world and the new. It was the explanation for why humans had shown up in Alaska before they appeared anywhere else in North America, and why the earliest cultures here bore such strong resemblance to those in Siberia.

And yet, there was no proof. This is both the fun and the torment of archaeology, trying to piece together the puzzle of human existence. It isn't an easy task. There is often no background information to go from, no timelines or frames of reference to guide you. It is slow and incremental, and riddled with uncertainty. Sometimes it takes a massive development project to fill in a big chunk of information. Like an eight-hundred-mile pipeline from the Arctic Ocean to the Pacific.

"You couldn't have done that for a hundred million dollars any other time," Mike said. "We were essentially looking at a cross-section of the aboriginal cultures that inhabited Alaska from 14,000 years ago up til last century."

As he bagged up artifacts and typed field reports, he thought about what it would have been like to live here 12,000 years ago, when mammoths and lions roamed the frigid plains.

Mike watched an operator drive a piling into the ground with an air hammer, and thought about how much the world had changed.

———————

As Josh and I looked around Galbraith Lake for a spot to camp, there were no remnants of D Barracks lying about. Or of the warehouses or any of the man-camp buildings that Mike had described. It was like it had all evaporated when the last section of pipe was laid. After setting up our tent by the lake, we headed out for a hike. I grabbed my rain jacket, even though the sky was the color of the little blue flowers sprinkled around our campsite. We followed a tiny creek up a draw, each step like sinking into a sponge. I scanned the horizon, keeping an eye out for the grizzlies and other critters that often shared the same trails as us.

Suddenly the ground in front of me exploded.

"Jesus!" I yelled, lurching back a good meter.

A blur of feathers blew up from the tundra and fluttered about 20 feet away from us, more of a big jump than what could actually be called flight. I placed a hand on my chest. It wasn't the first time I'd been startled by a ptarmigan, but it was perhaps the closest I'd come to a heart attack.

About halfway up the mountain, we sat down on a boulder to take in the view. A turquoise crescent of water spread out below us, shimmering in the sun.

"See the swans?" Josh pointed toward the right shore, where three slivers of white glided on the lake.

He always seemed to notice the small things, the fox tracks and birds' nests that I tended to walk right past. Maybe it's because I was always worried about bears. Or maybe Alaskans are just born with an extra sense for these things.

Behind the lake, past the wild sedges and the swans and our little blue tent, the pipeline snaked across the tundra and disappeared into the mountains. This view seemed to capture our time, I thought, showing our desire to preserve nature as well as our insatiable need to develop it. To move forward at any expense.

When I first came to Alaska, I didn't understand why people were so obsessed with oil. Why it came up at every editorial meeting at the newspaper, why the old guys in the diner were always talking about "throughput" and "dividends." Why the word "energy" was splashed across every campaign sign, from the U.S. Senate down to the race for city mayor.

It was the only way to get elected here. Our governor was a former Exxon lobbyist, and half of our state legislature came from the oil industry. Every member of Alaska's Congressional delegation supported drilling in the Arctic, even the lone Democrat (who would probably be considered a Republican in any other state). It wasn't really a partisan issue in Alaska. We relied on oil more than any other state relied on any other resource, more than Pennsylvania on coal or California on tech. It was our life-blood, holding up a third of the economy and financing ninety percent of government operations. Our tax policies were more like bait, bright spinning lures with beads and feathers dangling over a pool of global oil companies, tempting them north. We paid these companies millions of dollars in tax credits each year to scour our land and sea bed. They were eligible for all kinds of things, for drilling new wells or re-drilling old ones, building new pipes or storage facilities or even a shed. When the U.S. government tried to block drilling on federal lands, Alaska sued to pry them open. Anything to keep that pipe full. Sarah Palin may have been the one who made the saying famous, but "Drill, baby, drill" was the unofficial motto of Alaska long before she came around.

When oil had started flowing through the valley below us, it funda-mentally changed the character of Alaska, transforming it from a poor rural state to the richest in the nation. We built roads and bridges and prisons and hockey rinks. When prices spiked in the 1980s, Alaska's cup overflowed. With so much money pouring in, elected leaders started a savings account that would fund the government in the event the oil ever dried up. The Permanent Fund was invested in markets across the world, from power plants in China to agri-businesses in Africa. By the time I moved here, it had ballooned to more than $50 billion, a money-making machine that earned billions in interest every year, an industry in and of itself. The nice thing was, everyone got a cut. Not only did we not have to pay for government (the state income tax had been fully repealed in 1980), but we got our very own share of the oil profits—each and every Alaskan. The Permanent Fund Dividend, or the P-F-D, as it was affectionately known, was based on the oil fund's growth every year, a chunk of income that was sliced up like a giant blueberry pie and returned to the residents of Alaska.

In other words, Christmas came early in the Far North. Each October, when the amount was announced, Fairbanks trembled with anticipation. Headlines speculated, rumors swirled, and "PFD sales" popped up around town, from Alaska Airlines to Compeau's snowmachine shop. In 2011, the first year I qualified for a dividend, the mood was unusually gloomy. The economy was still recovering from the crash of 2008, and the dividend had slumped to historic lows. But when I received a check in the mail for $1,000, I was stupefied. A thousand dollars! It was a new computer, a ticket to Hawaii, a bonus I'd done nothing to earn. Just imagine what it would do for a family of six (each of whom, no matter what age, would get their own full PFD check).

The thing is, money changes people. It changed my college friends who went to Wall Street, and it changed Alaska. Not just the economy but whole mindsets. How can you be against oil development when it puts money directly in your pocket? The first year I got my check, I almost felt guilty. Was it blood money? Hush money? Or just enough to make you look the other way, to hold your tongue about things like oil spills and climate change and the need to move on to cleaner forms of energy.

But you get used to that cash, and what it can buy. A week on Maui. A new trailer. Or even just a fresh tank of heating oil. Pretty soon you start spending the check before it arrives. Then, within a few years, you're so wrapped up in oil it feels wrong to criticize it. You're called a hypocrite. Even worse, you feel like one.

In my view, that's what oil has done to so many Alaskans. Lavished us with jobs and infrastructure and lots of fun toys, while taking our voices away.

We stood up to make our final push to the ridge. No matter how much I criticized it, it was hard to imagine a future without oil. Who would pay for police and libraries and snow plows? What would we all do for work? Most of my friends depended on the oil industry in one way or another, whether they studied bears or cut trees or even bartended. The roads Josh built were paved with oil money. Even my work in sustainable housing was funded by the state, which meant it also relied on oil. Homes built from renewable materials and green technologies and good old hydrocarbons. In Alaska, nothing was clean.

But in the past few years, oil production had been shrinking. After peaking at two million barrels per day in the late eighties, it was down to less than half a million now. A glaring reality for anyone who counted on oil money to make a living. In other words, all of us. As we hiked farther uphill, I wondered if we would ever be able to get away from the pipeline. How many of us would really be able to live here without it? Certainly not the robust population of today.

At the top of the ridge, another layer of mountains rose from the horizon. We peeked into another gorgeous valley on the other side.

Josh took my hand.

"Can you believe we're getting married?"

He grinned. It was still a bit surreal. We had barely started planning the wedding, let alone talked about what would come next. House, kids, general zip code. I knew he didn't want to leave Alaska. He'd spent his entire life here, and he was fairly convinced the Lower 48 was a zoo. Honestly, the longer I lived here, the more I agreed. We had talked about Colorado, where we could live in the mountains and ski on the weekends. But every time I went back it seemed busier and busier, more like an amusement park than the quiet wilderness I had come to love.

Maybe this was it. Maybe I was stuck here forever. If so, I realized, peering into the valley, I would have to make peace with that pipe.

15
The Alaska Dream

Brooks Range • August, 1978

M

ike was tired of sitting in the rain. It was cold and misty, just
a few degrees above freezing, pretty typical for an August day
in the Brooks Range. Their pilot was late again. If he had a
nickel for every hour he'd spent waiting for the helicopter, Mike
thought, he could retire early and move up here for good. He
and Dale had just finished surveying some potential quarry sites. An
exploration well was slated to be drilled nearby to look for oil deposits.
But before building the well, they would need an airstrip, and to build
an airstrip they would need good rock. Engineers had found this intru-
sion of igneous rock thrusting up through the tundra that looked like
a good source of aggregate. But before drilling, shooting, and crushing
it to oblivion, first they had to make sure it wasn't sitting on an ancient
grave or some other cultural treasure.

Mike stood. If they were going to be stuck out here in the rain, he
might as well go for a hike. There was a mesa ahead he had always
wanted to climb. The table-shaped hill called to him because it looked
like a great spot for a hunting lookout. He turned to Dale.

"I'm gonna go check out that knoll over there."

"Have fun," Dale said, hunkered under his rain jacket.

Mike started up the talus slope. There were no trees or bushes to slow him down, and it didn't take very long to climb. The view from the top was well worth it. Just a couple hundred feet above the valley floor, he could see for miles in every direction. The Brooks Range spread out to the south in a beautiful panorama, and he could almost see to the Colville River to the north. Roughly twelve miles in any direction.

Archaeologists, though, are best known for their interest in the ground. When Mike glanced down, there was a shiny object lying by his foot.

Ooh, an artifact!

He stooped down, feeling the spark of discovery as he plucked the object from the soil. A projectile point, or at least the base of one. It was made of chert, about two inches in length, displaying the trademark flake scars of aboriginal tools. Though the tip was broken off, he could tell it had been used for hunting, probably attached to the end of a spear or throwing stick. Mike continued along the ridge, moving past some scruffy vegetation to another patch of exposed soil. He saw a reddish glint in the dirt.

Another one!

This one was in its complete form, long and slender, with a flat base and a pointy tip, almost like it could have fluttered from a willow tree. Mike turned it over in his hand. Both sides were covered in flake scars from the many quick flicks that had formed it. He studied the base closely. Interesting. He'd found hundreds of projectile points in these mountains, the notched points of the Northern Archaic tradition, the blades of the Denbigh Flint people, which were so intricate they could have been machined. But this one was different. It didn't look like any other point he'd seen here.

Shaped like a leaf, the lower edges were extremely smooth, as if they had been chiseled and then buffed by a stone. The base was tapered so it would fit right into the shaft of a spear or dart. In essence, it was just like the points he had found in New Mexico.

That's where Mike had first gotten hooked on New World archaeology. The oldest relic of human culture in the Lower 48 was a ten-minute drive from Portales, where he'd gone to school to study archaeology. He and his classmates had spent many days out in the field, roaming the dunes and sifting the dirt as they learned how to excavate sites and record information. The site had been home to the Clovis people at the end of the last Ice Age. Showing up around 13,200 years ago, it was the oldest civilization ever discovered in North America, or anywhere on the western hemisphere.

They were known as the Paleoindians, and they were considered the earliest of the Indigenous cultures of the Americas: the very first ones. For two thousand years, they had roamed the cool plains of the Southwest, hunting mammoth, horse, and bison. Mike had studied them extensively in college, chipping away at the questions of who they were, where they came from, and why. He knew their carefully formed points and other distinctive tools like the back of his own hand.

He turned the object in his palm. But why would he find this kind of technology up here? It didn't make sense. There had never been a Paleoindian site discovered in Alaska. Besides a few isolated projectile points, there was no reason to believe these prehistoric people had ever lived in the far north. While the earliest humans had almost certainly passed through this area on their way to the Lower 48, they would have been an entirely different culture at that time, with different tools bearing different marks. Archaeologists assumed that the Paleoindian culture had developed sometime later, as people migrated from Alaska down to the western plains over a period of hundreds of years. But maybe they were wrong?

Down in the valley, Dale was starting to wonder what his friend was up to. He and Mike had spent countless hours together during the pipeline days, digging through layers of substrate and piles of paperwork. Though the two history buffs didn't always agree, they had become close friends over the years. Dale started working his way up the mesa, ducking in against the rain.

"Hey, come check this out!"

Dale heard something in Mike's voice that perked his own antenna.

He looked down at his feet and saw tiny chert flakes dusting the ground like confetti. Byproducts of making stone tools, the flakes suggested that people had not only hunted in the area, but actually hung out there as well, making new tools and discarding old ones. In other words, it wasn't just a spot of passing interest, but an actual archaeological site. Dale said what they were both thinking.

"It's a lookout."

"Must be," Mike replied.

As Mike rotated the point with his fingers, as an appraiser inspecting the angles of a rare diamond, he could picture the aboriginal hunters sitting around a campfire, telling war stories while they chiseled their weapons.

He had a good feeling about this site. After years of exploring the Brooks Range, something about the mesa was new, different. Part of it was the sheer volume of artifacts littering the ground. They found half a dozen points in less than twenty minutes, almost unheard of for such a superficial examination. But the shapes were intriguing too. How did you explain lanceolate points in Alaska?

Despite the curiosity that had been lit inside him, it would be another decade before Mike realized just how special the mesa was. That it would become the first tangible proof of a connection between the Bering Land Bridge and the Paleoindians of the western plains, between the Old and the New World. It was a discovery that would help shape our understanding of human history. But at that moment, it was nothing more than a hunch.

Only fifteen years later, in the bright glare of a stage four thousand miles away, did the magnitude of the discovery sink in. He looked out at a hundred reporters and photographers crowded into a Washington D.C. press room. At the back wall covered in TV cameras, while BBC and Reuters waved their hands in the air. At Sam Donaldson from ABC News who he watched on TV every night.

"When I saw that, it was like, Jesus Christ, this is really a bigger deal than I thought."

Unfortunately for the others in the room, the New York Times already had the scoop. Mike had gone to dinner with their senior science reporter the night before and filled him in on the Mesa. He was expecting the story to run that morning, just before the press conference. But when he had opened the door of his hotel room and seen the newspaper lying on the floor, he was more than a little taken aback to see the article on the front page, above the fold!

The leading story of the world's most-read newspaper didn't take long to get around. By the next day, he was hearing from people all over—family and friends back in New York, buddies from the pipeline days, archaeology colleagues from around the world. Then the real media crush started—the limo rides to TV studios, the probing microphones thrust into his face by excitable reporters. News of the Mesa People was piped onto screens and radios across the country. These mysterious Arctic hunters had captured the imagination of America. It wasn't just the history wonks. People who had never laid eyes on a scientific journal wanted to know about this new chapter of the human story. Who were they and where had they come from? What did it all mean?

"What *did* it mean?" I asked Mike, leaning over my latte.

Clearly it was a big deal to find Paleoindians in Alaska, but why? How did it change the narrative?

We were sitting in a coffee shop on a Thursday afternoon, just across the street from my office. It was the one where retired guys loved to hang out and tell stories, and our table was surrounded by pilots and miners and professors, many of whom had lived in Alaska for half a century or more. Every once in awhile someone would tap Mike on the shoulder or call out from across the room.

"Well..." Mike paused to wipe a finger across his plate, cleaning up the last few crumbs of a blackberry scone. "I'm trying to keep this simple."

But in reality it wasn't simple. That's why it had taken more than a decade to identify those first projectile points. If it weren't for Mike's persistence, we may never have learned about the Mesa people. They could be another lost culture buried in the sediments of time. Shortly after the rainy day hike, Mike sent a few students back to the plateau to dig a quick pit. Finding stuff on the surface was great—it could tell you a lot about how a site was used—but it didn't give you a date. And without a date, a projectile point was little more than a neat paperweight to show off to your friends. A good date required two things. First, the artifact needed to be touching something organic. Rocks like flint or chert didn't contain organic material, so you couldn't date them directly. Charcoal left over from an ancient fire, on the other hand, would still contain carbon. That meant you could use a technique called radiocarbon dating to figure out the age. But second, and most importantly, the artifact needed to be in the right context. Not just touching the organic material incidentally, but situated in such a way that you knew they were related.

That's why Mike was so excited when his team unearthed an ancient campfire containing plenty of broken points and flakes. It painted a picture of a group of people circled around a fire working with the actual artifacts.

"So they're sitting around telling war stories to each other and working on their hunting equipment."

Mike pulled an imaginary arrowhead off a spear.

"They've got projectile points that were busted because they threw their dart at a critter and snapped the point off. So they take it out of the shaft and pitch it in the fire."

He pretended to toss it to the floor. The artifacts were still buried in the old fire pit, lodged in the burnt-orange earth like walnuts in the coffee cake in front of me. Furthermore, heat fractures on the rock showed they had been exposed to extremely high temperatures. It was just the confirmation Mike needed that the tools were the same vintage as the fire.

Things were looking good. So far, his instincts had served him well. I bet they're at least twelve thousand years old, he thought, as he bagged up samples and sent them off to the lab. If they were in fact Paleoindian, it was a big deal. Big enough to rearrange the understanding of how North America was settled. He couldn't wait to see the official date.

So he was not overjoyed when he tore open the lab report and read the results.

"It comes back at 8,640 years old," he said, the disappointment still dripping from his voice.

"Too young?" I said.

"Well, it took it out of the Pleistocene Age."

It was still a wonderful assemblage of prehistoric man, but not old enough to be from the Ice Age, that intriguing time period when wooly mammoths and saber-toothed tigers roamed the earth. That meant his hunters were not Paleoindians after all. Anyone younger than twelve thousand years old was from the Holocene Epoch, the beginning of the era we live in today.

"It was definitely younger than I thought it would be," Mike said.

It seemed like a lot of drama over a simple date, but dates mean everything in Mike's world. They're like DNA for biologists, or computer code for programmers. For archaeologists, they were as close as you could get to cold hard evidence. If you think of human history as an enormous puzzle, stretching across 150,000 years or so, every date is a single piece. Big or small, ragged or smooth, each one tells a bit of the story. When you have enough dates, a picture starts to emerge. That's how we know, for example, when the first humans appeared in Africa. How they migrated to Asia, Europe, and Australia. And that's how we know that sometime during the last Ice Age, they walked across the Bering Land Bridge to Alaska, and ultimately followed an ice-free corridor through Canada into the United States and then further south.

These dates are churned out by a little machine that counts how much radioactive carbon is held by an organic substance—such as a piece of charcoal or bone. When a living thing dies, whether it's a person or a tree or a mastodon, all life processes shut down and the radioactive carbon begins to disappear. Archaeologists know roughly how much carbon a living thing contains when it's alive. So once they figure out how much carbon is left, they just subtract it from the original amount, and voilà: you can say (roughly) how long your sample has been deceased.

Radiocarbon dating was still fairly new when Mike came to Alaska. It was revolutionizing the field of archaeology, allowing researchers to say with far more accuracy when certain events occurred. Like an acid test for gold miners, it held the key to the answers, to the story. The radiocarbon date was the difference between an epic discovery and another buggy day in the field, between an article in the New York Times and one in the university newsletter.

The date of the mesa sample put it in the Holocene Era. So it sat there for awhile. For almost ten years, in fact.

Until 1989.

Mike went back to the mesa with two colleagues to gather soil data. While he may not have discovered a new civilization, it was still an interesting slice of humanity that would tell them more about the peopling of the Arctic. When they dug a small test square, they happened to come down on the corner of another hearth. More charcoal.

"Let's test it again," said Rick Reanier, another archaeologist.

"What's the point?" Mike said. "We already know how old it is."

Plus, you needed a certain amount of charcoal for a radiocarbon date, and this small excavation didn't have enough. Rick persisted.

"You can use atomic mass spectrometry now," he said. "You don't need nearly as much to get a date."

This was a technology that hadn't existed ten years earlier, and one that was taking over radiocarbon dating. Mike wasn't expecting the results to be any different, but it didn't hurt to try.

"Okay," he relented.

It was twelve thousand years old. Ice Age old.

"I was like, 'Wow,'" Mike enunciated the word with his whole face.

His theory had been vindicated. The Mesa people were indeed Paleoindians, the same as the Clovis culture he had studied in New Mexico. While the ancient hunters were roaming the western plains of the Lower 48, they were also living in northern Alaska.

Now the fun part would begin—piecing together their life based on every tidbit of available info. These people were still a huge mystery. Mike wanted to know more about their activities, their food sources, their environment. So he launched a twenty-year study to reconstruct the local ecosystem—the landscape, grasses, climate, and wildlife. They took soil samples and studied the chemical composition. They recovered bones of prehistoric animals and dated them.

And they found some interesting stuff. Arctic Alaska was a different place nearly fourteen thousand years ago, when the Mesa people first showed up. It was cold, but not as extreme as today. There was less permafrost, because the ground was covered in grass, which doesn't insulate as well as tundra. The climate was even drier than it is now, which meant less standing water and, lucky for the locals, fewer mosquitoes.

Meanwhile, Ice Age megafauna roamed the plains. Hunters would have sought out high spots, like that mesa, to scope out the surrounding country. With no trees blocking the view, they would have been able to see herds of caribou fanning across the valley. But their main source of game was probably the horses and bison feeding on the grasslands.

And slowly the story came together. Mike saw how people had survived in the Arctic for thousands of years, back when they had to forge shelters and weapons from only the resources around them: rocks, bone, wood, animal skins. Before we had figured out how to produce steel or cement, or how to make energy from the vast amounts of petroleum lying under our feet.

16
Mining Camp

For some, going to the bush makes you appreciate the comforts of home, of coffee makers and computers and memory-foam mattresses. Not for Mike. Once he set foot in the Brooks Range, he didn't really want to leave. That's why, the same year he and Dale discovered the mesa site, and eight years after he started working at Galbraith Lake, he ended up paddling down an Arctic river, dodging ice jams at every turn. It was mid-September, and he hadn't expected ice to be forming so early. It was a little precarious given the eight-foot inflatable raft he was paddling with his friend, Andy Bateman.

The rubber boat was heavy with food and camping supplies. They sat on top of a mountain of gear, trying to steer clear of obstacles. It wasn't a very technical river. Fairly shallow and flowing about three miles an hour, it wouldn't have been challenging in normal conditions. But the ice shelves added a definite twist, jagged and irregular and totally unannounced, cutting off some channels entirely and sending water in new and unpredictable directions. Just the day before, they had hit ice on a hairpin turn and punctured one of the boat's main air tubes, leading to the coldest swim of Mike's life. Fortunately, he was able to grab the boat before it sank and repair the hole, but he had no desire to repeat the episode. So he was being extra careful about navigating now, using a long pole to push off the river bottom and keep them in the main channel. It would have been a lot easier with oars, except the ones they had built out of spruce boards had already been destroyed, snapped by the ice almost as soon as Mike and Andy started paddling. So now they were doing their best with two long spruce poles and a #2 miner's shovel. Mike thought wistfully of the small outboard motor he had attempted to bring on the trip. By the time they'd loaded up the Helio Courier with five hundred pounds of camping and hunting and surveying equipment, it was clear they wouldn't be able to bring it along.

But paddling wasn't the main purpose of the trip. Mike and Andy were actually on a prospecting mission. It was an idea Mike had gotten the year before, while working on a dig in the Brooks Range. He loved being out in the wilderness by himself, and figured mining would be a good excuse to do more of it. It also had some sentimental value; in a way, he was doing the thing his great grandfather never really had the chance to. Though Charles Miller had found his requisite gold flake, he had never had a chance to work the ground into production. For Mike, on the other hand, the opportunity still dangled. So he had scoped out a site with good mineral potential and talked his friend Andy into helping him stake some claims. On the last day of August, a bush plane dropped them on a gravel bar with their survival gear, plus the tools they would need to rough together a mining camp.

The first few days were spent surveying the local creeks for signs of gold. It had been a little tricky without maps. Mike had accidentally left them in the car back in Fairbanks, along with all the mining paperwork. So after brushing out property lines and setting corner markers, he drew out a rough map by hand. It wasn't perfect, but he'd be able to amend it in town before filing the claims with the recorder. Then this spot would be all his!

Besides a day of surveying and a couple days of hunting (quite a lot of bushwhacking, in reality, and no meat), most of the past two weeks had been spent building a cache, where Mike could leave a bunch of gear for the next time he came out. The small structure was elevated just out of reach of a large bear. It was nothing fancy, ten-by-ten-feet with a tarped roof. But like any bush project, it turned out to be more work than he'd expected, especially since they had to cut, peel, and fit the logs together with only a chainsaw and a drawknife. Mike was grateful to have Andy's help. The two met on the pipeline, and while Andy wasn't much of a woodsman, he was always game for an adventure. After about two weeks establishing a camp, Mike was happy with the results.

There was still lots of work to be done, of course, but it would have to wait until next year. The crisp autumn weather had finally given way to winter, and when they woke up on September 16, there were five inches of snow on the ground. Mike cursed when he opened the door of the tent.

This wouldn't make it easy for their plane to land. But that wasn't his most pressing problem, Mike thought, hearing his stomach growl. They were starting to run low on food. They'd been living on military rations the past two weeks, little plastic bags of freeze-dried spaghetti and stew and cornflake dessert bars. This was supplemented with duck, rabbit, and the occasional spruce grouse that came within shooting distance. Now that the weather had turned, though, it would be harder to hunt. Mike hoped they had enough rations to make it through.

That's why they weren't dawdling on the river. Their pilot, Lee, was probably already looking for them. He was planning to start at a lake about twenty miles south and fly upriver until he saw them. But their pace was somewhat stymied by this early crop of ice. Mike and Andy were portaging the bends whenever possible to avoid a blowout. Between that and the slow current, they were barely averaging one mile an hour.

The second day on the river, they enjoyed lunch on a gravel bar, sharing a duck breast cooked over a fire. It had warmed up to twenty-five degrees, a comfortable temperature in wool pants and boots. After a quick break, they nudged the raft off the rocks and started paddling again. There must be a good gravel bar around here, Mike thought. The Helio needed a strip at least six hundred feet long, and preferably straight. As they rounded a bend, Mike envisioned a nice stretch on the other side. Each turn was like a secret door, masking whatever beauty or treachery lay on the other side. Since Mike was up front, his job was to watch out for hazards. He raised halfway up to assess the next section. A series of riffles unfolded down the main channel. Nothing too serious.

But beyond that, something glistened in the sun, not moving with the flow of the river.

Uh oh.

The shelf of ice hovered a foot above the water, and it was right in their path.

The current carried them toward it like an unstoppable conveyor belt. There was nowhere to turn, nothing to do.

"Look out!" he called to Andy.

Before they could react, the ice snatched the raft from underneath them, and tore the soft floor with its sharp teeth.

Mike hopped off just time and landed on top of the ice shelf. He reached out for Andy.

"Jump!"

As the river sucked and slurped at their boat, trying to pull it under, Mike held it with everything he was worth. The wet material slipped and contorted in his grasp. Then with a sudden jerk it popped up on the shelf beside them. They dragged the boat to shore and slumped down beside it. Once they had caught their breath, they took stock of the situation. The float trip was over—that much was clear. The bottom of the raft had been shredded to pieces. But maybe their supplies were still intact. First things first, Mike thought. He tossed the tent to Andy.

"We better set up camp and start drying out."

While Andy put the tent together, Mike sorted through their gear. Clothes and cookstove and fishing box were accounted for. Whew. They still had the rifle and ammo. There was just one thing missing.

With both hands full, Mike looked at the empty boat, then at Andy.

"Do you see the food bag anywhere?"

Andy looked at him, then downriver.

All the freeze-dried meals had been stuffed in a large sack, along with the remaining duck breasts. Which was now gone. There were a couple more duck breasts in their backpack, but that was it. It would have to be enough.

Inside the tent, they fired up the Coleman stove and turned both gas burners on full blast, then hung their clothes on strings crisscrossing the ceiling. Everything was soaked—not just what they'd been wearing, but all their baggage as well. As the tent heated up, river water wafted from their coats and socks and long underwear, steaming up the tent like a spa. The warm mist was comforting.

But Andy still looked worried.

"Are we in danger?" he asked, squatting on the ground in his underwear. The lightheartedness he had maintained for most of the adventure had left his voice.

"Nah, we're fine," Mike assured him. It was a bump in the road, sure, but it could have been much worse. They were low on food, and it looked like it was about to snow any minute, but at least they still had the tent, and the gun. Plus, their pilot was on the way. All they had to do was find a good gravel bar and track down something to eat. It was the same mindset that had gotten him through the pipeline days—just deal with one crisis at a time.

Mike dumped the final sack and felt something hard in the bottom. He fished it out.

"Look!"

Finally something that would cheer up his poor friend. He held up a bottle of Worcestershire sauce as if it were a prize steak. "Let's make soup!"

But Andy's expression didn't change.

"I don't like that stuff," he said.

Unfazed, Mike started a fire outside and got some water boiling, then added a few drops of steak sauce and stirred with his finger. He drank down the salty tea. It actually wasn't bad.

And that's what he drank the next four days as they made their way downriver, scanning the sky for their pilot. It was exponentially more difficult on foot, not only because they were carrying heavy packs. Walking on an Arctic riverbank is kind of like walking on the moon, with awkward bumps and holes that could easily break an ankle. And with fresh snow on top, they were basically walking blind.

Now and then Mike would plunge down to his knee, then carefully stop, reposition his pack, and climb back out. Finally, they found a nice straight gravel bar. It looked long enough, but they would have to do something about the foot of snow on top. Mike flopped a spruce tree, limbed it, and tied a rope to both ends. He and Andy put the rope around their waists, and started plowing the beach like draft horses. They moved slowly and methodically, pouring their last bit of energy into this one task. For now, it was the only thing that mattered. The snow was light and fluffy, and difficult to plow, and by the end of the first day they were only half done.

Mike had never been so grateful for Worcestershire sauce, even if it was just enough for a salty broth. It warmed his stomach when the last freeze-dried meal was gone, and after they had polished off the dead rabbit they'd scavenged from a wolf kill. Even when the pilot was three days late, Mike clutched his mug of salty tea, dreaming of a thick broth full of chicken and potatoes. But Andy held strong to his aversion. He boiled the rabbit bones to squeeze the last few calories from it, but when that was gone, after two days with no food at all, he still didn't go near the steak sauce. When they eventually made it back to Fairbanks, Patty whipped up their special request of pancakes topped with syrup, ice cream, and whipped cream.

Andy never made it back to the Brooks Range. The prospecting trip had been adventure enough. For Mike, however, that little spot on the river would become his second home. He went up every year thereafter, the way many families go to the beach or a lake house. After spending the whole summer doing fieldwork on the tundra, he would climb in a little float plane and get dropped off on a clear lake surrounded by mountains. That's where he stayed for the next month and a half, until the berries had sagged into syrupy pouches and the peaks were as white as ice cream cones, until summer was officially over. He panned for gold and dredged in the creeks, but he never found much of value. That wasn't really the point. When he was up there, immersed in the woods, with no other soul for miles, it was the same magic he had felt as a boy in the Adirondacks.

Josh was six when he started going up to the mining camp. It's where he learned to paddle a canoe and shoot a gun. It was nothing like Cape Cod, where my family went every summer. Without an ocean or a boardwalk or saltwater taffy, most people wouldn't even consider it "vacation." But for Mike it was heaven.

17
The Alaska Reality

nd that's where Josh and his dad were hanging out in the fall of 2016, hiking in the mountains and fishing for pike and grayling in the lakes, when our wedding preparations were in full swing. Though Mike was 74 by then, he hadn't slowed down much. In fact, now that he was retired, he spent even more time at the mining camp, going for two months in the summer and another month in the winter to ride his old snowmachine around the valley, camp in forty-below, and "relax."

Meanwhile, back in Fairbanks, Patty was helping me with invitations. I had ordered them from a small artist I found online. They were decorated with colorful birch trees that reminded me of Fairbanks in the fall. Sitting at the kitchen table, Patty licked an envelope and dropped it on the pile.

"I can't believe it's only two months away," I said, feeling a flutter of excitement.

This was the period everyone had warned me about, when all the decisions and details were mounting up and the nearest courthouse started to look really appealing. The pile of invitations began to slide downhill, as if feeling the weight of my stress.

"I know. And I don't even have a dress," Patty said.

She had actually ordered a few dresses, but hadn't decided on one yet. Since Josh and I were getting married in my own parents' backyard, it was going to be a fairly casual affair. But I still had a strappy white dress, red ballet shoes, and an appointment at the hair salon.

Sitting in Patty's kitchen, sunlight streamed in the picture windows and soaked the enormous log walls in light. Mike had cut down the logs for their house himself, and dragged them out of the forest, some fifty years ago. It was a beautiful home, with a big fireplace, a bright clere-story, and a staircase made of knotty logs that Josh had built by hand.

And actually, we were living here too at the moment. It was just a temporary thing, while we waited for an offer to close with the bank. Yep, not just a wedding on the horizon, but a new house as well. Two major milestones, all in one month.

It was a little overwhelming if I thought about it too much, but life over the past year had gained a certain adult-like momentum. Josh had finished his engineering degree and was working for the state, building roads and bridges that society actually needed to function. He was paying off his student loans and saving up for the future. Meanwhile, I loved my job in sustainable design. The research itself was fascinating: we studied wall systems and windows, tested out ways to use solar in the Arctic and how to build foundations on thawing permafrost. But my favorite part was the human element, working with rural villages all over Alaska to design homes that reflected their climate and culture. I was getting to meet Indigenous people of all backgrounds, to ride in boats, bush planes, and four-wheelers through remote country, to join design charrettes and traditional potlucks and dances. These people lived in some of the most extreme places imaginable, on icy barrier islands and spits of land jutting into the ocean. The work was not only fascinating, but I actually felt like I was making a difference, helping people stay in their traditional homelands and continue their subsistence culture. On top of that, my office culture was hard to beat. I brought my dog in every day and had weekly meetings with my boss while skiing on the river.

When I wasn't working, I was packrafting and hiking, climbing mountains and skiing down them. In a way, I was living two lives: one of conference calls and deadlines and happy hours with friends, another of starry nights sleeping outside. It was the Alaska dream, something I couldn't imagine doing anywhere else. It was almost too good to be true.

Though I may not have realized it at the time, I was living in the reverie of boom-time Alaska. Ever since oil prices had spiked in 2008, the state had been raking in money from the pipeline, with huge budget surpluses every year to spend on highways and schools and nonprofits. To spend on the houses my organization designed and the roads that Josh's crew built. But Alaska hadn't always been this way. There had been booms before, sure. Gold, war, and oil had each brought tremendous windfalls to the state. But with each incredible high, there had followed an equally painful low.

All I had to do was look at the house I was sitting in. Behind Patty, the huge deck was drenched in sun, filled with flowers and tomatoes and sweet peas trellising up the railing. Though today it looked like an ad on the real estate channel, it hadn't always been that way. In fact, this house was almost unrecognizable compared to the one Josh grew up in. Thirty years ago, it had been just a shell, with no furniture or finishings or plumbing. The whole family lived down in the basement, a concrete box with plastic taped over the windows. They hauled water in five-gallon jugs and went to the bathroom just like the old sourdoughs did—in the outhouse.

Josh had told me plenty of stories about his rustic childhood—about hauling firewood in the sled and burrowing into his electric mattress when it was forty-below outside. But I'd never really heard it from Patty's perspective. Now that she was going to be my mother-in-law, it seemed like a good time to ask.

"What was it like living in the basement with two little kids?" After the friendly climate of New Mexico, living within spitting distance of everything she needed, suddenly she was in backwoods Alaska, largely on her own.

She laughed and licked an envelope slowly, buying herself some time. I'd asked too broad of a question, perhaps. Finally she spoke.

"Did I tell you about the black bear?"

"The black bear?"

"I never told you about that?"

Mike & Patty Kunz with kids Kelly and Josh (baby) when they were building their house in Fairbanks. PHOTO FROM KUNZ FAMILY COLLECTION.

"Um, no!" I said. I set down my pen to give her my full attention.

I had heard plenty of Mike's bear stories (he had accumulated quite a few from nearly fifty years in the bush), but never one from Patty.

"Well, it was summertime, and the kids were little. Kelly was five, so Josh must've just turned two. We had gone down to Anchorage for the weekend to go shopping and we got back really late."

She shuffled the cards as she eased into the story, playing a role that typically belonged to her husband.

They'd gone to bed after arriving home, and it was early morning when she was awoken by a rustling sound. Mike was out in the field doing archaeology work, just like every summer, leaving Patty alone with the kids. She threw off the sheet and sat up, peering into the kitchen. As her eyes adjusted, she could make out a black shape moving around the room. Must be Bruce the black lab, she thought. The neighbor's dog had a bad habit of breaking into their kitchen to rummage in the trash when she left the screen door open at night.

"Shoo!" she yelled.

Mike Kunz, 74, at his mining camp in the Brooks Range. PHOTO FROM KUNZ FAMILY COLLECTION.

That's usually all it took to scare him off, but she would have to call the neighbor again. She sat up and snapped on the bedside lamp. There was definitely still an animal in her kitchen. But the dark furry creature nosing through the trash was at least twice as big as a dog. She blinked to make sure it was real, that she was looking at a full-grown black bear inside the kitchen, steps away from her young children. She could feel her heart quicken as she grabbed the .45 special from the nightstand drawer. The rooms were separated by linen sheets, offering a tiny bit of privacy, but far from an ironclad barrier. As she crept toward the kitchen, she felt the fear turning into anger. What was this bear thinking, invading her home while her children were sleeping?

By the time she stepped into the kitchen she had worked up an uncharacteristic rage.

"Get out of my house!"

Startled by her voice, the bear pulled its head from the trash bin and dashed toward the door without even seeing her.

Patty set the gun on the freezer and ran to the door. Her tone, apparently, had worked. The bear had not only fled the house but had crossed the front yard and scrambled up a tree. As she slammed the door angrily, the bear looked back and got a glimpse of her: a petite woman in a nightgown, maybe half its size.

"It looked at me like, 'That's what I was running from? Why was I afraid of that?'"

The animal's fear vanished. Reinvigorated, the boar lept to the ground and around the corner of the house, disappearing from Patty's view. She brushed aside the sheet into the next room, where their cats had ripped holes in a plastic window so they could come and go as they pleased. It was just as she'd feared: the head of the bear was poking through the window, trying to crawl inside her living room.

This is why she had never liked black bears—their unruly passion for trash. She thought of the kids in their bunkbeds in the next room, behind another curtain, and then of the gun lying on the fridge, out of her reach. The only thing nearby was an old metal chair she'd bought from the Army surplus store. Acting on impulse, she grabbed the heavy chair with both hands and brought it down hard on the intruder, striking him right on the nose. The bear roared and retreated.

Thank god.

She took a breath, but she didn't let go of the chair. Moments later the long black nose reappeared, with nostrils that flared in anger. She smashed it once more. But this time the groan was eclipsed by an even more frightening noise.

"Mommy?"

Patty turned around and saw Josh shuffling into the room. He wore a T-shirt and diapers, sandy hair falling across his eyes, looking sleepy and confused.

"Joshua, get back in bed! It's a bear!"

Surprised by his mother's tone, Josh turned and ran back into his room. The bear had a similar reaction. When Patty faced the window, poised for another strike, all she saw was tattered plastic. She pulled back the window and saw a black rump disappearing in the trees. The message, it seemed, had finally been received.

"Ooooooh my gosh," I said, staring at Patty in an entirely new light.

As she sat at a table decorated in sunflowers, I tried to picture Patty as a young mom, defending her children from a dangerous predator. Suddenly it dawned on me—my mother-in-law was a badass. Not just because she had fought off a bear, but because of what came before it, all the decisions and actions that had led to that situation, one most of us will never face. She had moved to Alaska alone in a beat-up truck, had lived in an unfinished basement for decades, hauling water and heating it on the stove to give the kids baths in a big metal tub, just like they did in the 1700s. She and Mike were in their sixties by the time they moved upstairs, into this nice airy space with skylights and heated floors. How many people, given the choice, would have tolerated those conditions for so long?

"Why didn't you get out of the basement sooner?" I asked.

It was something that was never quite clear to me. I knew Josh's parents had run into some bad luck when they were young. But Mike had made good money during the pipeline days: enough, I would think, to afford a house with basic first-world amenities.

"It was the eighties," Patty said. "That was the first oil crisis."

Ah, the oil crisis. I had heard of it in abstract terms, how energy shortages had created painful price spikes around the nation. But I never really knew how it affected Alaska, a place that had been explicitly developed to stabilize the oil market and prevent these kinds of disasters. But oil was a global commodity, controlled by global forces. After the oil shortage of the 1970s that had fueled the creation of the Alaska pipeline, Middle Eastern nations started pumping more and more oil into the market. Pretty soon there was a glut, which, it turns out, is just as bad as a shortage. In the early 1980s, prices began to go down. And down and down and down.

This was bad news for Alaska's new economy, which was entirely built on oil. After the huge pipeline construction boom had died down, there simply wasn't much demand for workers anymore. While most of the pipeliners moved on, Mike wasn't ready to leave Alaska. He figured he could stick it out and find odd jobs until the next thing came along. There was talk of building a gas line from Prudhoe Bay to the Lower 48, and he was hired to do surveys for the project. But within a few years, that work had dried up too. Despite years of experience working in the oil industry and living in remote field camps, he found himself paging through the classifieds, looking for jobs. There were few listings for archaeologists.

But like so many Alaskans before him, he didn't mind doing some grunt work if it allowed him to stay in the place he loved. He and Patty had already bought property in Fairbanks and started building a house. Pouring the slab and putting up basement walls had eaten up most of their savings, and now he had a family to feed. So when a friend lined him up with a construction job on the North Slope, he readily accepted.

The week before leaving for Prudhoe Bay, Mike went to his last soft-ball game at the local Fairbanks fields. Though it was only "beer league," his team took it pretty seriously. Patty was sitting in the grass watching as Mike went to steal second. When he realized the ball was going to get there first, he stopped short.

"I felt my knee go 'pow pow,'" Mike said.

The guy on second base had heard it too. He rushed over to Mike, who lay crumpled in the sand. It took a few guys to carry him to his truck. When he got to the hospital, the diagnosis came back quick. He had blown out his left knee, the doctor said, ACL, MCL and meniscus all torn like a shoddy rope. He went into surgery that night, and five days later, as Mike was supposed to start his new construction job, he was still lying in a hospital bed hooked up to an IV. It would take months until he could walk without crutches, and even longer until he could attempt any kind of physical labor. While Mike did rehab and watched the kids, Patty supported the family from the reference desk of the public library.

Thus entered the period of Josh's childhood I had heard so much about—of ketchup and mayonnaise sandwiches, of long winter days huddled by the stove. There was enough money for food and gas and occasional doctor's visits, if necessary. But not enough to replace the TV when the cat threw up on it, and certainly no money to finish the beautiful log house they had started.

Crazy, I thought, how an attempt to steal second could take away so much.

But it wasn't really about Mike's ACL. In a healthy economy, he could have found another job, even with a sore knee. They could have rented a house and waited out the slump.

But there were no other industries here—no buffer or Plan B to fall back on. All of Alaska's eggs were stacked in the single basket of oil.

Just like today.

The same boom that had brought Josh's parents here, that had bestowed them with jobs and opportunities they couldn't find anywhere else, had also taken them away.

"Why did you stay?" I asked.

I waited for Patty to say something about the lifestyle, about how she could never go back to the Lower 48 after tasting the freedom of Alaska. The things most people say to this question.

"We couldn't afford to leave," Patty said. "After that first winter, I would have bought a one-way ticket to New Mexico if I could."

I was speechless. The narrative in my head all these years was wrong. She wasn't in love with Alaska; she was trapped here, boxed in by her circumstances. Josh's family didn't leave the state once in sixteen years. There was no money to take the kids to Disneyland or even visit relatives down south—they were too busy collecting water and firewood, just trying to get by. I knew the lifestyle didn't bother Mike one bit. He would live in the basement forever if it meant he could keep finding arrowheads in the Brooks Range.

But growing up poor had certainly had an impact on Josh. I thought of how he cozied up to the wood stove on cold winter days, how he never wanted to buy things from the store, like shelves or benches or even picture frames—but preferred to build them by hand, because he could. He took long showers and cooked elaborate meals using every pot in the kitchen, with the indulgence and appreciation of someone who had grown up without running water. It had molded him into the person he was—someone who didn't take anything for granted.

I could tell it had affected Patty as well. If she could go back in time, I'm pretty sure she would have gotten out while she could.

18
The Crash

As we approached the toe of the glacier, an immaculate arch popped out before our eyes, larger than the Arc de Triomphe but made of brilliant, blue ice. Even for nature, this color was hard to achieve; it could only be generated by the compression of ice over hundreds of thousands of years. We were at the foot of Mt. Deborah, a 12,300-foot peak I had admired countless times from Fairbanks, stenciled against the southern skyline. But up close it was ten times cooler.

We were right outside Denali National Park, in a stunning valley we had just discovered. It had taken three hours by snowmachine to get here, traveling on the smooth white highway of the Yanert River. The day before, we had set up camp about thirty miles in, on a wide gravel bar circled in mountains. Then today, we had followed the river another fifteen miles or so to get to its source—where water gushed from a glacier larger than most towns in Alaska.

Not long ago, it would have freaked me out being this close to a glacier. My first time hiking on one, I worried that every step would send me crashing through an ice bridge or plunging into a crevasse. The glaciers that bedazzle Alaska's mountains like jewels are as deadly as they are beautiful, living and moving things studded with traps and holes and invisible features covered in snow.

But today, as we skied along the foot of the glacier, I felt only awe. The large lake pooled below the mountain looked like something from a Christmas card. Sections of clear ice glinted in the sun where the snow had blown away, and chunks of copper speckled the valley like red rubies. But the coolest feature, by far, was the glacier itself, a frozen river that poured down from the mountain and erupted into stalagmites of ice. It was both ancient and ephemeral, holding dust from the days of cavemen as it melted before our eyes.

We explored the nooks and crannies, the tunnels and arches and flying buttresses of glacial ice, while keeping a safe distance. As lovely as it was, I knew not to get too close. Ice was fatally unpredictable.

I stopped in the blinding sunshine to take off a layer. It was strange to feel the heat of the sun again. After six months of winter, I felt like an early spring flower starting to bloom. As I stuffed my jacket in my backpack, I saw Josh working his way up a steep hill on the edge of the glacier. It was hard to tell if it was ice or rock.

"Careful!" I called.

He kept climbing, up up up, until he stood on top of a pyramid of ice. Ati was right on his heels, tracing the edge of the ice lip without a care in the world. I took off my glove to tap a picture with my phone.

Since our wedding last fall, life had been a happy blur. All the planning had been worth it for the joy of seeing my favorite people in one place, dancing under a full moon on the grassy hill where I grew up. I was so touched that friends from Manhattan and Boulder and London and Buenos Aires had all shown up to celebrate with us, while also reminding me of all the different lives I could have lived. There was my best friend from kindergarten who was a corporate lawyer in New York City; my college roommate who lived in the suburbs with her husband and two children; an old soccer friend who had started his own hedge fund. They all wanted to know if I was staying in Alaska for good.

"I'm pretty happy there," was all I could say.

We finished the night roasting marshmallows over a bonfire, on the field where we used to play soccer for hours and hours, overwhelmed with gratitude. Since then, so much more had happened. The day Josh and I got back to Fairbanks, we moved into our new house and started making it our own. Choosing paint, buying furniture, fixing gutters and drainages: all the "adulting" I had managed to put off for so long was finally catching up.

"You're nesting," my mom teased. "Just wait for the stork."

Maybe I was building a nest, but we were still having too much fun to call in the stork just yet. There were more rivers to float, more powder days and adventures to look forward to.

After getting our fill of the glacier-themed amusement park, we climbed back on our snowmachines. It took me a few tries pulling the starter rope before it chugged to life. I was still learning the ins and outs of the sled. We had bought two Ski Doos in the fall, after collecting our PFDs. The checks had been big this year. The recession of 2008 was now well behind us, and the stock market had bounced back with a vengeance, boosting the dividend to $2,000 for every person in Alaska. It was twice as much as the year before—and big enough to justify some new winter toys and a trailer to drag them around with.

I gripped the throttle and zoomed forward, following Josh back onto the trail. Traveling on frozen rivers—now this was still something that made me a little nervous. There were so many features to look out for—soft spots, overflow, open holes of water. But in early March, the ice was still nice and stable. Josh led the way since he liked to go fast, and I was pretty happy cruising at thirty miles an hour. I let Ati run behind until she faded into a black dot, then stopped to let her catch up. She was panting when she jumped in my lap, licking my face to thank me for the ride. Approaching our campsite, we stopped at an open slash of water to fill up our jugs. Just downriver, our yellow tent popped out against the snowy mountains, as bright as a lighthouse at sea.

The "Arctic Oven" was another recent purchase, a double-walled tent that kept you warm even at minus-forty. With a thick floor mat and a small wood stove, it was like sleeping in a little canvas igloo. For me, it was the key to winter camping, allowing us to venture out to amazing places without worrying about freezing to death. We'd gotten some good mileage out of it already—from local trips in the White Mountains to backcountry skiing in Valdez.

I laughed thinking back to my first winter, five years ago, when I walked around with frozen toes for three months because I was too cheap to buy real winter boots. At the time, I didn't think I'd be here long enough to invest in something that was more suited for space travel than for a place like Colorado. Look at me now, with a snowmachine, trailer, and an Arctic tent. I had lost track of how many pairs of skis I owned.

It wasn't that we were rich, but for the first time in my life I wasn't worried about money. Josh had been racking up fat paychecks working on remote construction sites the past two summers, doing fourteen-hour shifts seven days a week while living in a trailer. My car and student loans were finally paid off, and I'd picked up some freelance work. While I listened to friends in the Lower 48 complain about the economy, I had to admit, it was hard to relate. In Alaska, things were booming.

Later that night, I held a marshmallow over the fire. The stars twinkled against black canvas, the type of contrast you only get on a cold night, many miles from civilization. As my marshmallow drooped over the hot coals, I thought about the Halloween parties we used to have in Pennsylvania, telling ghost stories and making s'mores.

"They taste better burnt. More flavor," my mom used to say as she set her marshmallows on fire.

Pennsylvania would always be a part of me—the farms, the fields, the predictable turn of the seasons. But I had found a new home that stirred my passions and never failed to challenge me. After bouncing around for so long, it felt good to be committed to a place, with a husband and friends I loved. The future had so much potential I could almost feel it in the air. I looked to the west, where the mountains cut white triangles into the sky. Could life really be this good?

A few weeks later, I made my way to the conference room for a staff meeting, skipping down the stairs two at a time. My coworkers huddled around the long birch table, an assortment of architects, engineers, builders, and economists, the most idealistic group of people I had ever met. Just before 9:30, my boss Jack entered the meeting in jeans and a gray hoodie. Though he was in his sixties, he often seemed more like a ski bum than the CEO and founder of a successful engineering firm. But today the mood was grim.

"So you've all heard what's going on in Juneau," he said, shuffling his moccasins on the cork floor.

Somber nods all around. We knew that oil had crashed the week before. It was impossible not to. From airports to coffee shops to ski trails, it was the only thing people were talking about. The fracking boom that had exploded across the east coast had finally made landfall in Alaska: creating a glut of oil and gas on the market that had caused energy prices to tank. Great news for most consumers: cheaper fuel meant more money to spend on travel and shopping and home renovations. But not so bright for Alaska.

"Do we know what this means for our budget?" said Nathan, an energy economist who dreamed in numbers and spreadsheets.

There were murmurings that Alaska's capital budget might get zeroed out this year. Unfortunately, that's where most of our funding came from: the $1 million we relied on each year to test wall designs and energy systems and help people build good homes. An amount, Nathan had calculated, that paid for itself several times over in energy savings for Alaskans. We had other contracts as well, but our funding from the state was critical. Without it, I didn't see how we could keep the doors open.

Jack was clearly wondering the same thing.

"Not yet," he said. Through his ever-sunny veneer, I could see he was concerned. He had built this research center from the ground up, after working as a homebuilder for thirty years and seeing how poor most of the housing was in Alaska—moldy, drafty, and incredibly spendy to heat. He was convinced, like we all were, that energy efficiency was the first step in the movement to make our planet more sustainable. "It would be stupid to stop investing in us, but we never know what the Legislature will do."

When I shared the news with Josh that night, he didn't look surprised. "You guys too, huh?"

There was a rumor spreading through DOT about major cutbacks as well.

"They might cut all the design engineers."

"What?" I said. That was just crazy. "How will they keep the roads open?"

"Hire private contractors, I guess, even though it'll cost more."

As the days and weeks slid by, the panic seemed to spread like a crumbling pothole. It wasn't just agencies and nonprofits that were scared. It was like the whole economy was teetering on a cliff. Nobody knew what would happen to the price of oil, a global commodity controlled by global forces, or how our state would respond. By cutting services, using our savings, or reinstating an income tax? Each option came with strong emotions and grave political consequences.

Meanwhile, the oil industry, the golden child that supported a third of Alaska's economy, was shedding jobs like winter layers. Without money coming in at the top, we wouldn't need as many baristas or hairdressers or cab drivers. No one, it seemed, was safe.

Soon the fears turned to reality, and the barrage of layoffs began. They were slow and spotty at first, a few longtime professors, some contractors. My favorite local bookstore closed. Then it came faster. As oil companies scrambled to stem their losses, they laid off hundreds of workers on the North Slope. People put their homes on the market and headed south.

I could only look around and wonder, were we going back to the eighties again, that era that had so devastated Josh's family?

We hadn't seen the bottom yet. As we headed into summer, oil prices kept dropping, from $80 to $60 to $40 per barrel. It was like a fire sale that just wouldn't end. By 2016 we had lost thousands of jobs in the oil sector. Hundreds from the university. Plus many more in construction, business, and government. The state budget had been chopped in half.

The pain radiated throughout the economy, from top to bottom, and eventually to our group of friends. Furloughs and pay freezes and travel bans. The term "oil crisis" was resurrected to become a daily headline in the news. Soon we had the highest unemployment rate in the nation. It was official: we were in a recession, the dark place I had heard about from Mike and Patty, and all the others who lived through the oil era.

Surely things would go back to normal. Although the state's top economist said oil wasn't likely to rebound anytime soon, you could never underestimate the power of positive thinking. We were all hoping to wake up one day to $100 a barrel. Alas, it seemed that $50-a-barrel oil was the new normal.

Josh and I were lucky—we still had our jobs. But we had lost that golden feeling that growth was infinite, that the future spread out like the Yanert River on that beautiful spring day, glistening with opportunity.

Instead, it seemed rife with danger. Our mortgage was less an asset than an anchor. Who would want to move here now? The winter toys we had been enjoying so much suddenly seemed like a silly extravagance.

My eyes were open: I had been living in a boom time. And as any sourdough would tell you, one of the first rules of a boom was that it didn't last forever. Would we be able to weather the bust, as Josh's parents had done? As Clutch and Al and all the other old-timers had done at least once in their lifetime? Tighten our belts and go back to a simpler lifestyle? If I had learned anything from my jaunt through the past, it was that people had lived here with far less than we have today. But what about me? Was I capable of doing it? Did I want to try?

I had learned about the booms that had built Alaska, how gold and war and oil had brought an avalanche of money into the state, creating a life of comfort in one of the least hospitable places on earth.

Now I came face to face with a giant bust, which exposed the question that had always been just beneath the surface: Was it even possible to live here without oil?

PART FOUR

SUBSISTENCE

19
Visiting the Land of Caribou

A group of caribou freckled the bright red tundra, somewhere between the Yukon River and the Brooks Range. It was that precious window between summer and winter when Alaska turned into a splatter painting of fall colors, the creeks like golden brushstrokes against a fiery red tapestry. Even after four years, it still took my breath away. I pressed my forehead against the window of the small plane, feeling the land wash my stress and anxiety away. As panic spread about the future, I was going back to the bush for science camp.

A few minutes later we touched down in Arctic Village, a smattering of homes along the east fork of the Chandalar River. As I walked toward the village, a fang-shaped peak towered over the west of town. It reminded me a bit of Anaktuvuk Pass—a native village on a caribou highway, surrounded by beautiful mountains. Antlers littered the tundra in great knotted-up balls, and the pungent smell of meat drifted out from backyard smokehouses. But there was one major difference that jumped out as I walked down an empty dirt road. Unlike the first village I had visited, this one was really quiet. The streets weren't buzzing with brand new trucks or shiny yellow pieces of heavy equipment. There was no modern tribal hall or gleaming visitors' center. Small cabins and shacks stood side by side, as if huddling together to stay warm. No satellite TV dishes or outdoor freezers were parked outside. In fact, many didn't even have fuel tanks. Just piles of wood scrounged from the nearest forest, which was nowhere to be seen on this windswept tundra.

Huh, I thought. We were only 150 miles east of Anaktuvuk Pass, at the same latitude and same type of environment. Why did it seem so poor by comparison?

The groan of a four-wheeler interrupted my thoughts and a woman with long black hair zipped by, stopping a few yards in front of me.

"I'm Joanne. Are you Molly?"

Though I had never met her in person, Joanne White was the one who had invited me here. A Gwich'in Athabascan woman originally from Arctic Village, now she worked for the Fish and Wildlife Service in Fairbanks, and had organized this science camp for the past ten years. While there were hundreds of native villages scattered across Alaska, this one was quite unique. Practically a household name, in fact. That's because Arctic Village sat on the edge of the Arctic National Wildlife Refuge (ANWR), a chunk of wilderness the size of South Carolina crawling with polar bears and muskox and tens of thousands of caribou. It was one of the last intact Arctic ecosystems, a Mecca for hikers and paddlers and hunters and fishermen. But it was also the center of a furious debate over oil development, one that had spread from the quiet tundra to the busy halls of Capitol Hill and engulfed the entire nation. Everyone seemed to have an opinion on whether we should drill in ANWR, from South Dakota senators to Houston hunters. The Gwich'in people who lived here had been fighting for decades to keep the oil companies out. So far, it had worked. But pressure was building to open the refuge.

Now, with the price of oil stuck at historic lows, Alaskans were getting desperate. Many argued that drilling in the refuge was the only way to save the economy, to create jobs and revenue to pay for the state services we needed. With passions burning hot on both sides, ANWR had become a political lightning rod, not just a debate over how we should fix the deficit but something far deeper. A national flashpoint on development versus conservation.

"I'm going to Trimble's," Joanne said. She nodded to the back of the four-wheeler. "Hop on."

Though I had no idea who Trimble was, I climbed on behind her and grabbed the metal back-rack as we headed down the dirt road, across a small bridge and up a hill, toward the outskirts of town. Joanne pulled up to a hand-built log house where a group was gathered outside. An Elder with wispy black hair and a deeply lined face was holding up the frame of a canoe. About ten kids huddled around him.

"Tr'ih tsal," he said. "Means canvas canoe."

Trimble Gilbert was the traditional chief for the Tanana Chiefs Conference, a region that spanned the great midriff of Alaska, covering over a third of the state. He was also Joanne's uncle. At eighty years old, he still hunted caribou and built boats by hand.

The kids repeated the word slowly back to him.

Tree. Tsahl.

Unlike villages I'd visited in southwest Alaska, where you could hear kids speaking Yup'ik in the school hallways, most young people in the Arctic didn't know their native language. While they may have picked up a few words from hearing their grandparents speak it at home, it was something that had been mostly washed away by the tides of the western world. Now Elders were making a concerted effort to pass it on while they still could.

And they were doing the same with Indigenous skills, in fact, right before my eyes. Trimble bent a willow branch across his knee, demonstrating how they used to make the ribs of a canoe. They bound them with a piece of string until they were permanently curved, he explained, then attached them to the frame. Before screws were available, they used caribou hide strips to hold the joints together. The wooden boat was narrow and light, easy to carry between the lakes and rivers of the Yukon Flats.

"We used to paddle from here all the way to Ts'iivii T'it (hunting camp), forty, fifty miles upriver, before the motor or boat," he said, gesturing to the great nothingness that unfolded to the north. "And then if people got caribou, they put meat in there, and they paddled all the way down here."

The kids watched him silently, seeming to hang on every word. I was amazed at their respect. In Native culture, Elders weren't considered a burden to society but the leaders, the torchbearers. Today, the kids were helping Trimble finish the boat, sewing canvas strips to the exterior. They used to cover the boats in actual caribou skin, Trimble said, and seal the seams with animal fat, but had switched to canvas and thread when the white traders came along with their manufactured marvels.

After admiring the boat from various angles, I followed the crowd back to school, where the science camp was based. A group of shrieking girls spun on a Merry-Go-Round beside the river. The tundra behind them sparkled like a Christmas wreath with cranberries and little red leaves. Though school wouldn't officially start until next week, this week was filled with activities like stream ecology and snow sampling, as well as arts and crafts.

Since I worked at a research center that focused on housing, my plan was to do a construction project with the kids, at least on paper. I'd brought cutouts of the major building components—foundations, walls, windows, stoves—kind of like jumbo puzzle pieces. After we talked about the different parts of a home, they would get to assemble their own, thinking about whether to use logs or lumber for the frame, what type of fuel they wanted to burn. But that afternoon, when I stood in front of a gaggle of eight-year-olds trying to explain the instructions, it quickly dissolved into chaos. All I could do was watch as one boy chased his sister with scissors and a little girl made a snowflake out of my miniature laminated solar panel.

So instead of building a paper house in the gym, we ended up walking around the village looking at different houses, pointing out chimneys and roofs and windows, while all the kids held onto a string so I could keep track of everyone. Lesson learned: when it came to little kids, outdoor activities were clearly best.

Later that evening, thoroughly exhausted from my half-day stint as a teacher, I sat down next to Trimble in the school cafeteria. The mighty hunter looked kind of cramped sitting on a plastic fold-up bench where the children ate lunch. We had just finished an epic potluck of salmon and moose ribs. The school had cleared out as most of the community members drifted home, but a few kids were still zinging around the gym, playing dodgeball, basketball, and an amalgam of other sports.

Trimble looked as tired as I felt. He sat quietly, perfectly content. I, on the other hand, was bursting with questions. It was almost physically painful for me to sit so close to someone like Trimble without talking. But where to start—what could we possibly have in common?

"It's so beautiful here," I said. Let's go for the low-hanging fruit.

He nodded without really looking my way. I knew Arctic Village was relatively young. I wasn't even sure it existed when he was a kid.

"Were there lots of caribou when you were growing up?"

The mention of the sacred animal seemed to unlatch something, and Trimble started talking. For nearly an hour he told me about his childhood, and how they had lived before this village was even here. He was part of the last generation to live the old ways, sleeping in a canvas tent and following the food with the seasons. He spoke with a thick accent and a deep wisdom obtained not from books but from a lifetime on the land.

Trimble's family had harvested fish and muskrats from the many lakes dotting the Yukon Flats. In the winter they hunted with a small dog team, traveling up-valley for caribou and packing out meat in the sled. Nothing came easy in the Arctic.

"We are hard-working people, really hard," he said. "One good thing is, no sickness. Not really complaining about headache, no stomach problems, no leg problem either. Now it's change, a lot of sickness."

People didn't start settling in Arctic Village until the 1950s, when a store popped up, then a school. Trimble remembers coming to town when he was around fifteen years old.

"White people say 'What's your name?' I don't understand that. I don't understand nothing," he said.

Though he never attended school, he eventually learned to speak English when he traveled around the state and then joined the National Guard.

Today the Gwich'in have conformed to village life, like most of Alaska's Native communities. They have a school and a store and an Episcopal church, where Trimble preached every Sunday. Some kids, like Joanne, left the village for college, then got jobs in places like

Fairbanks or Anchorage. But for those who stayed, life still revolved around the land.

And around one thing in particular—the caribou. It was the foundation of life for the Gwich'in. For thousands of years, long before the first missionaries or trading posts appeared, Trimble's ancestors had subsisted on the husky reindeer. The Porcupine Caribou herd occupies an area the size of Wyoming, thundering across the landscape every spring and fall in search of food and favorable weather. They spend winters in the southern Brooks Range, feeding on vegetation underneath the snow. Then, in the spring, when the sun comes back and the tundra blooms, they begin their long journey north to their calving grounds, some four hundred miles away. By early June, pregnant females reach the Arctic coastal plain and give birth. To the untrained eye, this stretch of soggy ground could pass for a frozen wasteland, but it's actually teeming with life. The Gwich'in call it "Iizhik Gwats'an Gwandaii Goodlit"—the sacred place where life begins.

This is where they want to drill. When the refuge was formed back in 1960, a small area was set aside for the possibility of future drilling, on the notion that rich pockets of oil may lie beneath the tundra. For the Gwich'in, the past few decades have been an almost tireless fight to protect it. Not just in Alaska. People all over the country seemed to have an opinion about what should happen to the refuge, though most had never seen it. My mother was the perfect example. For people like her, it was symbolic. It should be protected for the sake of conservation, to show that we were capable of holding onto one of our true national treasures. If Big Oil could drill in ANWR, after all, it was hard to imagine there was any park, forest, or preserve on Earth that was safe.

But the pro-drilling crowd saw it differently. The refuge was an obstacle to growth, another sentimental example of putting wildlife before jobs, before people. Drilling would only happen on two thousand acres of land, the argument went, just one ten-thousandth of the entire refuge. To drive the point home, Don Young, Alaska's longtime Congressman, held up a blue pen in front of a row of U.S. senators. "This is how much of the refuge will be affected," he said, drawing a small dot on his nose. Developers would use a directional drill, a new technology that barely touched the surface. Just look at Prudhoe Bay, Alaska's governor added. We've already proven we can drill without scaring away the wildlife. What's the big deal?

Lisa Murkowski, Alaska's senior senator and chair of the Senate Energy Committee, tried to wipe away any remaining doubts of her colleagues.

"We can be confident none of this will come at the expense of the environment," she reassured them. "Development and environmental protection can and do exist in Alaska."

But do they?

Around July, when the ground begins to thaw, and mosquitoes seem to materialize out of thin air, the caribou calves are strong enough to travel. They gather in large groups, tens of thousands strong, and move as one, climbing mountains in leaps and bounds and overtaking swollen rivers. Sometimes they go to the coast, sometimes to the ice fields, sometimes to the foothills. They wander east and south, across the Canadian border or down to the southern part of the Arctic Refuge, where the Gwich'in live.

Every fall, during this migration, hunters from Arctic Village set out on the tundra to find the Porcupine herd, to provide for their families as they have for thousands of years. Before firearms were introduced, they built V-shaped fences out of spruce and willow to funnel the animals into a corral, then killed them with spears. Remnants of the miles-long fences still dot the tundra. Hunting techniques evolved over the years to bows, then muskets, and eventually to rifles. At the village store, I saw a young hunter heading out on a four-wheeler with an AR-15.

Life for the Gwich'in people has changed since Trimble was a kid, no doubt. But they still depend on the caribou. For them, it isn't just symbolic. It is their food supply for the whole year. It is the only way to live out here, in the land of near perpetual winter, where a gallon of milk costs $10 at the village store.

The Gwich'in people may be small, but they are strong, projecting the voice of their ancestors from the Arctic tundra to the power circles of D.C.: Please protect our sacred lands.

I looked at Trimble.

"What would happen if they drilled here?" I asked.

He looked down at his hands.

"It hurts us," he said. "We have a duty to protect the land and animals. We take care of them and they take care of us."

But not all of his Alaska Native brothers and sisters feel that way. Some are in favor of drilling, and are just as vocal about it. As lawmakers from around the country debated the fate of the faraway refuge, Matthew Rexford traveled from Kaktovik to make his case. He told lawmakers about his home, an Inupiaq village on the Arctic coast located inside the refuge, and how much they needed oil development.

"Qaaktugvigmiut and the Arctic Iñupiat will not become conservation refugees. We do not approve of efforts to turn our homeland into one giant national park, which literally guarantees us a fate with no economy, no jobs, reduced subsistence, and no hope for the future of our people."

Two powerful arguments from opposite sides, both claiming their survival hinged on whether or not there is oil development. Why the contradiction? Money, for one reason. Like so many issues that appear to be about something else on the surface, major dollars were at stake. While the people of Arctic Village had nothing to gain from drilling in the refuge, this isn't the case for Kaktovik, where opinion is much more divided on the issue. They would make a lot of money if oil were developed. It's a weird twist that dates back to the original oil boom of the sixties. When oil was struck at Prudhoe Bay, it wasn't just a bonanza for oil companies and the state budget. It was also a huge opportunity for Alaska Native people, who, at the time, had no ownership of their Indigenous land. While Native Americans in the Lower 48 had been granted land over the years in the form of Indian reservations, this issue had never really been resolved in Alaska. Indigenous people had been speaking out for decades—they'd even sued the U.S. government to try to get some type of recognition— but they never had any leverage. Now that billions of barrels of oil had been discovered beneath their feet, suddenly they held a hefty bargaining chip.

As oil companies circled like ravens on a fresh kill, tribes across the state banded together to fight for their land. It was an epic battle that lasted for years, as Native groups lobbied state and federal lawmakers, even President Nixon. Meanwhile, billions of dollars hung in the balance. Alaska's leaders squirmed as the pipeline project was put on hold until the issue was resolved. One year passed, then three, as both sides dug in their heels. Finally, in 1971, a settlement was reached. In exchange for handing over title to their land to the U.S. government, Alaska Natives would receive 44 million acres of land and $1 billion to share amongst themselves. The Alaska Native Claims Settlement Act, or ANCSA, was groundbreaking for Indigenous peoples the world over. The First Alaskans had taken on a colonial government and actually won. And it was structured very differently than the Indian land treaties in the Lower 48. Rather than being herded onto reservations, while the land was held in trust by the U.S. government, Alaska Native people were actually granted full title to their land. They owned it, inside and out. Not directly, but through a corporation that was allowed to use every tool and trick of free-market capitalism. ANCSA set up twelve Native corporations, one in each region of Alaska, to manage the land and money they had won for the best interests of the people.

While the victory was shared by tribes across the state, it was especially sweet for the North Slope, which was next door to the massive oil fields at Prudhoe Bay. As soon as the pipeline was up and running, the Arctic Slope Regional Corporation opened oil refineries and construction firms of their own, as well as IT services and hotels. They made hundreds of millions of dollars each year, buying stock and launching subsidiaries all over the world. At the same time, the local borough government collected property taxes on the oil fields, creating vast revenues and lots of high-paying jobs across the region. All this money was showered over the North Slope communities—Kaktovik, Barrow, Point Hope, and the first village I had ever visited— Anaktuvuk Pass. Residents received fat dividend checks each year, their individual share of corporate earnings. In a good year a family of six could bring in $60,000, without even punching the clock. By the time I met Trimble in 2014, the corporation had paid out nearly a billion dollars in dividends to its shareholders. Many of the North Slope Inupiat had become very wealthy people.

But that was not the case for all Native communities. Arctic Village, for example, saw none of these riches. Back in the 1970s, they had chosen to hold onto their land rather than hand it over to a corporation, one of just a handful of villages to make that decision. This meant they wouldn't receive any shareholder benefits—none of the dividends or scholarships or grand infrastructure programs offered by some corporations. But they owned their land, free and clear.

"We got 1.8 million acres," said Trimble, sitting up a little taller as he spoke. "We can do anything we want inside. Hunting and fishing and trapping. We know we own the land."

Ohhh. It finally clicked. *That's why it feels different here.*

I thought about Anaktuvuk Pass, with the fancy ATVs and the trucks air freighted in from Seattle. The breathtaking museum and modern city hall. That's why kids seemed to have the latest iPhone in their pocket, and why locals vacationed in Hawaii and Las Vegas, even though many didn't have jobs. They had something worth even more—shares in Alaska's top-grossing corporation.

Arctic Village, on the other hand, wasn't part of any corporation. There were no checks in the mail every quarter. No subsidized fuel or groceries. Most people couldn't even afford heating fuel. But in their eyes, they had something that was worth much more. Their homeland.

"Do you think it was the right decision?" I asked Trimble. "To choose the land over the money?"

Certainly they missed out on things. They didn't have toilets or sinks or handy thermostats. If you wanted to take a shower, you had to pay a couple dollars at the communal washeteria. But there was no doubt in Trimble's eyes or in the firm set of his jaw.

"I feel like this place, small area, it's only place might be safe later on, for the future generations," Trimble said. "We can pack water, nothing wrong with it."

The thing is—and this was a very new concept for me—Trimble's people had never defined being rich in terms of having money. Food and water and shelter were the only things that mattered. The people of Arctic Village had bountiful land and full freezers, and it's difficult to put a price tag on that.

Trimble rose from the plastic bench.

"I'm tired," he said kindly. "Maybe we can talk more tomorrow."

I smiled. "Goodnight."

I watched him walk across the gym in long, slow strides, then stood up and stretched my own legs. I was already home for the night. The school was the closest thing to a hotel in Arctic Village, and I would be sleeping on the floor tonight, with the other camp instructors.

I made my way back to the science classroom, where my sleeping bag was sprawled under a lab table full of microscopes. "Roughing it" by most standards. But I thought about how Trimble had grown up, curled up on a caribou skin atop the frozen ground. I wondered—would anyone choose to live that way now?

When I walked into the girls' bathroom to brush my teeth, I smiled at the woman standing at the sink. She had fairy-tale hair that fell in silver curtains to her knees, and she pulled a brush through it in long, luxurious strokes. It was hard not to stare as I set my toiletries on the counter beside her.

"Your hair is beautiful. How long have you been growing it?"

She gave a shy smile.

"Maybe thirty years," she said, with a Gwich'in accent. Julie Mahler was also here for science camp. Despite her shy presence, I could tell she had an incredibly sharp eye, as if she were taking note of everything and cataloguing it in her mind. I knew she lived out in the bush; I had heard her talking to kids earlier in the day about how to tie fishnets by hand. But that was about all I knew.

The next morning, after a pancake breakfast in the school cafeteria, we hiked down a four-wheeler trail leading out of town. Twenty-some kids fanned out on the trail, zipping into the brush and stomping on puddles crusted in ice. When we made it to the creek where the Elders used to gather water, Julie crouched on the tundra and called the kids over. They formed a big circle around her.

"What're you kids gonna do if you're stuck out here? What are you gonna eat?"

A third grader in a purple jacket chirped up.

"Pick berries!"

Julie smiled. "Berries are good but they're not gonna fill you up. You're gonna need some real food."

She snapped a branch from a willow tree.

"You can use willow to make a snare for ptarmigan," she said, twisting the end into a loop with a few quick flicks. Then she flipped her wrist as if waving a wand. "They just sit there and you put it around their neck and pull it down. We call them poor man's dinner." The kids laughed and pulled in a little closer.

As Julie talked about traps and snares and how to sneak around in the woods, I was just as fixated as the youngsters. This tiny woman was like a cross between Katniss Everdeen and Wonder Woman. She knew more about surviving than any crazy survivalist and more about the natural world than any biologist I knew.

As we scoured the tundra for edible herbs, it occurred to me why the kids were so drawn to her, why they listened to every word and watched her like some kind of magician. Unlike many Elders, Julie wasn't talking about how they used to live, about what they had done in the old days to survive. She still lived that way. She trapped and fished and hunted, and she did it all with boats and sleds she built by hand. At barely a hundred pounds, she could pull a sixty-pound Sheefish from the water and take down a moose ten times her size. She had raised a family in the Arctic wilderness without a store, a clinic, or any safety net at all, and had built a successful life without a job or a welfare check. She didn't need oil running through the pipeline any more than she needed a man to take care of her. If I was looking for an example of self-sufficiency, I didn't need to look any farther.

I watched Julie peel the bark off a willow branch with rough hands that had skinned too many animals to count.

If she could live without oil in the harshest land on earth, I realized, maybe there was still hope for the rest of us.

20
Fending for Myself

ulie Mahler was only ten when she decided she was going to live in the woods, by herself. She grew up in Fort Yukon, a Gwich'in community downriver from Arctic Village, tucked in the ice chest of Alaska's interior. The middle child of thirteen, there were always plenty of chores to keep her busy. She and her siblings hunted and fished, chopped firewood, and hauled water for the lodge that her parents ran.

"It would be cold, fifty, sixty below, and we'd still be out there packing water," she said.

When she wasn't helping out, she was exploring the creeks and sloughs around the village. The Upper Yukon was one of the richest fur-bearing regions in the world, producing animal skins that were used for fine hats and coats in Asia and Europe (where affluent ladies still liked to wear fox pelts around their necks). Julie and her older brothers trapped muskrats and martens from lakes on the south side of the river, and set snares in the snow for lynx and minks. No matter how cold it was, or how rough the trail, she never got tired of being out in the country, and feeling like she had the whole world to herself.

But what really made her want to live in the bush was seeing it from above. Julie's dad, Cliff Fairchild, ran a small air service out of Fort

Yukon. In fact, he was partners with Al Wright for a while—they shared a business, shuttling trappers around to their camps.

"Al used to stay at our lodge when he came to Fort Yukon. Sometimes he brought us candy from town," Julie said.

Guests showed up at their doorstep from all over the country. Julie's dad would fly them up to the Arctic Circle and take them to Chalkytsik, where they could see a small Alaska Native village firsthand. His Cessna-180 was usually reserved for customers, but once in a while, Julie managed to catch a ride.

Sometimes, early in the morning, when her dad was still eating breakfast, Julie and her sister would sneak onto the airplane and hide behind the backseats. It took all their self-control not to start giggling until they were in the air. When he yelled "Who's back there?" they emerged from their hiding spots and buckled in like proper passengers.

But they quickly learned one of the downsides of flying without a ticket: you couldn't always count on a ride home. The plane only had three extra seats, and they were usually spoken for. One time, Cliff landed in Circle, a neighboring village, and turned around in his pilot's seat.

"Well girls, I got passengers to pick up," he said. "I'll see you in a couple days."

Fortunately, they knew enough people in town that they could always find a place to stay. And though Cliff could have come back for them sooner, he was trying to teach them a lesson.

"That's how we learned to ask if we could fly and come back," Julie said.

As she watched the sun hit the icy tendrils of the Yukon and felt the country unfold beneath her, she looked for good places to live. At the foot of the Ogilvie Mountains, perhaps, or on a bluff over the Porcupine River. She wasn't sure where, exactly, but she would definitely end up somewhere out there, living on the land. Village life was great for some, with easy access to doctors and stores. That's why her people had settled down over the past generation and given up their nomadic way of life. But she knew it wasn't for her.

One day Julie was playing outside with her friends, talking in their secret spot about what they wanted to be when they grew up.

"I wanna live in the woods," she declared.

Though she was small for her age, Julie was as tough as any of the bigger kids and they knew better than to question her.

"Me too!" her best friend said.

They all agreed, then and there—as soon as they finished school, they would say goodbye to their families and move out in the woods, far away from civilization. They would build cabins and hunt and fish for food, just as their parents and grandparents had done. As the Gwich'in people had done for ages.

But like the dreams of many ten-year-olds, most would be forgotten, or replaced by more pragmatic plans. Except for one of them.

———————

A decade later, on a crisp fall day, Julie glided down the Sheenjek River. The small motor hummed as water lapped against the tin boat. She was looking for logs that had washed up on the banks. Not the driftwood that was steadily spit out by the Yukon, but nice fat logs that would be suitable for a cabin. Julie was still short and slight, but now, at twenty-two years old, she had long cinnamon hair and arms sculpted by a summer of labor. Her husband, Gene, steered in back while she kept an eye out for the wood. The leaves were already gold, a reminder that they had to start building soon if they were going to finish the cabin before winter.

Though he hadn't grown up in the bush, Gene Mahler loved the outdoors just as much as Julie. He came from Mishawaka, Wisconsin, and had moved to Alaska after college, looking for adventure. With blue eyes and dirty blond hair, it was hard to miss him in the mostly Gwich'in community of Fort Yukon.

Julie carried their son, Zeb, wrapped in a blanket on her back. Nearly two years old, he was looking more like his father every day. When Gene had first asked Julie to move to the bush, she couldn't quite believe it. After all, she used to babysit his kids when he was married to his first wife, a white lady also from Outside. But she wasn't cut out for village life, and one day she and the kids were gone, leaving Gene in Fort Yukon alone. It took Julie a while to realize he was interested in her.

"He just kept hounding the guy I was going out with. That's kinda how we met," she said.

But they hadn't even had a first date yet when he made a big proposition.

"Wanna move out with me?" he asked her.

"Move out where?"

"In the woods."

Huh? Julie thought. *Just like that?*

It was an enticing offer. It's what she had always wanted to do, after all, what she had promised in front of her childhood friends. This could be her chance. And there was no question she was attracted to Gene. He was tall and handsome, just the kind of outdoor man she wanted. Still, he was fifteen years older than her, and already had two kids.

Despite her reservations, Gene didn't give up. When he showed up at her house one night in the middle of dinner to seek her father's blessing, Julie finally said yes. Shortly after her twentieth birthday, they stood outside her parents' lodge in Fort Yukon and exchanged vows. Julie wore a silky pink dress that draped over her bulging belly. And now, two years later, they were doing just what they had promised one another, living on the great land, facing each challenge as it came.

Julie spotted a good stand of trees on the north bank of the river.

"Over there," she pointed.

But Gene was fixated on something else.

"Hey!" he yelled. "It's a grizz."

Julie jerked her head to the right. A coffee-colored grizzly, water dripping from his fur, was standing in the main channel of the river.

Gene kept his hand on the tiller.

"Shoot it!" he yelled.

Barely twenty feet away, the bear could take a running leap into the boat if it wanted to.

Julie tensed up. She had never shot a grizzly before, especially not with a baby on her back.

"No, turn around!" she yelled.

"Shoot it!" he repeated. It was only fifteen feet away now. "I don't want him coming in the boat."

Julie took a deep breath.

"Okay," she said.

She raised her shotgun, aimed and shot it right in the head. The bear went crazy.

"Turn out! Turn out!" she called to her husband.

She had knocked the muzzle off but hadn't killed it. The bear was thrashing around in the water, now only a couple boat lengths away.

"Shoot it again!"

"No, turn out!"

"You better shoot it, it's gonna go up on the bank."

Julie knew that the last thing you wanted was an injured bear near camp. Just as it was about to disappear in the willows, she fired again. The shot echoed through the valley. She scanned the brush. No sign of the bear. Gene drove to shore and marched into the willows, shotgun in hand. Julie waited in the boat with Zeb. After ten minutes had passed, she began to worry. Maybe she should go check on him?

Then Gene reappeared on the bank, holding a knife that had clearly been used.

"Aren't you going to come help me?"

She sighed and stepped off the boat, following him into the brush where the bear had stumbled before falling down for good.

Now it was lying face-up, legs splayed out. Dead.

"Hold his legs," Gene said.

He had already started skinning it out, making a cut straight up the belly. Julie just stood there, staring at the creature in awe. The claws were longer than her fingers.

"It's dead, you know," Gene told her.

It didn't matter. It was still terrifying. Julie stayed back, held by an invisible hand.

"My mother told me if you're afraid of it, don't touch it," she said.

But Gene was in no mood for philosophy. Skinning a grizzly was a lot of work, especially one this size.

"Shut the hell up and help me."

"Okay, okay, okay."

They worked carefully so they could keep the meat clean and save the skin for a rug. Gene cut two incisions on the inside of the back legs, from the tail out to the pads of the feet. He slit the skin and cut upward with quick flicks, then slid the blade along the stretchy white fascia. It easily peeled away. Julie could feel the power of the animal coursing through its leg, even in death. Gene sliced the tendons holding the feet and lifted the legs off the carcass.

Sitting there, hands stained in blood, Julie felt something blossom inside her. Not quite power, but confidence. She set aside her mother's words and decided she would not avoid the things that scared her. Rather, she'd have to face her fears head-on if she was going to live out here.

"That's when I said, 'Okay, I can handle anything.'"

"Wow," I said, looking up from the basketball court.

Julie and I were sitting on the bleachers watching the kids race back and forth. After a full day outside, somehow they still had energy to burn.

"And we lived out there ever since," she said.

"So Zeb grew up in the bush?"

"Yep. All five of em."

After Zeb, there was Gino and Elijah and Sunny and Earl Luis. Julie and Gene built a cabin on the Salmon Fork of the Black River, a hundred miles from the nearest village. Their only link to the outside world was by dog team or boat.

Julie's trapline ran in a twenty-five-mile loop around the cabin. Once a week, she hooked up the dogs to go check her traps, bundling the kids into the sled with furs stuffed around them like pillows. She set leg holds for martens and lynx. If she saw wolf tracks, she set out bait and laid snares around it. If they killed a moose, she would always set snares around the gut pile just in case a bear came by. Trapping was a means of survival for Julie, one of her only forms of income. But she also enjoyed it. It was a match of wits between human and quarry, a deadly game that was constantly changing. You had to know who was out there and what they were thinking, to understand the curiosity of the lynx, the suspicion of the wolf, and the fearlessness of the wolverine.

"If a wolverine comes around, they'll clean your whole trapline out," Julie said in a tone of warning.

When they stopped to camp overnight, she built a lean-to under the trees and made a big bonfire to keep everyone warm. As soon as the kids could walk, they started helping with every part of it, learning the subsistence way of life that Julie had been taught by her elders.

It took a lot of food to feed a family of seven, and fortunately there were plenty of moose around. It was a family-size animal, with a large bull providing about five hundred pounds of meat. They usually went through three moose per year. They would eat the heart and liver fresh, then make jars of burger and steak and dry the rest for winter. For cooking lard, Julie harvested a black bear and rendered the fat. "I like to get em in the fall when they're nice and fat, before they go in the hole," she said.

Meat and fish they could hunt and catch, but everything else they had to grow themselves. Though farming wasn't very common in the Arctic, it was a natural part of life where Gene came from. They built a big garden in the backyard and planted carrots and potatoes and cabbage. They raised horses and chickens and geese and goats.

"We milked goats and made cheese and butter. The kids would sit there doing their homework and shake the butter."

That part I could relate to, growing up in the heart of Pennsylvania's farm country. I thought of my mom gathering fresh eggs from the chickens every morning, and how she used to sneak goat milk into the store-bought cartons so we wouldn't complain about the taste.

Except it was a whole different thing up here in the Arctic.

"How did you get the animals up there?" I said, trying to picture a Cessna full of goats.

"We rode the horses up the river in wintertime. Everything else by boat."

It wasn't easy, but they managed. And in the process, Julie realized she could get just about everything she needed without going to the store. For the kids, they didn't know any better. By age seven or eight, they were hunting small game and camping in the woods by themselves. Before long, Julie and Gene could leave them at home when they went to town for errands, sometimes for a week at a time.

"Didn't you worry about them, on their own?" I asked.

The parents I knew fretted about everything, from diaper rash to screen time. My mom got nervous just thinking about me jogging on the trails by myself. While my siblings and I used to run wild in the woods behind the house, there hadn't been many predators in our area, and a very small chance of freezing to death.

"No. They're like little brushmen," Julie said proudly. "I never thought a bear's gonna get em or anything like that. Because they knew how to take care of em."

And that meant, often, thinking on their feet. One time, in the fall, Julie's two youngest were out hunting moose. They liked to get one right before winter, because they could hang the whole carcass outside to freeze, then slice off chunks as needed. Elijah and Luis were sitting by the river bank, not far from the house. Unlike tracking caribou or bear, moose hunting was more of a waiting game. Find a moosey area, sit still, make some calls, and let them come to you. Elijah heard distant rustling behind them. When he turned around, he saw a large bull moose across the meadow, emerging from the brush. The animal hadn't noticed them yet, so both boys crept to the ground to find a comfortable shooting position. At the same instant, they fired. It was hit! But instead of dropping, the moose started running, not full speed but in a kind of desperate trot. Straight at them.

Elijah kept his eyes fixed on the thousand-pound animal, growing larger as it got closer and closer.

"Hey!" he said to his younger brother. "I need more shells."

But Luis was nowhere to be seen. He had run down the trail and jumped the cutbank.

Elijah stood up to get a better look at the moose, which had stopped about ten feet away, just standing there. It had been hit in the chest and would eventually die, but he hated to see it suffer. His younger brother emerged from his hiding spot, looking a bit sheepish.

"I'm out too," he said.

Elijah would have to finish the job by hand, he decided. He couldn't get close enough to slit its throat—too risky—so he pulled a skinning knife from his belt and tied it to a long branch. First he pushed the moose over on its side, which was surprisingly easy in the animal's weakened state. Then, using the knife like an extended saw, he tried to cut the neck. But the blade was too dull.

He dropped the stick and wiped his forehead, then turned to his younger brother.

"I need you to hold him."

"No way!" Luis said.

"Come on! We need to finish this."

Reluctantly, Luis circled behind the moose and grabbed the rack. The magnificent animal lay still, its giant nostrils flaring. Elijah extended the saw and tried again. This time, when he poked the neck, the moose threw its head forward with the force of a half-ton slingshot. Elijah could only watch in shock as his younger brother sailed through the air, landing on the ground nearly twenty feet away. Then he quickly hunched over the moose and finished the job.

They had plenty of meat that winter, but that wasn't the end of the moose. Julie had raised her children to use every part of the animal, just as she had been taught. For the Gwich'in, the skins were just as valuable as the meat, fat, and organs—used to make clothing, blankets, bags, boots, even rope and cord. When all the meat was harvested and processed, the boys asked if they could tan the hide.

"Okay," she said. "Just get your schoolwork done first."

They were well into winter by now, so it would have to be an indoor project. There wasn't a lot of extra space in the cabin—just one room downstairs where the kids slept and a loft for Julie and Gene.

After hanging the hide on the wall to thaw (which took a few days), the boys prepared the ingredients they would need for tanning. They took the brains out of the freezer they had saved for this purpose, and boiled them into a thick mash on the stove. Then they mixed it with water in a giant trash can to create a magical moisturizing mixture that they would rub on the hide to prevent it from stiffening up.

Julie with her daughter Sunny at their home on the Salmon Fork Black River. PHOTO FROM MAHLER FAMILY COLLECTION.

When Julie got home from the trapline, she was greeted by a stench of brainwater so thick she could barely breathe.

"Wooooweeeeee!" she said. "When are you kids gonna be done?"

It was another few days until the skin was wrung out and dried and Julie had her cabin back to normal. After a week of wrestling with the gigantic hide, her boys had a rug that was softer than velvet, along with a lifelong appreciation for the art of tanning.

———————

Sitting on the bleachers, elbows resting on her knees, Julie could have been your average basketball mom. Yet there was nothing average about her. By the time she was my age, she had already built two houses and given birth to three kids, and she was spending her days not pecking away at a computer but gutting fish and skinning animals. She had given up plumbing, TV, and Internet in exchange for long nights filled with auroras and howling wolves. It sounded glamorous, in a way, but also incredibly hard.

"Were there any downsides to living out there?" I asked.

"There were hungry years," she said. "One time we lived on popcorn and beans all winter."

And of course, the inevitable mishaps that come with raising children in the bush. Like when they accidentally shoot themselves. Julie knew her youngest, Luis, liked to play with the six shooter, a small pistol the older kids were allowed to use for squirrels and grouse. One day Julie and Luis were hanging out outside, while the rest of the crew was in Fairbanks. Spring was when they did their big shopping trip of the year; with the river at its maximum height, they didn't have to worry about bottoming out the boat.

Julie was digging rows for her carrots when she heard a shot from the woods.

"Luis! Leave those squirrels alone!" she yelled.

A few minutes later he came hobbling over.

"Ah, mom." She looked up. "I shot myself."

"Cut it out," she said. She turned her attention back to the garden.

"No, I think I did." He hopped toward her. "My leg hurts."

She dropped the shovel and knelt beside him.

"Where? Show me."

"Down there," he pointed to his shin, underneath his boot. Julie didn't see a hole in the rubber, so she gently tugged it off.

"Ahh! Ahhh!" His face twisted in pain.

There was no entry wound on the shin. But when she rolled up his pants, she saw a little red hole just below the knee. The bullet had entered high and traveled down through the bone.

She touched the spot gently.

"Ow, ow, ow!"

There was no clinic nearby, and Julie wasn't going to remove the bullet herself. They would have to go to town. She tugged his boot back on.

"Come on, help me feed the animals," she said.

It wasn't the kind of homestead you could just walk away from. Once they had fed the horses and dogs and goats and chickens, they dragged the canoe down to the water. Luis had been on the river plenty of times, but never in the canoe. The Black River was fast, especially in the spring, as snowmelt came streaming down the mountains and showed little regard for travelers.

Julie got Luis settled into the middle of the boat, his leg perched on a wooden box, and handed him a paddle. She cupped the back of his neck and leaned in close.

"It's gonna be okay," she told him. "Just do exactly what I say."

The river was a rabid version of its normal self—with rapids churning over boulders and fragments of fugitive wood. Muddy water ripped trees from the banks and flushed them downstream. There were logjams stuffed into corners and sweepers hanging over channels like parking gates, blocking passage completely. After hours of paddling, they passed another boat going the opposite direction. Julie recognized the two men in the brand-new riverboat as Fish and Wildlife workers.

Ooh, Julie thought. *Maybe we could catch a ride!*

She waved her paddle in the air, high above her head.

But they didn't slow down. In fact, they kept driving toward her, coming so close that she had to dig in her paddle to stay upright. They waved and smiled as they motored by, totally unaware of that she was in distress.

"Thanks for nothing," she muttered from the back of the boat.

Luis' leg was pretty swollen by the time they arrived in Chalkyitsik three days later. The village health aide wanted to Medevac him to Anchorage.

"I don't got money to pay for Medevac," Julie told her. "We'll wait for a regular flight."

They made it to Fairbanks the next day and checked into the hospital. It didn't take long to remove the bullet and patch him up, and soon they were heading back upriver with a pair of crutches, to get ready for another summer.

———————————

Julie spent thirty years on the Salmon Fork, thirty summers putting up food and thirty winters trapping. There were hazards of living in the wilderness, of course, but they were hazards she understood.

"Why do you think more people don't live like that?" I asked.

We were working together in the school cafeteria, wiping down tables after dinner.

It was the last night of science camp. Julie had spent the week teaching kids the skills they needed to live off the land, skills that were fading from everyday life but still existed within them, deep inside.

On one level, I already knew the answer. We were creatures of convenience, lovers of technology. In our ever-advancing intelligence, we had figured out how to use our brains in order to preserve our bodies. I wondered how many people even mowed their own lawns anymore, let alone gathered food or chopped wood. And I was in no position to judge. My only glimpse of Julie's life came from backpacking trips, and only for a few days at a time. I had experienced the joys of living close to nature and the rewards of subsistence life, but like most people I still liked to come home and watch Netflix on the couch.

And yet the curiosity about this lifestyle is still alive, even in East Coasters like me. That's why we still go camping and fishing, why we spend our vacations visiting national parks and far-flung islands. It's part of the reason why two million people come to Alaska each year to escape the trappings of modern life.

We may embrace technology with open arms, but we still want to know what we are made of.

"I don't know why more people don't do it," Julie said. "It's a hard life, but it's fun."

After so much talk, it was time to see for myself. What was I really made of?

21
Filling the Freezer

'd only ever shot at targets before, at a coffee can perched on a tree branch or a paper bull's eye pinned up at a gravel pit. So I knew I hadn't been invited on this hunting trip because of my sharpshooting abilities. In the fall, I usually stayed home and picked berries while Josh went out chasing caribou with Jake. But this year, Kristin and I were going too. The plan was to spend the weekend camping in the Alaska Range and to hopefully get a caribou, maybe two. I didn't have a gun, of course, or a scope, or a single piece of camouflaged clothing, so I borrowed a .308 from Jake's arsenal and did my best to dress in neutral colors.

About four miles of vigorous hiking brought us to the top of the mountains: our base camp for the weekend. In an age when hunting had become so motorized—with packs of men in fatigues, cruising around on four-wheelers and airboats—it was nice to be far away from the craziness, with only the sound of the wind whispering in the hills.

We were just finishing dinner when the first caribou made an appearance. Full of chili and cheddar cheese, the four of us were sitting around the campsite chatting, feeling pretty inanimate. Kristin got up and walked over the ridge to pee.

"How do you like hunting so far?" said Jake, who grew up tracking caribou in these same mountains with his dad.

"It's not so bad," I said, plucking a mini Hershey's bar from my food bag.

So far it felt more like a hiking trip than anything. We'd spent the whole day climbing up various lookouts, then crouching low to scan the brush for movement. Nothing yet.

We gazed down at the Robertson River, gray channels braiding together like a cabled scarf, before emptying into the Tanana.

"It's not always like this," Jake said, looking at Josh. "Remember last year?"

"Ha," Josh laughed. "When the wind was blowing sixty miles an hour, and I thought I was gonna get speared by your tent pole?"

I had heard all about it. After nearly getting blown off the mountain, they had aborted the trip and come home early. As a result, our freezer was almost empty this year.

Suddenly Kristin came running back toward us, gesturing wildly as she zipped up her pants.

CARIBOU, she mouthed soundlessly. Jake and Josh sprung up and grabbed their rifles. I followed them toward the ridge.

As we approached the ridgeline, the others started walking in big, exaggerated steps. So this is what stalking was like. I felt slightly ridiculous, like the wily coyote creeping up on his prey, but didn't want to be the one to spook the caribou on my very first hunt.

Despite our attempts at stealth, the caribou must have smelled us, because by the time we made it over the ridge it was gone. Kristin pointed down a rocky slope. A nice-sized bull was standing there, staring at us. In an instant, he took off up the other side.

Suddenly everyone started moving like it was a military drill. Kristin trotted down the gully while Jake stayed high and followed the rim. Josh made his way to the next valley over, in the direction the caribou had headed.

And then I was alone, standing on the side of a mountain holding a rifle I barely knew how to use. *So...What now?*

I figured loud noises were probably frowned upon, so there was really no way to communicate with the others. And since I had no idea where I should go, I decided to hold my ground. Maybe the caribou would come back in this direction, right into my path. The hillside happened to be covered in blueberries, so I crouched down and started picking. Between handfuls, I watched Jake's silhouette traverse the valley in the age-old pursuit of man versus prey.

It was a good forty-five minutes before everyone showed up in camp again, looking just like they had when they left. No empty shell casings or blood-soaked hands. No caribou. Still, it was exciting. As we boiled some water for tea and debriefed about the chase, suddenly I felt wide awake. A new energy coursed through the air—we knew they were out there.

As the mountains merged with the darkening sky, Josh and Jake talked about their rifles, comparing weights and triggers and bullet trajectories. Kristin ducked over the ridge for one last look, this time taking her gun along. I went in the tent to change into long underwear and socks. Even in the summer, I usually slept in a full layer of wool when we went camping, especially in the mountains. I laid my rifle in the vestibule, barrel pointed out, to keep it dry and protected. For once, I wasn't too worried about bears—not with the firepower in our camp. But it had been a full day, and I was ready for bed. As I molded my puff coat into a pillow, I called out to the guys.

"Goodnight!"

Instead of a reply, a shot echoed through the valley. Jumping up, I unzipped the tent door and poked my head out. Josh and Jake hadn't moved, and were looking in the direction of the shot.

"Dammit Kristin," Jake said, pushing himself up with a sigh. But he was smiling.

I threw on a rain coat and stuffed my feet back in my shoes, not bothering with socks. Following the sound, we found Kristin on the other side of the ridge, rifle slung over her shoulder, crouched beside a large bull. Her curly hair was tucked under a green hat and she had a big smile on her face.

She had taken it down in one shot.

Jake raised his hand to give her a high five, looking very proud of his wife. He pulled out his knife as she started telling the story.

"I peeked over the ridge and it was just standing there eating," Kristin said. "Maybe a hundred yards away."

She had dropped to her stomach and crawled toward it, Army style (yes, this bridesmaid of mine is a badass). When she was nice and close, about fifty feet away, she propped up on her elbows and carefully set up the shot, as her dad had taught her years ago. The caribou never saw her coming.

"Damn! I'm impressed!" I looked at her in admiration. I never would have known what to do in that situation.

Night was falling fast on the mountain, and we had a lot of work to do. The caribou's stomach was inflating like a balloon as the belly contents turned to gas, and it was best to skin it while the muscles were warm.

This was the part of hunting that had always turned me off. But as Jake started working with his knife, making a line down the center of the belly, there was no squirting blood or strange odor, nothing that could really qualify as "gross." He held the sides open as Josh used a hacksaw to cut the sternum, opening up the rib cage. Jake reached into the chest and cut the windpipe and esophagus and all the soft tissue attached to the chest cavity, while Josh used both arms to scoop out the organs. A pile of guts spilled onto the ground.

Now for the skin. Following Kristin's lead, I cut up the inside of a back leg, then slid my knife along the soft white membrane under the skin and peeled it back. It gave away easily. As I continued working on the leg, I couldn't get over how warm it felt in my hands, how the heart had stopped beating just minutes ago. I thought back to Julie's first bear, of what it was like standing at the gate between life and death, being the one that holds the key. Once we had skinned the whole caribou— from the legs up to the neck and shoulders, the guys cut along the major muscle groups to divvy up the meat. We separated out the big hunks, the neck, the backstrap, the ribs, and then cut the remainder into four parts. Two front quarters and two hind quarters, which held the majority of the meat.

Less than an hour after Kristin fired the shot, four game bags sat on the tundra, stuffed with fresh, organic meat. And the last daylight had been snuffed out.

We were dirty and exhausted when we finally crawled in our tents. But sleep didn't come. Not because I was having nightmares about vengeful caribou, but because the wind kicked up to gale force, nearly blowing our tent off the mountain. So this is what Jake and Josh had been referring to. I guess they weren't exaggerating after all. We finally surrendered and moved downhill, nestling our tents in a small hole beside the ridge, which offered a little more protection.

Lying awake in my sleeping bag that night, as the wind hammered the thin nylon walls, I had lots of time to think. *We killed something.* Well, technically Kristin had, but there was blood on my hands as well. It was hard to describe the feeling of seeing something so alive one second and dead the next. It was sad, certainly, but also satisfying. We had worked hard to get our meat, had taken one life to feed others.

The concept was still on my mind as we continued hunting the next day. I didn't really process it until a few days later. After packing out two caribou, driving back to Fairbanks, and processing meat for ten hours into one-pound packets of burger and stew, we sat around Jake and Kristin's kitchen table to taste the spoils.

Kristin whipped up Thai curry with fresh caribou steak and veggies from the garden. I took a bite with a scoop of brown rice. It was so fresh it almost popped in my mouth. So much better than anything I could buy at the grocery store, and without the preservatives or growth hormones of our modern-day meat.

I guess this is what it would take to live more sustainably. I didn't need to be a master hunter like Julie, but I would need to be able to feed myself. Despite my small part in the hunting experience, it had made me feel much more independent.

Our outdoor freezer would soon be filled to the brim with steaks, burger, Italian sausage, and ribs, enough meat for an entire year. As Kristin and I divvied it up, tossing packages into cardboard boxes, I asked her what it felt like to pull the trigger. It wasn't her first time killing something—she had grown up hunting deer with her dad in Wisconsin. And her enthusiasm had been obvious—she was the first one up in the morning, glassing the hillsides at dawn, and the last one back to camp at night. She wanted to spot the caribou, and she wanted to shoot it herslf. Still, I knew she felt the impact.

"Was it hard?" I said.

"Ya know, it is a little sad. But mainly I just felt thankful." She lowered her voice almost to a whisper, as if she were telling me a secret. "After I took the shot I said, 'Thank you, caribou.'"

22
Oil vs. Food

Another summer solstice passed, the days shrunk to hours, and suddenly it was time for science camp again. Winter had been impatient this year, and there was already a skin of snow on the ground when I landed in Arctic Village in late August. I found Julie and Trimble in the school gym with the kids, who were all a size bigger than I remembered. I recognized many of the teachers and scientists from last year, too, but there were a few new faces in the crowd.

Wearing a Carhartt vest over a navy blue fleece, I would never have guessed that Tim Kaine was a U.S. Senator, or that he would soon be one step away from Vice President of the United States as Hillary Clinton's running mate in 2016. Up here, he just looked like another hiker or hunter passing through the refuge. Kaine was traveling with another senator from New Mexico, Martin Heinrich, and the head of the U.S. Fish and Wildlife Service. They had left their cushy offices on Capitol Hill to fly to the top of the world for one main reason. Drilling was back on the table in Congress again, as Republicans made another push to open the Arctic National Wildlife Refuge. It seemed crazy to me, especially now. With oil prices so low, companies weren't even developing their existing reserves, choosing to sit on them until the value rose. Why bother opening a remote Arctic site that would cost ten times more to develop? But it was the principle, I knew, as much as the oil itself—the belief that we should get something out of our public lands rather than let them "waste away" as national parks. Like most of their fellow Democrats, Kaine and Heinrich were opposed to drilling in the refuge. But rather than just toeing the party line, they had actually come here to see it for themselves.

It wasn't every day their kind of VIP showed up in Arctic Village, and the gym was decorated with colorful Gwich'in posters welcoming the visitors to town.

Kaine sat down across from me at the folding table, where the kids were weaving baskets of various shapes and colors. They smiled shyly as he attempted to break the ice, then showed him how to lace the wooden strips together. I introduced myself and asked how he was enjoying his trip so far.

"Oh, it's wonderful." His southern accent reminded me of my college days in Richmond, where Kaine had served as city mayor, and even taught at my alma mater, the University of Richmond, before moving up the political ladder.

They had camped the night before, at a spot deep in the refuge called Red Sheep Creek, and woke up covered in four inches of snow. Up close, I could see his eyes were puffy from lack of sleep, and he looked more like a Survivor contestant than a U.S. Senator. While he loved the outdoors, he and his colleagues hadn't come just to say they'd spent the night above the Arctic Circle. Rather, he wanted to meet the people who lived in the refuge, the ones who would be most affected by oil development, and hear what they had to say.

The potlatch was extra special that night, with with luscious salmon fillets and platters of barbecued moose ribs covering the school cafeteria tables. After dinner, community members formed a big circle in the gym. Standing in the middle, Trimble looked sharp in a leather vest adorned with Gwich'in beads and tassels, like the distinguished tribal chief he was. He welcomed his guests to Arctic Village and told them about its history. Their people had lived in these mountains for thousands of years, he said, long before the land and animals were controlled by the federal government, long before the United States was even founded.

The senators listened respectfully as the village Elders spoke of their connection to the land and the birds and the caribou, stepping into the circle one by one. While they each had different stories to share, the theme was consistent: they had managed to live off these resources for hundreds of generations, to maintain them in a responsible way. Now they were asking the senators to do the same.

If only the rest of Congress could be here, I thought, to hear this plea directly. It was far more powerful than the ads on this issue seen by so many Americans on TV. It seemed so clear out here on the tundra, so completely unambiguous. This was their home. These resources were all they had. It was the reason their ancestors had settled here in the first place, and the reason they'd stayed for millennia. How could we put oil companies ahead of real people, to concentrate more wealth in the hands of those who already had so much?

After everyone had spoken, the skin drums came out and the singing began, songs about ravens and wolves and the most sacred creature of all—the caribou. I danced along in the circle, following the moves of the woman in front of me—the arm waving and foot stomping to a simple and timeless rhythm.

The senators joined the circle too. Like me, they came from a totally different culture, one that was incredibly young compared to the Gwich'in Athabascans. Our ancestors had moved to this continent only a few hundred years ago, had come from Europe looking for a better life. We were products of the western world, a world of books and philosophy and science, where people didn't worship nature so much as study and try to manipulate it. Far removed from our nomadic days, we lived in a world of Costcos and Home Depots, where everything we needed was just a click away.

We were clearly visitors in this land of ice and tundra, immersed in a whole new universe of food and language and music. And yet our two worlds could not be separated anymore. Over the past century, they had crashed together and become one. It was evident not only from the diesel generators burning day and night to power this small village, but it was written on the land as well. In the melting sea ice and thawing permafrost, in the sinkholes that dented the tundra from here all the way to the Arctic Ocean. Climate change is transforming the Arctic faster than anywhere else on earth, a direct result of the cars we drive and the food we eat and the products we manufacture. Of the way we live. These first-world conveniences are not free. They are changing the oceans. Changing the atmosphere. Changing the animal migrations. Our lifestyle is changing the balance of life on the planet.

Of course, it's not like the Indigenous people are outside of it. Over the past century, they have adopted the technologies of the western world as well, a world fueled by oil. Julie bought flour and coffee at the village store; Trimble put gas in his snowmachine.

But just because we all need oil to some extent, is that really an excuse to suck every last drop out of the earth? To drill in our wildlife refuges even if it means tearing open Indigenous lands, jeopardizing the food source they need to live? The pro-development crowd has framed it as a black and white issue: open the refuge or doom the economy. And I had to admit, I'd almost bought into it. Living in Alaska had shown me how much I depended on oil, how complicit I was in the resource economy. After seeing what Alaska was like before these booms, and seeing how hard people had to work to meet their basic needs, I could no longer pretend that I was somehow living a sustainable lifestyle. The recent bust had driven it home: without oil, I had so much to lose.

But coming to Arctic Village, dancing and eating and picking berries with the local people, was a blast of fresh air. It wasn't one versus the other: oil or economic ruin. That was what my media ethics professor would have called a false binary, an artificial choice. BP and Exxon weren't knocking down the door to get into the refuge, not with oil prices at $40 a barrel. It was just a ploy, a well-worn political argument by those who wanted to trade wilderness for something more valuable—like a tax cut for the wealthy. If we were to sustain Alaska's resources for everyone, we needed to take a more nuanced approach, to put a real value on wilderness and wildlife that could be held up against commodities. To truly appraise the worth of clean water or the millions of pounds of fish and moose generated by the subsistence economy.

The question was, was there any stopping this movement? In the past, it had taken a huge public outcry to block drilling in the Arctic

Refuge, not just in Alaska but in voting districts across the nation. We were clearly in a different place today. Would the American people be willing to give up a couple hundred dollars in tax relief to protect a slice of northern Alaska, a place they would probably never see? And what about Alaskans—could they turn down the prospect of another boom?

I had seen the connection between resources and quality of life. Oil was important, yes, but we *could* live here without it. Just as Trimble and Julie had done. Just like Clutch and Al. It wasn't the glamorous life we had come to enjoy, but a simpler, rougher version. We would have to hunt and fish and haul water. We'd have to sacrifice some of the luxuries we took for granted, like high-speed Internet or fresh raspberries in the middle of winter. If we jeopardized our food and water, on the other hand, there would be nothing left to protect. And if we paved the wilderness with roads and mines and drill pads, who would want to live here anyway?

That's what the Gwich'in people were trying to tell us, and so many others as well, who had the benefit of perspective. We weren't locked into an oil future. We could transition away from the path we were on, could return to the things that were most important. The things that made Alaskans who we are.

Just like the people of Arctic Village couldn't have it both ways, couldn't afford to live out here on the tundra with toilets and showers and central heating, neither could I. I couldn't support drilling and also support climate action, not in any genuine way. Opening the refuge wouldn't just place the Porcupine Herd into the hands of the oil industry. It would commit us to fossil fuels for the next sixty years, at a time when we needed to be moving to more sustainable sources of energy.

I had to make a choice, to take a stand and live with the repercussions. Even if it meant risking the things that had become so essential.

———

Julie sat on the couch bouncing her granddaughter on her lap. She was almost two, with round cheeks bulging with a piece of moose fat. Julie was in Fairbanks this week staying with her son, who happened to live

Julie harvesting a moose at her homestead in the Arctic after a recent fall hunt. PHOTO FROM MAHLER FAMILY COLLECTION.

just a few miles from me. A group of Washington bureaucrats was in town to talk about climate change, and they wanted to hear an Indigenous perspective. Though Julie wasn't fond of the city, she had traveled here to share her story, using what currency she had to defend her home.

I had learned a lot from Julie since running into her in the school bathroom over a year ago, and not just about hunting and trapping. She had shown me what it meant to live a sustainable life in this day and age, had helped me realize what I was capable of. Since meeting her, I had skinned a muskrat and butchered a caribou, things that had seemed not just foreign but unthinkable before living in Alaska.

Julie had also inspired me to face my fears. Not just fear of bears or cold or darkness, but something deeper: a fear to commit to a certain set of values. It wasn't enough to speak up among like-minded people. If I wanted things to change, to really have an impact, I had to reach those who saw the world differently, people like Clutch Lounsbury and

Al Wright, and even my father-in-law. I don't know why it was so hard to take a stand, but it had been. Choosing one side meant rejecting another; it was much more comfortable to float around the issues, analyzing them endlessly from every angle. And journalists are experts at this. We aren't supposed to have a point of view, after all, but to show "both sides" of every story (as if there are only two sides to anything). Perhaps that's why I had chosen that path. I didn't really like to disagree with people; I'd rather keep jumping from point to point, to try to land on common ground.

It was scary to stand up in the line of fire, and say something controversial, but that's what needed to happen. I had done the research, examined the points of view, digested the various arguments ad nauseum. I had peeled back the curtains of my own biases and exposed them to the most contrary views I could find—had walked into a proverbial fire wearing a suit of untested ideals. Some had burned away, while others had survived—tempered by the flames into something new, something sturdier. Now I needed to commit to this new self. If I truly believed we were pushing our planet too hard, melting the ice that held the whole thing together, I couldn't look away. At the risk of sounding alarmist, I had to tell the world.

23
The Next Bend

lurched forward as Julie pulled the stick, barely able to hold on. Our hands gripped the smooth tree branch in alternating formation, four sets of knuckles strained white with effort. After a couple minutes writhing and twisting on the ground cross-legged to try to win control of the branch, I was getting tired. The stick pull was a scrappy, free-form battle of strength and will, kind of like Athabascan arm wrestling. When Julie wrenched it toward the ground in one quick motion, my grip failed and I plunged into the dirt.

Wow, beaten by a sixty-year-old woman.

Julie laughed and helped me up. "You had me. You let go too soon."

Well, I consoled myself, she had been playing this game since she was five.

When I shared my secret with her later that day by the river, she swatted me in a motherly way.

"Pregnant!" She put her hand over her mouth. "And you're wrestling with that stick!"

I wasn't showing yet. I was only a couple months along and hadn't publicized it. But for some reason, out in the woods with Julie, I felt the urge to tell her.

We were at fish camp on the Porcupine River, ten miles from Fort Yukon, the village where Julie grew up.

Julie was hosting a culture camp for the local youth, and I had come out to help. It was the perfect spot for a camp, a broad forested area on a straight strip of river. A dozen teepee-style tents were propped up in a clearing and a big tarped kitchen was slung by the river, where Julie's niece cooked over a wood fire pretty much all day, churning out enough food to feed thirty kids and another ten adults. There was a fish wheel nearby and a big beach littered with driftwood.

I had spent four days out here with the kids, some still in diapers and some who were old enough to drive the riverboat. Though we were nine miles above the Arctic Circle, in the hot July sun it felt more like Arizona. Fortunately, the Porcupine River was clear and cold, better than a swimming pool. We usually jumped in right in front of camp and floated downstream to a large gravel bar, where the kids splashed around in the turquoise water and sprawled on the sunny beach. It was a good way to pass the hottest hours of the day. And since it never got dark this far north, we usually went back for an evening swim.

In some ways it reminded me of my own childhood camp, where we used to build lean-tos and roast marshmallows, and swim until our lips turned blue. But there were some clear differences too. For starters, the days here revolved around subsistence activities, starting with the giant salmon the kids pulled out of the fish wheel each morning, then gutted, filleted, and sliced into strips. Once the long orange ropes were hanging in the smoke house, it was on to the next project. This morning, Julie had shown them how to tan the muskrats she had helped them catch this spring, just a few miles from here.

We had huddled around as she plied the skin, using the shin bone of a moose as if it were a pastry knife to peel away bits of flesh and fat. It was a delicate process—press too hard and you could poke a hole in it, too soft and you wouldn't get the nice leathery feel.

Julie had been trapping along this river since she was kid. Now she was passing it on to the next set of youngsters. That was the whole point of being out here, to teach the kids about their Athabascan roots, the skills that had kept them alive for thousands of years, but were slowly disappearing to the modern world. In the age of bypass mail and

Amazon Prime, there were easier ways to get food and clothing, even out here in the bush.

After dealing with the fish and the muskrat, going for a swim and eating hamburgers for lunch, it felt good to just relax in the sun with Julie, and to have a minute to share my news. Behind the kitchen, a group of campers pulled firewood off a dead spruce tree. An older boy sawed the trunk into rounds while two others carried them over to the cook pit and dumped them in a pile. With a never-ending list of chores, there was no time for texting or Instagram, even if they had managed to sneak a phone past Julie.

Alaska's future depended on these kids. Not just on the skills they were learning here, but on how they wanted to live. Would they choose to continue the traditions of their grandparents, to live off the land and its riches, or would they rather cash in on the resources surrounding them, and make a down payment for a more comfortable life? Elders like Julie and Mike and Clutch and Al had lived their lives, had made their choices, and left their mark on Alaska. Now it was up to the next generation.

Much of our day was focused on traditional skills, like setting a fish net or making salve out of spruce bark. But a big part of this camp was simply building confidence. These kids were living in a very different world than their Elders had known—a world that was both bigger and smaller, much easier in some ways and incredibly hard in others, as they tried to navigate the endless paths laid out before them. In some ways, I saw the beauty of the old way, when your course was set, and you knew you would follow in the footsteps of your parents and grandparents. A time before you were bombarded with images from the outside world, constantly reminded of all the things you were missing, all the opportunities you couldn't quite reach. Before the cruel perception of choice.

"What I see now is, kids are lost," Julie said. "They walk around on their phone listening to music, they can't even see."

And yet here they were, surrounded by grizzly bears and blizzards and all the other extremes of the Arctic. If it weren't for airplanes showing up daily, hauling food and fuel, they would be totally separate from the supply chain that was keeping them alive.

"If they're gonna live in a village," Julie said, "they better learn how to survive."

For me, life was already feeling profoundly different. Even though I was months away from being a parent, I was beginning to see the world through new eyes. As a group of girls zipped around me on the beach, I placed a hand on my still-flat belly. No kicks yet, but I knew she was in there, slowly growing into a person. My daughter would be part of the next generation, the ones who would inherit this busy, wonderful, distressed planet. The planet we left them. I looked out at the river, running with wild salmon, crawling with moose and black bear. It still felt clean and healthy and full of life. Would she ever get to see it that way?

———————

That night, as we waited anxiously for dinner, a boat came from the direction of the village. The purr of the motor grew loud, and the kids raced to the bluff to see who it was. Each arrival created a ripple of excitement, a message from the civilized world. Julie's son, Gino, was behind the wheel. He had a golden colored dog with a wagging tongue and, even more intriguing, a pair of water skis. The kids mobbed him.

"Daddy!" said his five-year-old son. "I wanna ski!"

The others joined into a chorus.

Can I go? Can I go?

Gino pulled his son up in a big hug.

"After dinner," he said.

He made his way through the pack to find his mom. I could see he had Julie's smile, with the wiry build and blue eyes of his father.

He grabbed a plate and piled it with fresh salmon and green beans. Dinner had an extra sense of urgency that night. When the kids had washed their dishes and set them on towels to dry, they scurried down the footpath to the beach. Water skiing at twilight—yet another thing I hadn't expected at Gwich'in culture camp.

Gino drove close to shore and tossed the skis toward his son. It clearly wasn't his first time, I could tell, as he popped up right away and had no problem holding on as his dad carved figure eights in the water. He was finally trapped in a triangle of wakes and went down in a tangle of skinny arms and legs. Gino circled around and offered a hand, lifting him into the boat.

An older boy went next, then another. They had varying degrees of skill and experience, but all managed to stand up and cruise for a while. Man, it looked fun.

It was getting late, close to ten, the coolness of night creeping in even as the sky stayed bright. Most of the kids had gotten out of the water and air dried. They roasted s'mores over a fire, still in bare feet.

A tall streaky-haired girl named Lauren approached Julie as she threw more driftwood on the fire.

"Can I do it?" she asked.

Despite the courage of her stance, I could hear in her voice she was slightly unsure.

Julie looked at her.

"What do you mean, can you do it?" she said. "Of course you can do it."

They waded into the river together. Julie held onto the skis as Lauren wriggled her feet into them, then handed her the rubber handle. Once situated, Julie gave Gino a thumbs up. He hit the gas and the boat sprang forward.

Lauren had barely straightened her legs before she crashed into the water, like a newborn calf trying to take its first steps.

Gino made a big circle back to shore. Julie grabbed the skis.

"Try again," she said, holding them in place for Lauren. "Remember, straighten up as soon as you feel tension on the line."

Lauren tried but went down again. This time she surfaced with a resigned look that reminded me of my first time waterskiing, when you realize how much harder it is than it looks.

"I can't do it," she said.

But Julie didn't budge. She was up to her waist in the river, her basketball shorts and green T-shirt soaking wet.

"Again," Julie said. "You *can* do it."

Lauren looked frustrated, but couldn't bring herself to say no to Julie. She stuffed her feet back in the skis.

Gino pulled the throttle. The boat roared to life, quickly eating up the slack in the nylon rope. It pulled Lauren up. Her legs wavered ever so slightly, then straightened. She was up!

"Whoot!" Julie cried.

Lauren glided over the water, quaking a little at first before finding her center of gravity. Then she was solid. Gino smiled over his shoulder and a cheer rippled across the beach—the first girl to water ski at camp, a memorable moment for us all. Though I barely knew Lauren, I couldn't suppress a swell of pride as I watched her zip around the river, catching air like an old pro.

Julie was elated too. This is what culture camp was all about, and for that matter, life too: learning skills, testing your limits, and seeing if you can push a little farther. Maybe that's the appeal of Alaska—it reminds us constantly that we are only human, while giving us occasional glimpses of the divine.

Wow, I thought. I hope my daughter has an ounce of Julie's spirit. She may not grow up and live in the bush, she may not shoot grizzlies or trap lynx. Who knows, maybe she will. But I hope she has the option to live out here, to fall asleep to howling wolves and dancing auroras, and know she is part of their world.

The next morning I threw my backpack on the boat and turned around to give Julie a hug. I was ready to get home and see Josh and Ati, but also sad to leave. Before she let me go, Julie placed a hand gently on my belly.

"Take good care of that baby girl," she whispered.

I smiled at her.

"I will."

Index

About the Author

Molly Rettig grew up in Hershey, Pennsylvania and attended the University of Richmond, where she played soccer and studied sociology. After a short break ski-bumming, she earned an MA in Journalism from the University of Colorado Boulder with a focus on Environmental Policy.

She moved to Alaska to work at the *Fairbanks Daily News-Miner*, and in 2010 wrote a story about a sustainable home in Anaktuvuk Pass. That introduced her to the Cold Climate Housing Research Center, which is part of the U.S. National Renewable Energy Laboratory, where she now works as communications director, producing stories and multimedia about housing, energy, and culture.